Lecture Notes in Economics and Mathematical Systems

continuation on page 221

Lecture Notes in Economics and Mathematical Systems

Managing Editors: M. Beckmann, Providence, and H. P. Künzi, Zürich

Operations Research

95

M. Zeleny

Linear Multiobjective Programming

Springer-Verlag
Berlin Heidelberg GmbH

Dr. Milan Zeleny
Graduate School of Business
Uris Hall
·Columbia University
New York, NY 10027/USA

AMS Subject Classifications (1970): 90-04, 90 A 05, 90 C 05, 62 C 25

ISBN 978-3-540-06639-2   ISBN 978-3-642-80808-1 (eBook)
DOI 10.1007/978-3-642-80808-1

Offsetprinting and bookbinding: Julius Beltz, Hemsbach/Bergstr.

Acknowledgment

Parts of this study derive from a thesis defended at the University of Rochester in 1972. I am immensely indebted to my advisor, Dr. P. L. Yu, now at the University of Texas, for his continuous encouragement, patience and reassurance. He has generated the persistence and faith which has proven to be absolutely essential for completing the work.

Most of the research and technical efforts were carried out at the University of South Carolina which had provided the computing facilities. My thanks go to Dr. J. Eatman for his programming assistance.

I dedicate the work to my wife, Dr. Betka Zeleny, who helped to transform countless discouragements into strong motivational impulses.

Milan Zeleny
Columbia University,
New York, Autumn 1972

ABSTRACT

One of the more persistent criticisms of current decision-
-making theory and practice is directed against the traditional
approximation of multiple goal behavior of men and organizations
by a single, technically convenient criterion.

This criticism extends also against traditional decision-
-making tools like mathematical programming, game theory, etc.,
where a single objective function is often used to approximate
essentially multiobjective situations.

In this research we develop theory and algorithms which may
be applied to linear programming problems involving multiple,
noncommensurable objective functions. Such a multiplicity of
objectives induces substitution of a single optimal solution
(which can no longer be safely determined) by the whole set of
nondominated solutions.

In Part I of this paper we explore the first method for locating all nondominated extreme points which is based on multiparametric programming. The ℓ- dimensional parametric space, which
can be interpreted as the set providing all possible wighted combinations of ℓ objectives, is decomposed into a finite number of
subspaces. These subspaces provide sets of optimal weights imput-
ed to each objective function by corresponding extreme point solution. The decomposition also provides a criterion upon which
the decision about nondominance of any particular extreme point
can be based.

In Part II, A Multicriteria Simplex Method, we introduce
second method for locating all nondominated extreme points, independent of any parametric considerations. It represents simple
generalization of the conventional single-objective simplex method. It appears that the decomposition of the parametric space
can be viewed as a significant byproduct of this method.

In Part III, Generating of All Nondominated Solutions, we

develop a technique for generating <u>all</u> nondominated solutions
from a given set of nondominated extreme points. In multiobjective
situations the superiority of an extreme point solution, over
one which is non-extreme, no longer applies.

In Section 5 some important topics indicating future developments are treated. Alternative approaches, allowing potentially
faster and simpler generation of nondominated extreme points, are
discussed. Problems of nonlinearity and "nondominance gaps" are
analyzed and their general resolution suggested. An important
problem of choosing the final solution among possibly large
number of nondominated solution is analyzed extensively.

Appendices contain a short note on redundancy among linear
constraints, printout of FORTRAN code for multicriteria simplex
method, and some examples of outputs.

Table of Contents

VIII

LINEAR MULTIOBJECTIVE PROGRAMMING III.

List of Figures

1. Introduction

1.1. The origin of the multiobjective problem and a short historical review

The continuing search for a discovery of theories, tools and concepts applicable to decision-making processes has increased the complexity of problems eligible for analytical treatment. One of the more pertinent criticisms of current decision-making theory and practice is directed against the traditional approximation of multiple goal behavior of men and organizations by single, technically-convenient criterion. Reinstatement of the role of human judgment in more realistic, multiple goal settings has been one of the major recent developments in the literature.

Consider the following simplified problem. There is a large number of people to be transported daily between two industrial areas and their adjacent residential areas. Given some budgetary and technological constraints we would like to determine optimal transportation modes as well as the number of units of each to be scheduled for service. What is the optimal solution? Are we interested in the cheapest transportation? Do we want the fastest, the safest, the cleanest, the most profitable, the most durable? There are many criteria which are to be considered: travel times, consumer's cost, construction cost, operating cost, expected fatalities and injuries, probability of delays, etc.

It might be an impossible task to tie all these criteria into a single unifying trade-off function which could serve as the objective function for the associated mathematical programming problem. It may be better for us to look at such a problem as one with <u>multiple</u>

<u>objectives</u> which are all to be at their "best" possible values under

the given conditions.

Given a <u>vector-valued objective function</u> $\theta(x) = (\theta_1(x),\ldots,\theta_\ell(x))$

and a set of feasible solutions $X \subseteq E^n$, the vector maximum problem

$$\text{v-Max } \theta(x) \text{ subject to } x \in X$$

is the problem of finding all solutions that are nondominated. Instead

of a single optimal solution we seek <u>a set of "nondominated" solutions</u>

(efficient set, admissible set, Pareto-optimal set). We prefer the

term "nondominated" because of its unambiguity.

The main property of the set of nondominated solutions is that for

all solutions outside the set we can find a nondominated solution at

which all objective functions are unchanged or improved and at least one

strictly improved.

It might be worthwhile to support these statements with two quota-

tions related to our subject:

Howard Raiffa[1]: "Personally I feel that this quest for a "scientific"
and "mathematically objective" rule [decision criterion,
objective function, M.Z.] is all wrong!......; we should
limit formal analysis to the characterization and determi-
nation of the efficient set [set of nondominated solutions,
M.Z.] and let unaided, intuitive judgment take over from
there."

---

[1] Raiffa, Howard: "Decision Analysis", Addison-Wesley, 1970, pp. 155-156.

John von Neumann[2/]: "....This [multiple objective situation, M.Z.]
is certainly no maximum problem, but a peculiar and discon-
certing mixture of several conflicting maximum problems....
This kind of problem is nowhere dealt with in classical
mathematics. We emphasize at the risk of being pedantic
that this is no conditional maximum problem, no problem of
the calculus of variation, of functional analysis, etc. It
arises in full clarity, even in the most "elementary" situations, e.g., when all variables can assume only a finite
number of values."

The problem of the formation of a single optimality criterion from
a number of essentially noncomparable elementary criteria first appeared
in [Pareto, 1896].

The concept of "Pareto optimality" (here nondominated solutions)
found its way into operations research in the pioneering work of [Koopmans,
1951]. This was, of course, in connection with the activity analysis of
production and allocation. A more general approach, viewed as a vector
function maximization problem of mathematical programming, can be found
in [Kuhn,Tucker, 1951]. We should also mention the work of [Markowitz,
1956], who applied the concept of a nondominated set in portfolio selection problems.

After a decade of "nontechnical" discussions of multiple versus
single objective function on pages of Operations Research [represented,
for example, by Klahr, 1958] the direct extensions of Koopmans' ideas

---

[2/] von Neumann, J., and Morgenstern, O.: "Theory of Games and Economic
Behavior", 3rd ed., Princeton University Press, Princeton, 1953,
pp. 10-11.

appeared in [Charnes,Cooper, 1961]. Here we can find the first algorithmic approach, the "spiral method", still heavily influenced by the activity analysis framework.

In recent years the problem of vector function maximization has been approached from the more general viewpoint of Kuhn and Tucker. Most authors deal with general optimality conditions. For example, [Zadeh, 1963], [Klinger, 1964], [DaCunha,Polak, 1967], [Geoffrion, 1968].

An algorithm for maximizing two objective functions via parametric linear programming is presented in [Geoffrion, 1967].

1.2. Linear Multiobjective Programming

In this work we try to extend the theory of vector function maximization, especially in the direction of algorithmic developments. We will concentrate our efforts on linear structures only. The reasons are essentially twofold. First, we have found that the linear case is sufficiently complex to merit concentrated attention. Though the interest in the linear case has increased substantially in recent years, satisfactory algorithms have not been published yet. Also, the possibility of utilizing the existing concepts of the simplex method and parametric linear programming is very attractive and, from a practical viewpoint, most applicable.

Second, nonlinear cases are uncomparably more difficult to solve. All difficulties of the nonlinear programming theory are compounded here together with complex characterization of the nondominated set in nonlinear cases. Before the nonlinear case may be approached efficiently, more experience is needed not only with multiobjective programming, but also with interpretations of nondominated solutions. It is due to the persuasion of the author that the complete nondominated set will not be of primary interest from the practical viewpoint. A concept of "representative" nondominated solutions might be technically, as well as practically, more attractive.

1.3. Comment on notation

It is important to distinguish the following notation: Let $x \in E^n$ and $y \in E^n$, where $x = (x_1,\ldots,x_n)$, and $y = (y_1,\ldots,y_n)$. Then

(i) $x > y$ if and only if $x_j > y_j$, $j = 1,\ldots,n$

(ii) $x \geq y$ if and only if $x_j \geq y_j$, $j = 1,\ldots,n$ and $x \neq y$

(iii) $x \geqq y$ if and only if $x_j \geqq y_j$, $j = 1,\ldots,n$

(iv) $x \sim y$ if and only if $x \ngeqq y$ and $y \ngeqq x$

(v) $x = y$ if and only if $x_j = y_j$, $j = 1,\ldots,n$.

We shall denote a set by a capital character and use superscripts
to indicate the index of a set of vectors. For example, a set of k
vectors will be denoted as

$$X = \{x^1, x^2, \ldots, x^k\},$$

where

$$x^i = (x_1^i, x_2^i, \ldots, x_n^i), \quad i = 1, \ldots, k.$$

Also, given $\{x^1, x^2, \ldots, x^k\}$ we shall define a convex hull of
$x^1, \ldots, x^k$ as

$$[x^1, x^2, \ldots, x^k] = \{x | x = \sum_{i=1}^{k} \lambda_i x^i, \lambda_i \geq 0, \sum_{i=1}^{k} \lambda_i = 1\}$$

or, in abbreviated form, as $C[X]$ or $C[x^1, \ldots, x^k]$.

Similarly,

$$[x^1, x^i] = \{x^i + \lambda(x^1 - x^i); \ 0 \leq \lambda \leq 1\}$$

indicates a closed line segment or a convex combination of x^1 and x^i.

An open line segment will be denoted as $(x^1, x^i) = \{x^i + \lambda(x^1 - x^i);$
$0 < \lambda < 1\}$.

Given a set X, its interior will be denoted by Int X and its
boundary by ∂X. We will need to distinguish between the interior points
and interior points with respect to the relative topology. A fine discussion of these concepts is in [Stoer,Witzgall, 1970]. Considering a

convex polyhedron $X \subseteq E^n$, a point is called a __relative interior point__
of X if it is an interior point of X with respect to the relative
topology induced by the minimal manifold containing X, i.e., with
respect to the relative topology induced in

$$M(X) = \{x \mid x = \sum_i \lambda_i x^i, \ x^i \in X, \ \sum_i \lambda_i = 1\},$$

the manifold generated by X. We will denote the relative interior of
X as X^I.

For simplicity, we shall often denote a linear combination in
vector notation as follows:

$$\sum_{i=1}^{\ell} \lambda_i \theta^i(x) = \lambda . \theta(x).$$

Other more specialized notations will be introduced in the text when
needed.

LINEAR MULTIOBJECTIVE PROGRAMMING I.

2. Basic Theory and Decomposition of the Parametric Space

One of the theoretical approaches which appears repeatedly in the literature is based on reduction of a vector-valued objective function to a family of scalar-valued objective functions [see, e.g., Geoffrion, 1968, and DaCunha,Polak, 1967].

The approach works quite well for bicriterial cases [see Geoffrion, 1967]. However, its multicriterial extension has not been successfully analyzed for an algorithmic development.

In this section we shall explore multiobjective linear programming problems through multiparametric programs.

Let us denote a set of ℓ (possibly incommensurate) objective functions as

$$\theta(x) = (\theta^1(x),\ldots,\theta^\ell(x))$$

where $\theta(x)$ is a vector-valued objective function, $x \in E^n$ is the decision variable, and let $X \subseteq E^n$ be a set of all feasible solutions.

The vector maximum problem

$$v - \text{Max } \theta(x) \quad \text{subject to} \quad x \in X \tag{2-1}$$

is the problem of finding all points $\bar{x} \in X$ which are nondominated,

that is,   there exists no other $x \in X$ such that $\theta(x) \geq \theta(\bar{x})$ and $\theta(x) \neq \theta(\bar{x})$.

We may denote the set of all nondominated solutions as N and define $D = X - N$ as the set of all dominated solutions. It is seen that

$$\bar{x} \in N \iff \theta(x) \geq \theta(\bar{x}) \implies \theta(x) = \theta(\bar{x}). \qquad (2\text{-}2)$$

Definition 2.1. Let Λ be the set of all vectors λ, defined as follows:

$$\Lambda = \{\lambda \mid \lambda \in E^{\ell}, \ \lambda_i \geq 0, \ \sum_{i=1}^{\ell} \lambda_i = 1, \ i = 1,\ldots,\ell\}. \qquad (2\text{-}3)$$

Definition 2.2. Given $\lambda \in \Lambda$, let $P(\lambda)$ denote the following problem:

$$\underset{x \in X}{\text{Max}} \ \sum_{i=1}^{\ell} \lambda_i \theta^i(x)$$

or find a point $\hat{x} \in X$ such that

$$\lambda.\theta(\hat{x}) \geq \lambda.\theta(x) \quad \text{for all} \quad x \in X.$$

Definition 2.3. Let

$$L = \{x \mid x \in X, \ x \text{ solves } P(\lambda) \text{ for some } \lambda \in \Lambda\},$$

$$(L) = \{x \mid x \in X, \ x \text{ solves } P(\lambda) \text{ for some } \lambda \in \text{Int } \Lambda\}.$$

Remark 2.4. The conclusion $(L) \subseteq N \subseteq L$ allows one to solve (2-1) by means of $P(\lambda)$. It has been proven repeatedly in the literature:

(a) $(L) \subseteq N$ [e.g., Geoffrion, 1968, DaCunha,Polak, 1967].

(b) $\theta[X]$ convex $\implies N \subseteq L$ [Arrow,Barankin,Blackwell, 1953].

(c) X closed and convex, $\theta(x)$ concave for all $x \in X$, one component of $\theta(x)$ strictly concave for $x \in X$, then $N \subseteq L$ [DaCunha,Polak, 1967].

The conclusion of Remark 2.4. is explored and derived in complete generality by [Yu, 1971,1972]. Some of his results are discussed in the next section, 2.1. Notice that $\theta[X] = \{\theta(x)\,|\,x \in X\}$ is the image of X through θ. Observe, when X is a polyhedron and θ is linear, then $\theta[X]$ is also a polyhedron. Thus $(L) \subseteq N \subseteq L$. By solving $P(\lambda)$ for all $\lambda \in \Lambda$, we can get a set of solutions containing the entire set N.

Remark 2.5. N may not be equal to L. This can be easily resolved by considering the following lemma.

Lemma 2.6. If for some $\lambda \in \Lambda$, $\bar{x}$ is the unique solution of $P(\lambda)$, then $\bar{x} \in N \cap L$.

Proof. Suppose $\bar{x} \in \mathcal{D}$. Then there exists $x \in X$ such that $\theta(x) \geq \theta(\bar{x})$. Since $\lambda \geq 0$, $\lambda \cdot \theta(x) \overset{\geq}{=} \lambda \cdot \theta(\bar{x})$. Thus $\bar{x}$ cannot uniquely solve $P(\lambda)$, a contradiction. Q.E.D.

The dominated solutions contained in L occur only when there are more alternate optimal solutions to $P(\lambda)$ for some $\lambda \in \Lambda$. By comparison on objective space $\theta[X]$, the dominated solutions in L could be discarded.

2.1. Basic Theory-linear case

The following is based on some results described in [Yu, 1971,1972]. In particular, the following theorem will be useful:

Theorem 2.1.1. Let $cx = (c^1 \cdot x, \ldots, c^\ell \cdot x)$ be an ℓ-dimensional linear vector function, $X \subseteq E^n$ be a convex polyhedron (set of feasible solutions),

$\lambda \in E^{\ell}$ and let the set of $x \in X$ which maximizes the function $\lambda.cx$ over X be denoted by $X^*(\lambda)$. Then

(a) $\underset{\lambda>0}{\cup} X^*(\lambda) \subseteq N \subseteq \underset{\lambda\geq0}{\cup} X^*(\lambda)$

(b) If $c[X^*(\lambda)]$ is a singleton for all λ, λ not strictly larger than 0, then $N = \underset{\lambda\geq0}{\cup} X^*(\lambda)$.

Remark 2.1.2. Notice $c[X] \equiv \theta[X]$ for $\theta(x) = cx$.

Remark 2.1.3. Let $N^> = \underset{\lambda>0}{\cup} X^*(\lambda)$ and $N^{\geq} = \underset{\lambda\geq0}{\cup} X^*(\lambda)$. Then the (a) part of Theorem 2.1.1. is reduced to

$$N^> \subseteq N \subseteq N^{\geq}.$$

Because of the above inclusions, we could call $N^>$ and $N^{\geq}$ the _inner and outer approximation of_ N. Notice that the statements (L) $\subseteq N \subseteq$ L of Remark 2.4. and $N^> \subseteq N \subseteq N^{\geq}$ of this Remark, are essentially equivalent. In $N^>$ and $N^{\geq}$ we use positive cone $\Lambda^>$ and non-negative (non-zero) cone $\Lambda^{\geq}$. In (L) and L we use a hyperplane of $\Lambda^>$ and $\Lambda^{\geq}$ to represent them. Under the maximization, both approaches yield the same solution. The approach using (L) and L allows us to reduce the dimensionality of Λ by one, as discussed in section 2.2.

The following Figure 2.1.1. should clarify Remark 2.1.3.

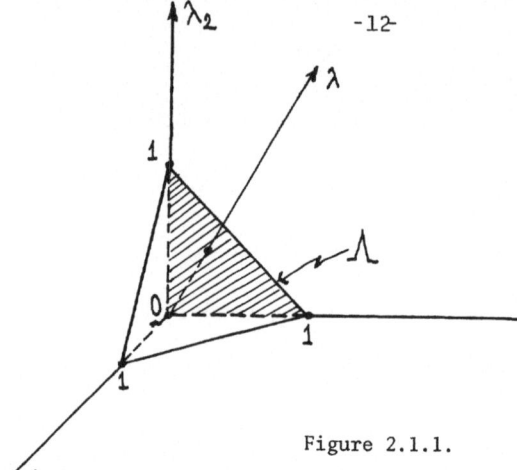

Any $\lambda \in \Lambda^2$ may be represented in Λ as in Figure 2.1.1. Λ-space itself may be reduced to the shaded two-dimensional polyhedron.

Figure 2.1.1.

Remark 2.1.4. In general, the nonempty polyhedron $X \subseteq E^n$ is defined by

$$X = \{x \mid x \in E^n; \; Ax \leqq b\} \tag{2-1-1}$$

where b is a fixed vector in E^{m+n}, and A is a given fixed $(m+n) \times n$ matrix.

Given $\lambda \geq 0$, a point $x^* \in X$ is a solution of $\underset{x \in X}{\text{Max}} \; \lambda . cx$ if and only if there exists a multiplier $\mu \in E^{m+n}$, $\mu \leqq 0$, such that

$$Ax^* \leqq b$$

$$\mu . A + \lambda . c = 0 \tag{2-1-2}$$

$$\mu . (Ax^* - b) = 0.$$

Notice that the definition (2-1-1) differs from that in (2-2-3). Also, the non-negativity constraints are incorporated in general inequality constraints.

Let the set of <u>active</u> constraints at x^* be denoted by

$$R(x^*) = \{r \mid r \in R, \; A_r x^* = b_r\}, \tag{2-1-3}$$

where A_r is the rth row of A, and $R = \{1,\ldots,m+n\}$.

We may distinguish two cases:

(1) $R(x^*) = \phi$. Then $x^* \in$ Int X, $\mu = 0$, $\lambda.c = 0$

(2) $R(x^*) \neq \phi$. Let $\mu_{R(x^*)}$ and $A_{R(x^*)}$ be the vectors derived

from μ and A by deleting all components not in $R(x^*)$.

Then from (2-1-2), we get

$$\mu_{R(x^*)} \cdot A_{R(x^*)} + \lambda.c = 0$$

or

$$\lambda.c = -\mu_{R(x^*)} \cdot A_{R(x^*)}, \tag{2-1-4}$$

where $\quad -\mu_{R(x^*)} \geq 0.$

Let us define

$$H^> = \{h | h = \lambda.c, \lambda > 0\}$$

$$H^{\geq} = \{h | h = \lambda.c, \lambda \geq 0\} \tag{2-1-5}$$

$$G(x^*) = \{h | h = \mu_{R(x^*)} \cdot A_{R(x^*)}, \mu_{R(x^*)} \geq 0\}.$$

From (2-1-1), (2-1-2), and (2-1-4) we have:

Theorem 2.1.5. Given the conditions stated in Theorem 2.1.1., we have

(a) $x^* \in N^>$ if and only if $0 \in H^>$ or $H^> \cap G(x^*) \neq \phi$

(b) $x^* \in N^{\geq}$ if and only if $0 \in H^{\geq}$ or $H^{\geq} \cap G(x^*) \neq \phi.$

Remark 2.1.6. $H^>$ and $H^{\geq}$ are the positive and semipositive cones generated

by the gradients $\{c^1,\ldots,c^{\ell}\}$, and $G(x^*)$ is the non-negative cone defined by the gradients $\{A_r | r \in R(x^*)\}$, i.e., by $A_{R(x^*)}$. Given $N^>$ and $N^=$ it

is then easy to identify N from the definition of nondominance or from

Theorem 2.1.1.(b).

<u>Remark 2.1.7.</u> If $0 \in H^> \Rightarrow x \in N$ for all $x \in X$.

2.2. Reduction of the dimensionality of the Parametric Space

By fixing $(\ell-1)$ parameters λ_i in Λ (Definition 2.1.) the ℓth para-

meter is automatically determined because of the normalization condition.

So we can decrease the dimension of parametric space Λ by one. For sim-

plicity, let us consider $(\ell+1)$ objective functions to begin with.

Let

$$c^i \cdot x = c^i_1 x_1 + \ldots + c^i_n x_n, \quad i = 1, \ldots, (\ell+1).$$

Then

$$P_\lambda = \lambda \cdot cx = \sum_{i=1}^{\ell+1} \lambda_i c^i \cdot x = (1 - \sum_{i=1}^{\ell} \lambda_i) c^{\ell+1} \cdot x + \sum_{i=1}^{\ell} \lambda_i c^i \cdot x$$

$$= [(1 - \sum_{i=1}^{\ell} \lambda_i) c^{\ell+1} + \sum_{i=1}^{\ell} \lambda_i c^i] \cdot x = [c^{\ell+1} + \sum_{i=1}^{\ell} \lambda_i (c^i - c^{\ell+1})] \cdot x.$$

To simplify our notation, let $(c^i - c^{\ell+1}) = c^i$ for $i = 1, 2, \ldots, \ell$. Then

$$P_\lambda = (c^{\ell+1} + \sum_{i=1}^{\ell} \lambda_i c^i) \cdot x = \sum_{j=1}^{n} (c^{\ell+1}_j + \sum_{i=1}^{\ell} \lambda_i c^i_j) x_j \qquad (2\text{-}2\text{-}1)$$

Set $(c^{\ell+1} + \sum_{i=1}^{\ell} \lambda_i c^i) = c(\lambda)$. Then

$$P_\lambda = c(\lambda).x = \sum_{j=1}^{n} c_j(\lambda)x_j \ . \tag{2-2-2}$$

Observe that P_λ is a __bilinear function__ defined on $X \times \Lambda$. By fixing $\lambda^* \in \Lambda$ we obtain a linear function P_{λ^*} to be maximized over X.

Let X be defined by

$$X = \{x \,|\, x \in E^n; \ \sum_{j=1}^{n} a_{rj}x_j = b_r; \ x_j \geq 0; \ r = 1,\ldots,m;$$
$$j = 1,\ldots,n\}. \tag{2-2-3}$$

We shall assume $1 \leq m < n$, $X \neq \phi$, and the rank of $[a_{rj}]$ is m. Thus X is a convex polyhedron. Notice the equality constraints in X. (All slack and surplus variables are included).

__Convention 2.2.1.__ To avoid a separate treatment of degeneracies, let us agree that a different basic feasible solution means a different extreme point of X. Let N_{ex} denote all nondominated extreme points of X.

__2.3.__ __Decomposition of the Parametric Space as a Method to Find Non-__
__dominated Extreme Points of X.__

Let

$$\Lambda = \{\lambda \,|\, \lambda \in E^\ell; \ \lambda_i \geq 0; \ \sum_{i=1}^{\ell} \lambda_i \leq 1\}.$$

For a fixed $\lambda^* \in \Lambda$, let $x^o(\lambda^*)$ be a maximal solution of $\underset{x \in X}{\text{Max}} \ P_{\lambda^*}$, where P_{λ^*} is given by (2-2-1) and by (2-2-2) with $\lambda = \lambda^*$. For simplicity we shall use only x^o to represent $x^o(\lambda^*)$. Similarly, we shall use c^* to represent $c(\lambda^*)$.

We shall also denote as J the index set of the basic variables, while $\bar{J}$ will indicate the index of currently nonbasic variables. Note $J \cup \bar{J} = \{1,\ldots,n\}$.

For simplicity, let $J = \{1,\ldots,m\}$. Then a <u>general simplex tableau</u> for x^0 is:

r	Basis	c^*	b^0	c_1^* x_1	$\cdots$	c_m^* x_m	c_{m+1}^* x_{m+1}	$\cdots$	c_j^* x_j	$\cdots$	c_n^* x_n
1	x_1	c_1^*	y_1^0	1	$\cdots$	0	y_{1m+1}	$\cdots$	y_{1j}	$\cdots$	y_{1n}
.	.	.	.	.		.	.		.		.
.	.	.	.	.		.	.		.		.
.	.	.	.	.		.	.		.		.
m	x_m	c_m^*	y_m^0	0	$\cdots$	1	y_{mm+1}	$\cdots$	y_{mj}	$\cdots$	y_{mn}
			z_0^*	0	$\cdots$	0	z_{m+1}^*	$\cdots$	z_j^*	$\cdots$	z_n^*

Table 2.3.1.

If x^0 is nondegenerate, then $x^0 = \{x_1,\ldots,x_m, 0,\ldots,0\}$, where $x_j = y_j^0 > 0$ for $j \in J$ and $x_j = 0$ for $j \in \bar{J}$.

Looking at the tableau we see that

$$z_j^* = z_j^* - c_j^* ,$$
(2-3-1)

where

$$z_j^* = \sum_{r=1}^{m} c_r^* y_{rj}, \quad j = 1,\ldots,n$$

and

$$z_0^* = \sum_{r=1}^{m} c_r^* y_r^o .$$

Observe that the optimality condition for x^o to be a maximal solution

for $P_{\lambda *}$ is

$$z_j^* = z_j^* - c_j^* \geqq 0 \qquad \text{for } j = 1,\ldots,n. \tag{2-3-2}$$

Notice if x^o is unique or if $\lambda_i^* > 0$, $i = 1,\ldots,\ell$, then $x^o \in N$.

Remark 2.3.1. Notice that z_j^* may be expressed by

$$z_j(\lambda*) = \sum_{r=1}^{m} c_r(\lambda*) y_{rj} - c_j(\lambda*),$$

using the notation of section 2.2.

Substituting $c(\lambda*) = (c^{\ell+1} + \sum_{i=1}^{\ell} \lambda_i^* c^i)$ we get:

$$z_j(\lambda*) \equiv z_j^* = \sum_{r=1}^{m} (c_r^{\ell+1} + \sum_{i=1}^{\ell} \lambda_i^* c_r^i) y_{rj} - (c_j^{\ell+1} + \sum_{i=1}^{\ell} \lambda_i^* c_j^i)$$

$$= (\sum_{r=1}^{m} c_r^{\ell+1} y_{rj} - c_j^{\ell+1}) + \sum_{i=1}^{\ell} \lambda_i^* (\sum_{r=1}^{m} c_r^i y_{rj} - c_j^i). \tag{2-3-3}$$

Observe, if for each $\lambda \in \Lambda$ we could find $x^o(\lambda)$ or show that P_λ has an

unbounded solution, according to Theorem 2.1.1., essentially all the

N-points have been located.

Substituting in (2-3-3)

$$\gamma_j \equiv \sum_{r=1}^{m} c_r^{\ell+1} y_{rj} - c_j^{\ell+1} \quad \text{and}$$

$$\delta_j^i \equiv \sum_{r=1}^{m} c_r^i y_{rj} - c_j^i$$

we get

$$z_j(\lambda^*) = z_j^* = \gamma_j + \sum_{i=1}^{\ell} \lambda_i^* \delta_j^i \geq 0, \quad j \in \bar{J} \tag{2-3-4}$$

for the optimality conditions expressed as a linear function of λ_i^*.

Observe that for $j \in J$, the index associated with basic variables, $z_j(\lambda^*) = 0$. Notice also that $z_j(\lambda^*)$ is a linear function of λ whenever x is fixed at x^o. So, the set $z_j(\lambda^*) \geq 0$, $j \in \bar{J}$, generates a closed convex polyhedron $\Lambda(x^o)$ in Λ, such that for each $\lambda \in \Lambda(x^o)$, x^o is the maximal solution to P_λ. This observation yields:

<u>Theorem 2.3.2.</u> Let $\lambda^* \in \Lambda$ and let x^o solve

$$\underset{x \in X}{\text{Max } P_{\lambda^*}} .$$

Let

$$\Lambda(x^o) = \{\lambda | \lambda \in E^{\ell}; \; \gamma_j + \sum_{i=1}^{\ell} \lambda_i \delta_j^i \geq 0; \; j \in \bar{J}\}. \tag{2-3-5}$$

Then $\lambda^* \in \Lambda(x^o)$, and the extreme point x^o solves $\underset{x \in X}{\text{Max }} P_\lambda$ for all $\lambda \in \Lambda(x^o)$.

Remark 2.3.3. Let us reemphasize that x^o represents a basis rather than an extreme point. So two bases corresponding to the same extreme point are considered to be different extreme points.

Notice the following properties of $\Lambda(x^o)$ which will be useful in further developments:

1) $\lambda \in \text{Int } \Lambda(x^o)$ and $\delta_j^i \neq 0$, for all $j \in \bar{J}$ and all $i=1,\dots,\ell$, imply that x^o is the unique solution of P_λ.

2) $\lambda \in \partial\Lambda(x^o)$ => there is at least one alternative optimal solution (other than x^o) to P_λ.

3) If $y_{rj} \overset{<}{=} 0$ for all r and $z_j(\bar{\lambda}) = 0$ for $\bar{\lambda} \in \partial\Lambda(x^o)$, then a polyhedron adjacent to $\Lambda(x^o)$ may be constructed such that it corresponds to an unbounded solution.

The following Theorem 2.3.4., can clarify (3) of Remark 2.3.3..

Theorem 2.3.4. Let $x^o \in X$ be an extreme point of X such that $\Lambda(x^o) \cap \Lambda \neq \phi$ and $\Lambda \notin \Lambda(x^o)$. Let $\bar{\lambda} \in \partial\Lambda(x^o)$ and $k \in \bar{J}$ be such that $z_k(\bar{\lambda}) = 0$ and $z(\lambda)$ is a nonzero function of λ. If all the elements of the pivot column k, $y_{rk} \overset{<}{=} 0$, $r \in R$, where $R = \{1,2,\dots,m\}$, then there exists in E^ℓ an unbounded polyhedron Λ_k such that

(i) $\Lambda(x^o) \cap \text{Int } \Lambda_k = \phi$

(ii) $\Lambda(x^o) \cap \Lambda_k \neq \phi$

(iii) for $\lambda \in \text{Int } \Lambda_k$ the solution to $\underset{x \in X}{\text{Max }} P_\lambda$ is unbounded.

Proof. Since $\bar{\lambda} \in \Lambda(x^o)$, x^o is a maximal solution to $P_{\bar{\lambda}}$, which is defined by (2-2-2) for $\lambda = \bar{\lambda}$. The corresponding optimality conditions (2-3-4) can then be written as

$$\gamma_j + \sum_{i=1}^{\ell} \bar{\lambda}_i \delta_j^i \geq 0, \ j = \bar{J} \ . \tag{2-3-6}$$

Let us consider the kth column.

·Recall that all the elements of the pivot column $y_{rk} \leq 0$, $r \in R$, where $R = \{1,2,\ldots,m\}$. Let

$$\Lambda_k = \{\lambda \,|\, \gamma_k + \sum_{i=1}^{\ell} \lambda_i \delta_k^i \leq 0\}.$$

Then for each $\lambda \in \text{Int} \ \Lambda_k$ there is no bounded solution to P_λ on X. Note Λ_k is an unbounded halfspace. Since for all $\lambda \in \Lambda(x^o)$

$$\gamma_k + \sum_{i=1}^{\ell} \lambda_i \delta_k^i \geq 0,$$

and for all $\lambda \in \text{Int} \ \Lambda_k$

$$\gamma_k + \sum_{i=1}^{\ell} \lambda_i \delta_k^i < 0,$$

we have

$$\Lambda(x^o) \cap \text{Int } \Lambda_k = \phi.$$

Note, $\bar{\lambda} \in \Lambda_k$. Thus

$$\bar{\lambda} \in \Lambda(x^o) \cap \Lambda_k, \text{ i.e., } \Lambda(x^o) \cap \Lambda_k \neq \phi. \qquad\qquad \text{Q.E.D.}$$

Given $x^o \in X$, let $\Lambda(x^o)$ be constructed in the sense of Theorem 2.3.2. Let $J_o = \{j_1, j_2, \ldots, j_m\}$ be the index set of basic columns and the index set of nonbasic columns with respect to J_o be denoted by $\bar{J}_o = \{j_{m+1}, j_{m+2}, \ldots, j_n\}$. Then

$$\Lambda(x^o) = \{\lambda | \lambda \in E^\ell; \; \gamma_j + \sum_{i=1}^{\ell} \lambda_i \delta_j^i \geq 0; \; j \in \bar{J}_o \}. \qquad (2\text{-}3\text{-}7)$$

Let the kth column represent the pivot column, and y_{pk} is the pivot element chosen. The following simplified simplex tableau describes the situation:

Basic Cols.	Nonbasic Columns		
J_o	$\bar{J}_o$		
$\overset{\downarrow}{p}^{th}$	$\overset{\downarrow}{j}^{th}$	$\overset{\downarrow}{k}^{th}$	b^o
----0----	----y_{1j}---------	--y_{1k}----	y_1^o
----1----	----y_{pj}--------	(y_{pk})---	y_p^o
----0----	----y_{mj}--------	--y_{mk}----	y_m^o
----0----	--$z_j(\lambda)$-------	-$z_k(\lambda)$---	z_o

where z_o is defined by (2-3-1) and $z_j(\lambda)$ by (2-3-4).

Remark 2.3.5. Notice that $\Lambda(x^o)$ of (2-3-7) may be rewritten simply using (2-3-4) as

$$\Lambda(x^o) = \{\lambda | \lambda \in E^\ell; z_j(\lambda) \geq 0; j \in \bar{J}_o\}. \tag{2-3-8}$$

After the simplex iteration we get x^1 and $\Lambda(x^1)$. Notice that $p \in J_o$ is the leaving column vector. We shall denote the new basic and nonbasic columns by:

$$J_1 = J_o \cup \{k\} - \{p\} \tag{2-3-9}$$

and $$\bar{J}_1 = \bar{J}_o \cup \{p\} - \{k\}. \tag{2-3-10}$$

By simplex method (or by Gaussian elimination technique) we get

$$z_p^1(\lambda) = \frac{-1}{y_{pk}} \cdot z_k(\lambda), \quad p \in \bar{J}_1 \tag{2-3-11}$$

and $$z_j^1(\lambda) = z_j(\lambda) - \frac{y_{pj}}{y_{pk}} \cdot z_k(\lambda), \quad j \in \bar{J}_1 - \{p\} \tag{2-3-12}$$

Let x^1 be the solution corresponding to the basis J_1. Then

$$\Lambda(x^1) = \{\lambda | \lambda \in E^\ell; z_j^1(\lambda) \geq 0; j \in \bar{J}_1\}. \tag{2-3-13}$$

Note $y_{pk} > 0$. Then (2-3-11) and (2-3-12) can be rewritten as they appear in (2-3-13):

$$z_k(\lambda) \lessgtr 0 \quad \text{for} \quad j = p \tag{2-3-14}$$

and $\qquad z_j(\lambda) - \dfrac{y_{pj}}{y_{pk}} \cdot z_k(\lambda) \gtreqless 0 \quad \text{for} \quad j \in \bar{J}_1 - \{p\}. \tag{2-3-15}$

Note, $k \in \bar{J}_o$. Then (2-3-8) and (2-3-14) imply that

$$H_k = \{\lambda | \lambda \in E^\ell; \ z_k(\lambda) = 0\} \tag{2-3-16}$$

is the separating hyperplane for $\Lambda(x^o)$ and $\Lambda(x^1)$ respectively, so that

$$\Lambda(x^o) \subset \{\lambda | \lambda \in E^\ell; \ z_k(\lambda) \geqq 0\} \tag{2-3-17}$$

and $\qquad \Lambda(x^1) \subset \{\lambda | \lambda \in E^\ell; \ z_k(\lambda) \leqq 0\}. \tag{2-3-18}$

Clearly the following is true:

$$\text{Int } \Lambda(x^o) \cap \Lambda(x^1) = \Lambda(x^o) \cap \text{Int } \Lambda(x^1) = \phi.$$

If $\lambda \in H_k$ then $z_k(\lambda) = 0$. For example, for
$\lambda^* \in \partial\Lambda(x^o)$ and $\lambda^* \in H_k$, $z_k(\lambda^*) = \gamma_k + \sum\limits_{i=1}^{\ell} \lambda_i^* \delta_k^i = 0$.
Then from (2-3-8), (2-3-14) and (2-3-15) we have

$$H_k \cap \Lambda(x^o) = \{\lambda | \lambda \in E^\ell; \ z_k(\lambda)=0; \ z_j(\lambda) \gtreqless 0; \ j \in \bar{J}_o - \{k\} \tag{2-3-19}$$

and $\quad H_k \cap \Lambda(x^1) = \{\lambda | \lambda \in E^\ell; \ z_k(\lambda)=0; \ z_j(\lambda) \gtreqless 0; \ j \in \bar{J}_o - \{k\} \tag{2-3-20}$

because $\bar{J}_1 = \bar{J}_o \cup \{p\} - \{k\}$ (see (2-3-10)).

Then from (2-3-19) and (2-3-20) we have

$$H_k \cap \Lambda(x^0) = H_k \cap \Lambda(x^1) = H_k \cap \Lambda(x^0) \cap \Lambda(x^1).$$

Thus

$$H_k \cap \Lambda(x^0) = H_k \cap \Lambda(x^1) \subset \Lambda(x^0) \cap \Lambda(x^1). \qquad (2\text{-}3\text{-}21)$$

On the other hand, since H_k is the separating hyperplane for $\Lambda(x^0)$ and $\Lambda(x^1)$ we have

$$\Lambda(x^0) \cap \Lambda(x^1) \subset H_k \cap \Lambda(x^1) = H_k \cap \Lambda(x^0). \qquad (2\text{-}3\text{-}22)$$

From (2-3-21) and (2-3-22) we get

$$H_k \cap \Lambda(x^0) = H_k \cap \Lambda(x^1) = \Lambda(x^0) \cap \Lambda(x^1).$$

The above discussion may be summarized by the following theorem:

Theorem 2.3.6. Let x^0 be a basic feasible solution associated with a basis J_0 and let $\Lambda(x^0)$ be constructed according to Theorem 2.3.2. For $\lambda* \in \partial\Lambda(x^0)$ there is at least one $k \in \bar{J}_0$ for which $z_k(\lambda*) = 0$. Define

$$H_k = \{\lambda | \lambda \in E^\ell; \; z_k(\lambda) = 0\}.$$

Introducing the kth column into the basis according to Theorem 2.3.4. two possibilities can be distinguished:

(1) all $y_{rk} \leqq 0$, $r \in R$ and Λ_k is constructed. Then $\Lambda(x^0) \cap \Lambda_k = H_k \cap \Lambda(x^0)$.

(2) let $y_{pk} > 0$ be the pivot element. Then a new basis
$J_1 = J_0 \cup \{k\} - \{p\}$ is constructed, associated with basic

feasible solution x^1. Also $\Lambda(x^1)$ is constructed. Then

(a) H_k separates $\Lambda(x^0)$ and $\Lambda(x^1)$ so that

$$\Lambda(x^0) \subset \{\lambda | \lambda \in E^\ell; \, z_k(\lambda) \geq 0\} \quad \text{and}$$

$$\Lambda(x^1) \subset \{\lambda | \lambda \in E^\ell; \, z_k(\lambda) \leq 0\}.$$

(b) $\Lambda(x^0) \cap \text{Int } \Lambda(x^1) = \text{Int } \Lambda(x^0) \cap \Lambda(x^1) = \phi.$

(c) $H_k \cap \Lambda(x^0) = H_k^\cdot \cap \Lambda(x^1) = \Lambda(x^0) \cap \Lambda(x^1).$

Proof.

For (1). According to Theorem 2.3.4.

$$\Lambda(x^0) \cap \text{Int } \Lambda_k = \phi.$$

Then,

$$\Lambda(x^0) \cap \Lambda_k =$$

$$= \Lambda(x^0) \cap [\text{Int } \Lambda_k \cup H_k] =$$

$$= [\Lambda(x^0) \cap \text{Int } \Lambda_k] \cup [\Lambda(x^0) \cap H_k] =$$

$$= \Lambda(x^0) \cap H_k.$$

For (2). The parts (a), (b), (c) have been shown by (2-3-17), (2-3-18), and (2-3-21) and (2-3-22) respectively. Q.E.D.

Remark 2.3.7. The following Figure 2.3.1. shows the relations of Theorem 2.3.6. in the two-dimensional case.

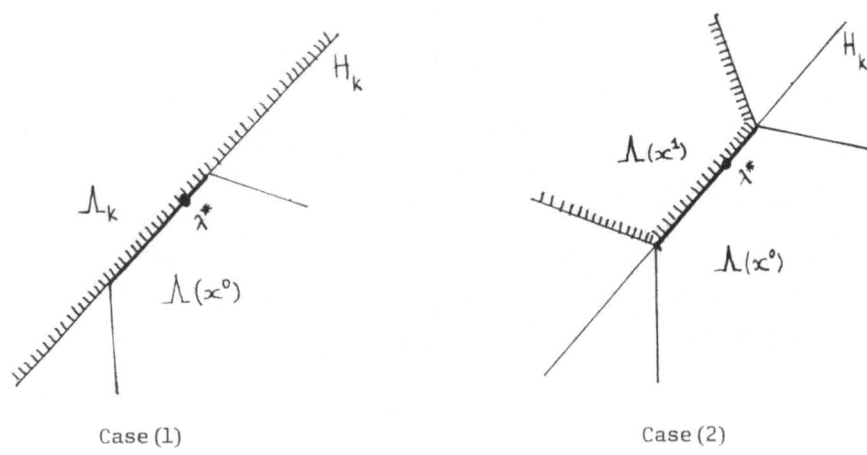

Case (1)   Case (2)

Figure 2.3.1.

In Figure 2.3.2. some three-dimensional representations of Theorem 2.3.6. are analyzed.

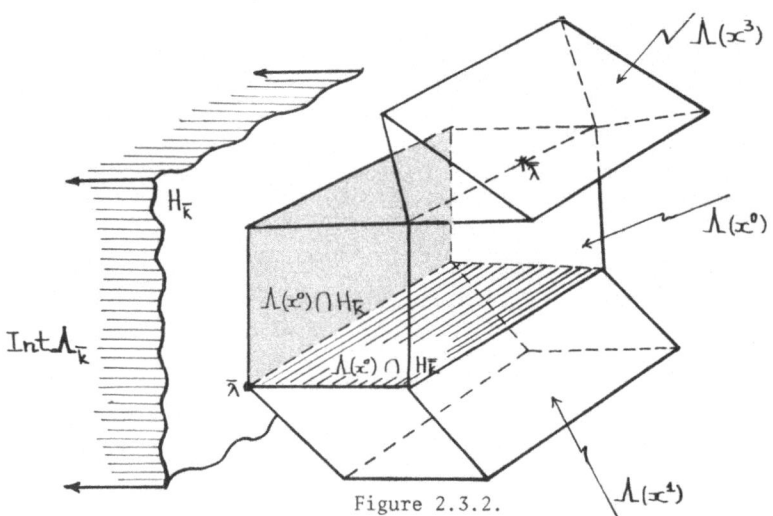

Figure 2.3.2.

In Figure 2.3.2. notice that for $\bar{\lambda} \in \partial\Lambda(x^o)$ by choosing $\bar{k}$ or $\bar{\bar{k}}$ both $\Lambda_{\bar{k}}$ and $\Lambda(x^1)$ are constructed. We see that $\Lambda(x^o) \cap \Lambda_{\bar{k}} = \Lambda(x^o) \cap H_{\bar{k}}$ and $\Lambda(x^o) \cap \Lambda(x^1) = \Lambda(x^o) \cap H_{\bar{k}}^a = \Lambda(x^1) \cap H_{\bar{k}}^a$. Notice also that at $\bar{\bar{\lambda}} \in \Lambda(x^o)$ the $\Lambda(x^3)$ cannot be constructed in the adjacent sense because only two hyperplanes pass through $\bar{\bar{\lambda}}$. However, $\Lambda(x^3)$ can be constructed from $\Lambda(x^o)$ if there would be another effectively bounding hyperplane through $\bar{\bar{\lambda}}$, as it is demonstrated in the numerical example. (Tableau 2-5-1-10)

__Definition 2.3.8.__ Referring to the theory of simplex method, for $j \in \bar{J}$, if $y_{rj} > 0$, we define

$$\theta_j = \underset{r}{\text{Min}}\left\{\frac{y_r^o}{y_{rj}} \; ; \; y_{rj}' > 0\right\}. \tag{2-3-23}$$

According to the simplex method theory, given $\lambda^* \in \Lambda$, the problem of maximization of P_{λ^*} (see (2-2-2))   has   two possible outcomes:

(i)   there is a maximal solution. In this case there exists a
      basis J such that all $z_j(\lambda^*) \geq 0$ for all $j \in \bar{J}$.

(ii) P_{λ^*} has an unbounded solution. Then there exists a basis J
      such that there is at least one column $k \in \bar{J}$ such that
      $y_{rk} \leq 0$ for all r and $z_k(\lambda^*) < 0$.

In the case (i) we could construct $\Lambda(J)$ such that $\lambda^* \in \Lambda(J)$ and J is the optimal basis for all P_λ, $\lambda \in \Lambda(J)$.

In the case (ii) there is an open halfspace Λ_k defined by $z_k(\lambda) < 0$ such that $\lambda^* \in \Lambda_k$ and if $\lambda \in \Lambda_k$ the P_λ is unbounded.

Thus, it is seen that each $\lambda \in \Lambda$ is covered by either a polyhedron $\Lambda(J)$ or by an open halfspace Λ_k. Since the number of bases is finite, they produce only a finite number of polyhedra $\Lambda(J)$ and open halfspaces Λ_k. This shows that Λ can be covered by a finite number of polyhedra and open halfspaces. The above discussion may be summarized by:

Theorem 2.3.9. (1) Maximization of P_λ for all $\lambda \in \Lambda$ produces a finite covering of Λ.

(2) There are no "holes" in the covering of Λ.

(3) The polyhedra corresponding to a bounded solution form a convex set.

(4) There is no "barrier" problem which would prevent us from reaching adjacent polyhedra.

Proof. Parts (1), (2) and (4) follow directly from the previous discussion. For the part (3):

The set $\tilde{\Lambda} = \{\lambda \mid \lambda \in E^\ell; \text{ a solution to } \underset{x \in X}{\text{Max }} P_\lambda \text{ is bounded}\}$

may be expressed by

$$\tilde{\Lambda} = \text{complement } \{\underset{k}{\cup} \Lambda_k\} =$$

$$= \underset{k}{\cap} \{\text{complement } \Lambda_k\}$$

which is a convex polyhedron. Also, $\Lambda \cap \tilde{\Lambda}$ is a convex polyhedron. Q.E.D.

Before discussing the algorithmic implications in section 2.4. we shall state another theorem which will help us to decide the nondominance of a given basic solution.

Definition 2.3.10. Let

$$\text{Int } \Lambda = \{\lambda \mid \lambda \in E^{\ell}, \; \lambda_i > 0; \; \sum_{i=1}^{\ell} \lambda_i \leq 1\} \qquad (2\text{-}3\text{-}24)$$

In view of the notation used in Theorem 2.3.6., let us state the following:

Theorem 2.3.11. If $H_k \cap \Lambda(x^o) \cap \text{Int}\Lambda \neq \phi$, the x^1, constructed by introducing the kth column into the basis, is a nondominated solution.

Proof. We assume from the statement of the Theorem that $x^o \in N$. Since $\gamma_k + \sum_{i=1}^{\ell} \lambda_i \delta_k^i \geq 0$ is a binding constraint for $\Lambda(x^o)$, then

$$H_k \cap \Lambda(x^o) \cap \text{Int}\Lambda \neq \phi \text{ implies that}$$

$$H_k \cap \Lambda(x^1) \cap \text{Int}\Lambda \neq \phi$$

according to Theorem 2.3.6. Q.E.D.

Remark 2.3.12. If $H_k \cap \Lambda(x^o) \cap \text{Int } \Lambda = \phi$ then x^1 may not be a nondominated solution. An example of Remark 2.3.12. is given in section 2.5.1.

2.4. Algorithmic Possibilities.

We have started with the fact that any nondominated extreme point $x^j \in N$ can be obtained by solving $\underset{x \in X}{\text{Max }} P_\lambda$ for some $\lambda \in \Lambda$.

To each $x^j \in N$ the corresponding polyhedron $\Lambda(x^j)$ therefore must have at least one point in common with Λ. (See also Theorem 2.3.11.)

Remark 2.4.1. We would like to be sure that a set of all nondominated

extreme points is a "connected set." If the set of such points is not

connected, then there are at least two different nondominated extreme

points which cannot be reached one from the other through a series of

adjacent nondominated extreme points.

Theorem 2.4.2. A set of nondominated extreme points is a "connected

set."

Proof. The proof follows directly from Theorem 2.3.9. and Theorem 2.3.11.

      Let x^V and $x^W \in N_{ex}$ Then each of the corresponding $\Lambda(x^V)$ and $\Lambda(x^W)$

has at least one point in common with Λ.

      Choose $\lambda^V \in \Lambda(x^V) \cap \Lambda$ and $\lambda^W \in \Lambda(x^W) \cap \Lambda$. Because of the convexity

of Λ we can write:

$$[\lambda^V, \lambda^W] \in \Lambda.$$

      We know also that the line segment $[\lambda^V, \lambda^W]$ is contained in
the union of all polyhedra which are associated with bounded solutions. Because of a finite covering of Λ, we can select a finite
sequence of distinct polyhedra $\{\Lambda(x^V), \Lambda(x^{V+1}), \ldots, \Lambda(x^{V+k})\}$, such
that $\Lambda(x^{V+k}) = \Lambda(x^W)$. Furthemore, $\Lambda(x^{V+i})$ and $\Lambda(x^{V+i+1})$ are connected in the sense of Theorem 2.3.6.   Q.E.D.

      Figure 2.4.1. provides graphical interpretation of Theorem
2.4.2.

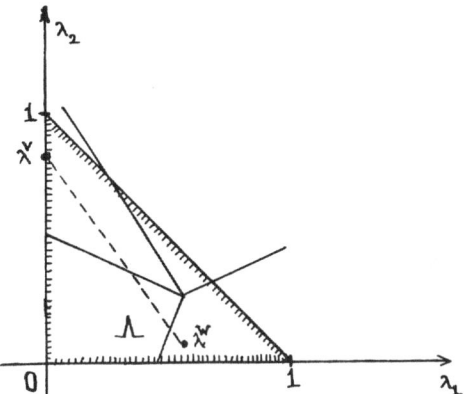

Figure 2.4.1.

Consider some $x^o \in N_{ex}$ and corresponding $\Lambda(x^o)$. Let the corresponding basis of x^o be J.

The goal is to construct all adjacent polyhedra to $\Lambda(x^o)$. By considering all $k \in \bar{J}$ (for which $z_k(\lambda) = 0$, for some $\lambda \in \Lambda(x^o)$) the corresponding columns may be introduced successively and all required polyhedra constructed.

We would like to limit our choice of $k \in \bar{J}$, however, only to such nonbasic columns which, being introduced, would not result in

(a)   a polyhedron already computed.

(b)   a polyhedron which has an empty intersection with Λ (since it corresponds to a dominated solution).

Graphically, we mean the following (see Figure 2.4.2.):

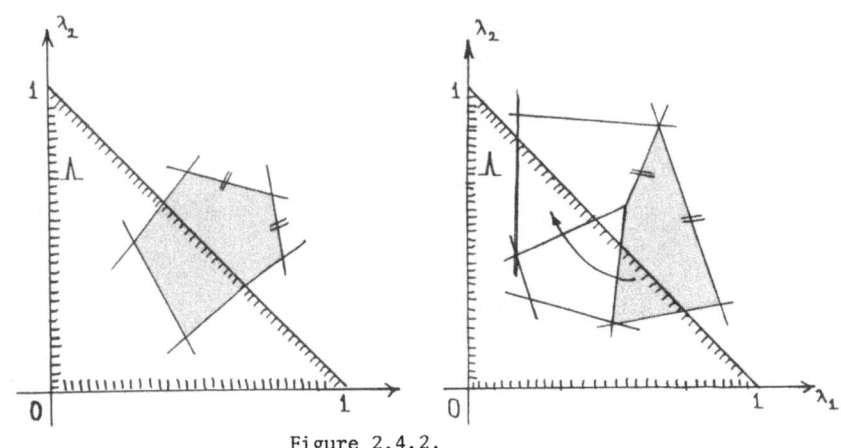

Figure 2.4.2.

Shaded polyhedra are $\Lambda(x^o)$. Crossed are the faces (and their corresponding nonbasic columns) which are not to be introduced in the basis. Notice
that in the second example we could actually move to a nondominated basis,
but this is also reachable without leaving Λ.

To determine whether a particular nonbasic column should go in the
basis we solve the following (see Theorem 2.3.11.):

$$\gamma_k + \sum_{i=1}^{\ell} \lambda_i \delta_k^i = 0 \quad k \in \bar{J}$$

$$\gamma_j + \sum_{i=1}^{\ell} \lambda_i \delta_k^i \geq 0 \quad j \in \bar{J}-k \qquad (2\text{-}4\text{-}1)$$

$$\sum_{i=1}^{\ell} \lambda_i < 1$$

If the system (2-4-1) has a feasible solution, then the introduction of the kth column will result in a polyhedron having a nonempty intersection with Λ.

Using the described multiparametric approach, we have basically two strategies available to generate a set of nondominated extreme points (more exactly, nondominated basic solutions). Both strategies assume an availability of some efficient method to generate adjacent extreme points.

Simple block diagrams for both strategies follow in Figures 2.4.4. and 2.4.5.

Remark 2.4.3. Notice that using the Strategy II we construct all adjacent polyhedra to $\Lambda(x^i)$ for which the intersection with IntΛ is nonempty. For that we do not need to find all the extreme points of $\Lambda(x^i)$. We consider only all faces of the highest dimension which, in turn, correspond to nonbasic columns of the associated simplex tableau. From these we select only those which have required properties (the face intersects with Int Λ, it does not lead to a basis already considered, etc.). The calculation of all extreme points might be redundant or insufficient in different situations. For example, let $\Lambda(x^i)$ be represented by two polyhedra in Figure 2.4.3.

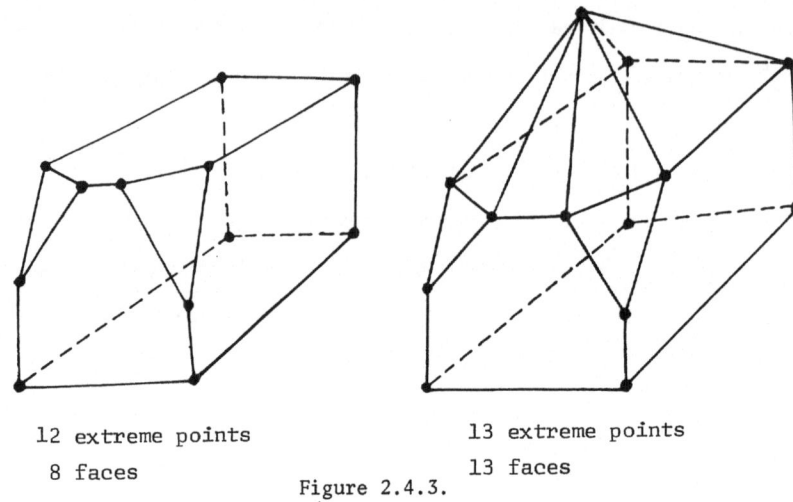

12 extreme points   13 extreme points

8 faces   13 faces

Figure 2.4.3.

From the previous discussion we may conclude that the available algorithmic possibilities would not lead to an efficient method, if finding all nondominated extreme points is our primary goal.

STRATEGY I

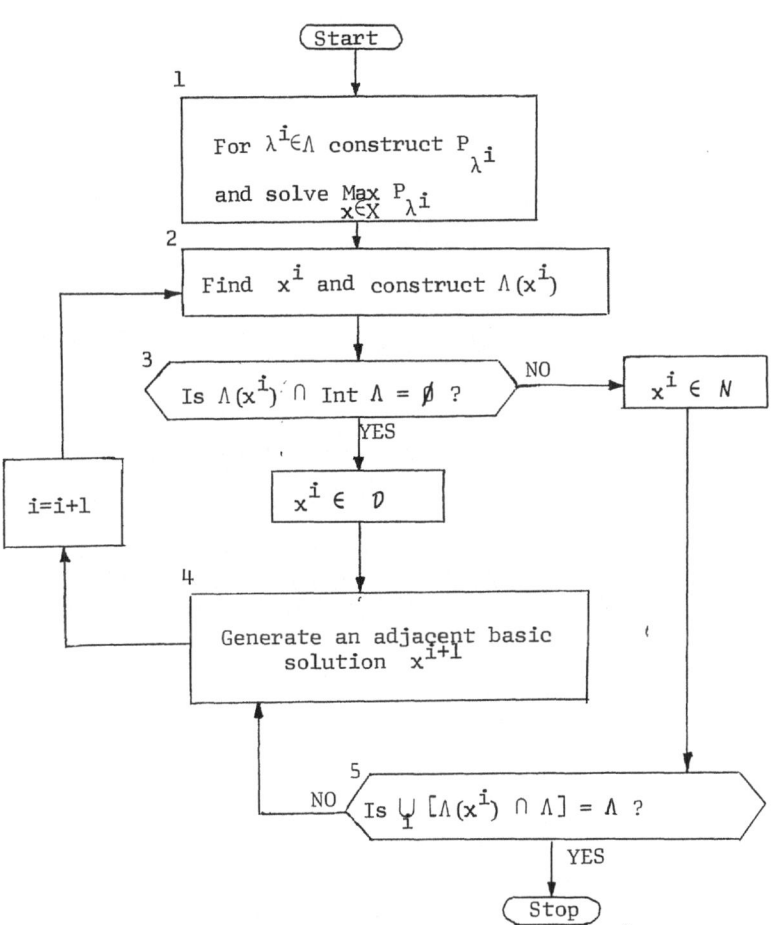

Figure 2.4.4.

STRATEGY I

(Comments)

1. It is convenient to start with $\lambda^i = 0$. Then $\lambda^{\ell+1} = 1$ and we solve $\underset{x\in X}{\text{Max}}\ c^{\ell+1}.x$. If the solution is unique, we start with $\Lambda(x^i) \cap \text{Int}\Lambda \neq \phi$, i.e., $x^i \in N$.

2. Construct $\Lambda(x^i)$ in the sense of Theorem 2.3.2. The construction of $\Lambda(x^i)$ might be simplified by following the approach in Remark 2.5.1.

3. To show that $\Lambda(x^i) \cap \text{Int}\Lambda = \phi \Rightarrow x^i \in D$ let us state the following:

    (a) $\Lambda(x^1) \cap \Lambda =, \phi$ implies clearly $x^1 \in D$.

    (b) $\Lambda(x^1) \cap \Lambda \neq \phi$ and $\Lambda(x^1) \cap \text{Int}\Lambda = \phi$ imply that there is some $\overline{\lambda} \in \partial\Lambda$ at which an alternate solution to x^1, say x^0, may be constructed such that: (See Theorem 2.4.2.)
    $$\overline{\lambda} \in \Lambda(x^0) \quad \text{and} \quad \Lambda(x^0) \cap \text{Int}\Lambda \neq \phi,$$
    i.e. $x^0 \in N$. Thus, for all $\lambda \in \Lambda(x^0)$, we have
    $$\lambda.cx^0 \geqq \lambda.cx^1$$
    and $\overline{\lambda}.cx^0 = \overline{\lambda}.cx^1 \quad \overline{\lambda} \in \Lambda(x^0) \cap \Lambda(x^1)$.
    Since $\Lambda(x^1) \cap \text{Int}\Lambda = \phi$ there is no $\lambda \in \Lambda$ such that $\lambda.cx^1 > \lambda.cx^0$. Notice $\text{Int}\ \Lambda(x^1) \cap \Lambda = \phi$. Thus, for all $\lambda \in \Lambda$,
    $$\lambda.cx^1 \leqq \lambda.cx^0.$$

    We may distinguish four possibilities:

    (i) $cx^1 \geq cx^0$

    (ii) $cx^1 \leq cx^0$

(iii) $cx^1 = cx^0$

(iv) $cx^1 \sim cx^0$

The possibility (i) must be excluded by definition of $x \in N$.

Possibility (iv): $cx^1 \sim cx^0$ implies there is at least one

$i = 1,\ldots,\ell$, with $c^i.x^1 > c^i.x^0$. Choose $\lambda \in \Lambda$ such that

all $\lambda_i > 0$ if $c^i.x^1 > c^i.x^0$ and $\lambda_i = 0$ otherwise. Then

$\lambda.cx^1 > \lambda.cx^0$, a contradiction. So, only $cx^1 \leq cx^0$ or

$cx^1 = cx^0$ are possible. If $cx^0 = cx^1$, then $\Lambda(x^0) \subseteq \Lambda(x^i)$

(degeneracy, see Remark 2.5.1.). If $cx^0 \geq cx^1$, then $x^1 \in \mathcal{D}$.

4.   We generate an adjacent basic solution to x^i, say x^{i+1}. We

must choose the method which would lead us only to an as yet

unexplored basis. Any of the two approaches discussed in

Section 3.3. would be applicable here.

5.   We must check whether Λ space has been completely decomposed by

$\Lambda(x^i)$ generated up to this point. Direct application of this

criterion would lead us to nontrivial computational difficul-

ties. However, because of "connectedness" and finiteness of

the decomposition (see Theorems 2.3.9. and 2.4.2.) whenever

we cannot find an unexplored adjacent basis to any x^i's gener-

ated up to this point, such that $\Lambda(x^i) \cap \mathrm{Int}\Lambda \neq \phi$, then the de-

composition is completed. In the view of the point (3) above,

the criterion may be

$$\bigcup_i [\Lambda(x^i) \cap \Lambda] = \mathrm{Int}\ \Lambda$$

for the linear case.

STRATEGY II

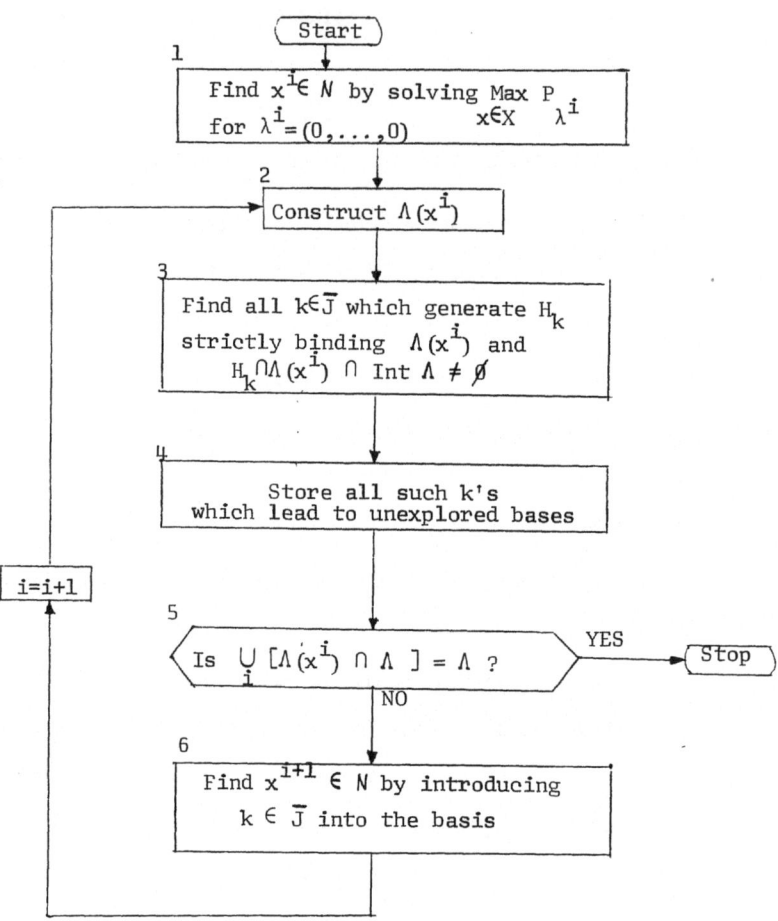

Figure 2.4.5.

STRATEGY II
(Comments)

The steps (1) and (2) are the same as for STRATEGY I.

3. In this step we use conclusions of Theorem 2.3.11. Now we have
    to explore all $k \in \bar{J}$ by solving the problem (2-4-1). Notice
    that simultaneously we determine whether the constraint corre-
    sponding to $k \in \bar{J}$ is effectively binding $\Lambda(x^i)$. Thus we make
    only the transformations leading to nondominated solutions.
    Since the set N_{ex} is connected, we can always make the tra-
    versal.

4. We always choose $k \in \bar{J}$ which would lead to an adjacent basis.
    If the only unexplored bases are not adjacent to x^i, we choose
    the "next closest", etc., in the sense of the distance between
    bases defined in section 3.3.

5. The same comments as for (5) of STRATEGY I apply here; i.e., if
    the storage in (4) is empty, we stop.

6. Obvious.

2. 5 Discussion of difficulties connected with the decomposition method.

In this section we shall discuss and give examples of some difficulties which might result in an inefficiency of the decomposition technique.

1. Degeneracy. The one-to-one correspondence between an extreme point
x^j and $\Lambda(x^j)$ can be destroyed. For example, in Figure 2.5.1.to x^o both
$\Lambda(x^{o'})$ and $\Lambda(x^{o''})$ may be computed. This might result in that although
all N-points have already been discovered, the Λ may not be fully decomposed.

2. Redundant constraints. Redundant constraints of $\Lambda(x^j)$ may cause
difficulty. Introduction of corresponding columns may lead to D-point
as well as to N-point. However, an effectively binding constraint of
$\Lambda(x^j)$, say k^{th}, for which $H_k \cap \Lambda(x^j) \cap Int\Lambda \neq \phi$ always leads to N-point
(see Theorem 2.3.11.). To use this fact we should have an efficient
subroutine to identify nonredundant constraints (see, for example,
(2-4-1)). Consult also Appendix Al on page 187.

3. Alternative solutions. The one-to-one correspondence between basis
x^j and $\Lambda(x^j)$ may be destroyed. That is, for all $\{x^j\}$ such that $\{x^j\}$
are optimal solutions to P_λ for all $\lambda \in \Lambda(x^j)$ the $\Lambda(x^j)$ are identical,
independent of x^j. This would imply that although Λ has been fully
decomposed, we still may not have all N-points.

Remark 2.5.1. The above difficulties are consistent with Theorem 2.1.5. If we assume $0 \notin H^\geq$ then

$$x^j \in N^> \iff H^> \cap G(x^j) \neq \phi$$

and $\qquad x^j \in N^\geq \iff H^\geq \cap G(x^j) \neq \phi.$

Then in degenerate cases there are two or more bases associated with the same extreme point x^j. Notice that $G(x^j)$ is uniquely defined, independent of different bases. This means that if $x^{j(1)}, \ldots, x^{j(r)}$ are the bases associated with x^j, then there is a possibility that $\Lambda(x^{j(k)}) \subset \Lambda(x^j)$, where $\Lambda(x^j)$ is a representation of $H^\geq \cap G(x^j)$ in Λ. See Figure 2.5.1. for graphical interpretation.

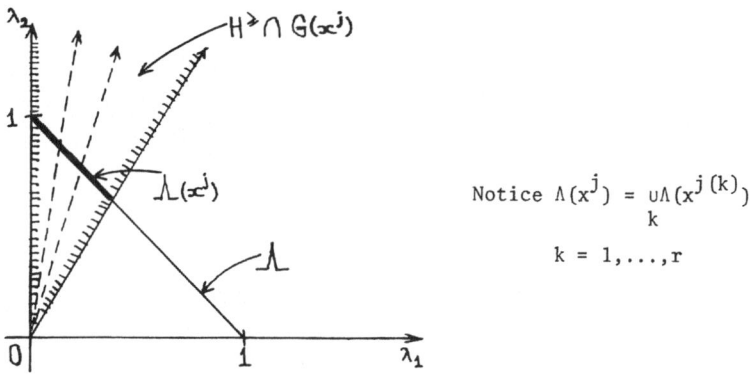

Notice $\Lambda(x^j) = \cup_k \Lambda(x^{j(k)})$

$k = 1, \ldots, r$

Figure 2.5.1.

Also, the problem of alternative solutions may be explained in terms of Theorem 2.1.5. We shall use Figure 2.5.2. to explain.

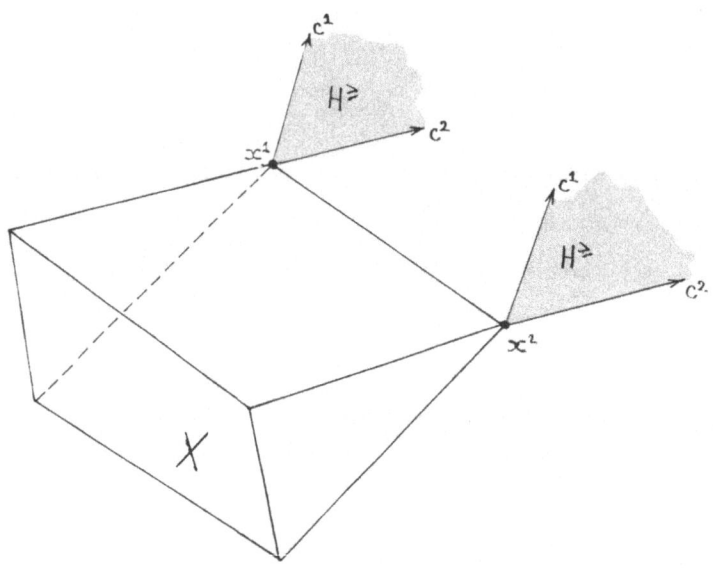

Figure 2.5.2.

Notice that though X is three-dimensional, $H^{\geq}$ may be two-dimensional. Then, although $G(x^1) \neq G(x^2)$, we may see that $G(x^1) \cap H^{\geq} = G(x^2) \cap H^{\geq}$ which implies that $\Lambda(x^1) = \Lambda(x^2) \neq \phi$. Also, $\lambda \in \Lambda(x^1) \cap \Lambda(x^2)$ implies that x^1, x^2 are two alternative solutions of P_λ.

2.5.1. <u>Some numerical examples of the difficulties.</u>

We will introduce a more complex numerical example for the demonstration. Let us consider the following problem:

v-Max cx, where cx = $(c^1.x, c^2.x, c^3.x)$, where

$$c^1.x = \quad x_2 + x_3 + 2x_4 + 3x_5 + x_6$$

$$c^2.x = x_1 \quad + x_3 - x_4 \quad - x_6 - x_7$$

$$c^3.x = x_1 + 2x_2 - x_3 + 3x_4 + 2x_5 \quad + x_7$$

subject to

$$x_1 + 2x_2 + x_3 + x_4 + 2x_5 + x_6 + 2x_7 \overset{\le}{=} 16$$

$$-2x_1 - x_2 \quad + x_4 + 2x_5 \quad + x_7 \overset{\le}{=} 16$$

$$- x_1 \quad + x_3 \quad + 2x_5 \quad - 2x_7 \overset{\le}{=} 16$$

$$x_2 + 2x_3 - x_4 + x_5 - 2x_6 - x_7 \overset{\le}{=} 16$$

$$x_i \overset{\ge}{=} 0, \ i = 1,\ldots,7$$

Let

$$P_\lambda = x_1 + 2x_2 - x_3 + 3x_4 + 2x_5 + x_7$$

$$+ \lambda_1(-x_1 - x_2 + 2x_3 - x_4 + x_5 + x_6 - x_7)$$

$$+ \lambda_2(-2x_2 + 2x_3 - 4x_4 - 2x_5 - x_6 - 2x_7)$$

The objective function coefficients are given by the following table:

j	1	2	3	4	5	6	7
c_j^3	1	2	-1	3	2	0	1
c_j^1	-1	-1	2	-1	1	1	-1
c_j^2	0	-2	2	-4	-2	-1	-2

Let us start with $\lambda^0 = 0$, i.e.,

$$P_{\lambda 0} = x_1 + 2x_2 - x_3 + 3x_4 + 2x_5 + x_7$$

is to be maximized. The initial tableau is:

	x_1	x_2	x_3	x_4	x_5	x_6	x_7	y_1	y_2	y_3	y_4		
y_1	1	2	1	①	2	1	2	1	0	0	0	16	
y_2	-2	-1	0	(1)	2	0	1	0	1	0	0	16	
y_3	-1	0	1	0	2	0	-2	0	0	1	0	16	
y_4	0	1	2	-1	1	-2	-1	0	0	0	1	16	(2-5-1-1)
	-1	-2	1	-3	-2	0	-1	0	0	0	0	0	
	1	1	-2	1	-1	-1	1	0	0	0	0	0	
	0	2	-2	4	2	1	2	0	0	0	0	0	

Introducing the fourth column we obtain the following solution x^0:

x_4	1	2	1	1	2	1	2	1	0	0	0	16
y_2	-3	-3	-1	0	0	-1	-1	-1	1	0	0	0
y_3	-1	0	1	0	2	0	-2	0	0	1	0	16
y_4	1	3	3	0	3	-1	1	1	0	0	1	32
	2	4	4	0	4	3	5	3	0	0	0	48
	0	-1	-3	0	-3	-2	-1	-1	0	0	0	-16
	-4	-6	-6	0	-6	-3	-6	-4	0	0	0	-64

$$(2\text{-}5\text{-}1\text{-}2)$$

$$x^o = (0,0,0,16,0,0,0,0,)$$

Next we calculate the corresponding $\Lambda(x^o)$:

$$\Lambda(x^o) = \begin{cases} 4\lambda_2 \lessgtr 2 & 1. \quad \leftarrow \\ \lambda_1 + 6\lambda_2 \lessgtr 4 & 2. \\ 3\lambda_1 + 6\lambda_2 \lessgtr 4 & 3. \\ 3\lambda_1 + 6\lambda_2 \lessgtr 4 & 5. \\ 2\lambda_1 + 3\lambda_2 \lessgtr 3 & 6. \\ \lambda_1 + 6\lambda_2 \lessgtr 5 & 7. \\ \lambda_1 + 4\lambda_2 \lessgtr 3 & 8. \end{cases}$$

Notice that x^o is a degenerate solution. Let us explore the situation when the cell (2,4) of Tableau (2-5-1-1) is the pivot element. We get:

y_1	③	3	1	0	0	1	1	1	-1	0	0	0
x_4	-2	-1	0	1	2	0	1	0	1	0	0	16
y_3	-1	0	1	0	2	0	-2	0	0	1	0	16
y_4	-2	0	2	0	3	-2	0	0	1	0	1	32
	-7	-5	1	0	4	0	2	0	3	0	0	48
	3	2	-2	0	-3	-1	0	0	-1	0	0	-16
	8	6	-2	0	-6	1	-2	0	-4	0	0	-64

$$(2\text{-}5\text{-}1\text{-}3)$$

Remark 2.5.1.1. Notice that Tableau (2-5-1-3) represents degenerate solution. Because λ_1 and λ_2 are considered zero, the first criterial row indicates that we have to introduce the first column before the corresponding polyhedron can be calculated. We get the following:

x_1	1	1	$\frac{1}{3}$	0	0	$\frac{1}{3}$	$\frac{1}{3}$	$\frac{1}{3}$	$-\frac{1}{3}$	0	0	0
x_4	0	1	$\frac{2}{3}$	1	2	$\frac{2}{3}$	$\frac{5}{3}$	$\frac{2}{3}$	$\frac{1}{3}$	0	0	16
y_3	0	1	$\frac{4}{3}$	0	2	$\frac{1}{3}$	$-\frac{5}{3}$	$\frac{1}{3}$	$-\frac{1}{3}$	1	0	16
y_4	0	2	$\frac{8}{3}$	0	3	$-\frac{4}{3}$	$\frac{2}{3}$	$\frac{2}{3}$	$\frac{1}{3}$	0	1	32
	0	2	$\frac{10}{3}$	0	4	$\frac{7}{3}$	$\frac{13}{3}$	$\frac{7}{3}$	$\frac{2}{3}$	0	0	48
	0	-1	-3	0	-3	-2	-1	-1	0	0	0	-16
	0	2	$-\frac{14}{3}$	0	-6	$\frac{5}{3}$	$-\frac{14}{3}$	$\frac{8}{3}$	$\frac{4}{3}$	0	0	-64

$$(2\text{-}5\text{-}1\text{-}4)$$

The corresponding set of constraints is:

$$\Lambda(x^o) = \begin{cases} \lambda_1 - 2\lambda_2 \leqq 2 \\ 3\lambda_1 + \frac{14}{3}\lambda_2 \leqq \frac{10}{3} \\ 3\lambda_1 + 6\lambda_2 \leqq 4 \quad \leftarrow \\ 2\lambda_1 + \frac{5}{3}\lambda_2 \leqq \frac{7}{3} \\ \lambda_1 + \frac{14}{3}\lambda_2 \leqq \frac{13}{3} \\ \lambda_1 + \frac{8}{3}\lambda_2 \leqq \frac{7}{3} \\ \frac{4}{3}\lambda_2 \leqq \frac{2}{3} \quad \leftarrow \end{cases}$$

Notice that in both sets of constraints $\Lambda(x^o)$ is determined by

$$3\lambda_1 + 6\lambda_2 \leqq 4$$
$$\lambda_2 \leqq \frac{1}{2}$$

which are the only nonredundant constraints. Note, $\overline{\Lambda}(x^o) = \Lambda(x^o) \cap \Lambda$ is given by

$$\overline{\Lambda}(x^o) = \begin{cases} 3\lambda_1 + 6\lambda_2 \leqq 4 & 3. \\ 3\lambda_1 + 6\lambda_2 \leqq 4 & 5. \\ \lambda_2 \leqq \frac{1}{2} & 1. \\ \lambda_1 + \lambda_2 \leqq 1 \\ \lambda_1, \lambda_2 \geqq 0 \end{cases}$$

This polyhedron $\bar{\Lambda}(x^o)$ is graphically represented in Figure 2.5.1.1. Looking at original Tableau (2-5-1-2) we see that the first and the third or fifth columns may be introduced. Before we do this, let us make the following remark.

Remark 2.5.1.2. The problem of redundant constraints is a very important one. Returning to Tableau (2-5-1-2), let the second column be introduced into the basis. Notice the 2nd column is corresponding to the redundant constraint $\lambda_1 + 6\lambda_2 \leqq 4$ of $\Lambda(x^o)$. We get tableau (2-5-1-5):

x_2	$\frac{1}{2}$	1	$\frac{1}{2}$	$\frac{1}{2}$	1	$\frac{1}{2}$	1	$\frac{1}{2}$	0	0	0	8
y_2	$-\frac{3}{2}$	0	$\frac{1}{2}$	$\frac{3}{2}$	3	$\frac{1}{2}$	2	$\frac{1}{2}$	1	0	0	24
y_3	-1	0	1	0	2	0	-2	0	0	1	0	16
y_4	$-\frac{1}{2}$	0	$\frac{3}{2}$	$-\frac{3}{2}$	0	$-\frac{5}{2}$	-2	$-\frac{1}{2}$	0	0	1	8
	0	0	2	-2	0	1	1	1	0	0	0	16
	$\frac{1}{2}$	0	$-\frac{5}{2}$	$\frac{1}{2}$	-2	$-\frac{3}{2}$	0	$-\frac{1}{2}$	0	0	0	-8
	-1	0	-3	3	0	0	0	-1	0	0	0	-16

(2-5-1-5)

$$\tilde{x} = (0,8,0,0,0,0,0)$$

Actually $\tilde{x}$ is a dominated extreme point and the corresponding $\Lambda(\tilde{x})$ is as follows:

$$\Lambda(\tilde{x}) = \begin{cases} \frac{1}{2}\lambda_1 - \lambda_2 \gtreqless 0 & \quad 1. \\[2mm] \frac{5}{2}\lambda_1 + 3\lambda_2 \lesseqgtr 2 & \quad 2. \\[2mm] \frac{1}{2}\lambda_1 + 3\lambda_2 \gtreqless 2 & \quad 3. \\[2mm] 2\lambda_1 \lesseqgtr 0 & \quad 4. \\[2mm] \frac{3}{2}\lambda_1 \lesseqgtr 1 & \quad 5. \\[2mm] \frac{1}{2}\lambda_1 + \lambda_2 \lesseqgtr 1 & \quad 6. \end{cases}$$

Notice that $\Lambda(\tilde{x})$ is an empty set as could be seen in Figure 2.5.1.2.

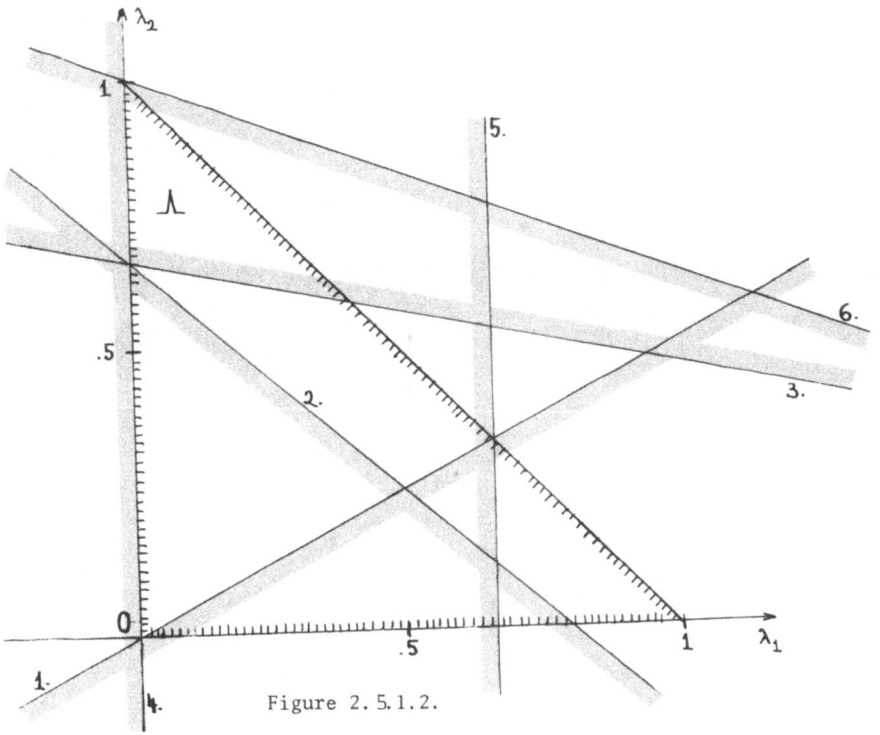

Figure 2.5.1.2.

Therefore, no linear combination of $c^1 \cdot x$, $c^2 \cdot x$ and $c^3 \cdot x$ can reach its maximum at $\tilde{x}$.

Let us go back to Tableau (2-5-1-2) and introduce the first column. We get:

x_1	1	2	1	1	2	1	2	1	0	0	0	16
y_2	0	3	2	3	⑥	2	5	2	1	0	0	48
y_3	0	2	2	1	4	1	0	1	0	1	0	32
y_4	0	1	②	-1	1	-2	-1	0	0	0	1	16
	0	0	2	-2	0	1	1	1	0	0	0	16
	0	-1	-3	0	-3	-2	-1	-1	0	0	0	-16
	0	2	-2	4	2	1	2	0	0	0	0	0

$$(2\text{-}5\text{-}1\text{-}6)$$

$$x^1 = (16,0,0,0,0,0,0)$$

Construct $\overline{\Lambda}(x^1) = \Lambda(x^1) \cap \Lambda$ and after discarding the redundant constraints we get:

$$\overline{\Lambda}(x^1) = \begin{cases} 3\lambda_1 + 2\lambda_2 \leq 2 & 3. \\ 4\lambda_2 \geq 2 & 4. \\ -3\lambda_1 + 2\lambda_2 \geq 0 & 5. \\ \lambda_1 + \lambda_2 \leq 1 & \\ \lambda_1, \lambda_2 \geq 0 & \end{cases}$$

See Figure 2.5.1.1.

Notice at $\lambda_1 = \frac{1}{3}$, $\lambda_2 = \frac{1}{2}$ the constraints corresponding to the third,
fourth and fifth columns are active and may be introduced into the basis
according to Theorem 2.3.4. However, only the third and the fifth are
eligible since the fourth would lead us back to x^0. Choose the third
column first:

x_1	1	$\frac{3}{2}$	0	$\left(\frac{3}{2}\right)$	$\frac{3}{2}$	2	$\frac{5}{2}$	1	0	0	$-\frac{1}{2}$	8
y_2	0	2	0	4	5	4	6	2	1	0	-1	32
y_3	0	1	0	2	$\left(3\right)$	3	1	1	0	1	-1	16
x_3	0	$\frac{1}{2}$	1	$-\frac{1}{2}$	$\frac{1}{2}$	-1	$-\frac{1}{2}$	0	0	0	$\frac{1}{2}$	8
	0	-1	0	-1	-1	3	2	1	0	0	-1	0
	0	$\frac{1}{2}$	0	$-\frac{3}{2}$	$-\frac{3}{2}$	-5	$-\frac{5}{2}$	-1	0	0	$\frac{3}{2}$	8
	0	3	0	3	3	-1	1	0	0	0	1	16

$$(2\text{-}5\text{-}1\text{-}7)$$

$$x^2 = (8,0,8,0,0,0,0)$$

$$\text{construct } \bar{\Lambda}(x^2) = \begin{cases} -\frac{3}{2}\lambda_1 + 3\lambda_2 \geqq 1 & 4. \\ -\frac{3}{2}\lambda_1 + 3\lambda_2 \geqq 1 & 5. \\ \frac{3}{2}\lambda_1 + \lambda_2 \geqq 1 & 11. \\ \lambda_1 + \lambda_2 \leqq 1 \\ \lambda_1, \lambda_2 \geqq 0 \end{cases}$$

See Figure 2.5.1.1.

Remark 2.5.1.3. Tableau (2-5-1-7) may be used to demonstrate the 3rd difficulty discussed in section 2.5 . Notice that for the fourth and fifth columns we have obtained identical constraints. Introducing any of these two we get identical polyhedra, say $\Lambda(x^3)$ and $\Lambda(x^4)$. However, the associated extreme points will be different, i.e., $x^3 \neq x^4$. This is in agreement with the theory, since no two polyhedra may have a common interior point, unless they are equal.

Let. us demonstrate the Remark 2.5.1.3. Introduce the fourth and fifth columns subsequently to move from x^2 to x^3 and from x^2 to x^4:

x_4	$\frac{2}{3}$	1	0	1	1	$\frac{4}{3}$	$\frac{5}{3}$	$\frac{2}{3}$	0	0	$-\frac{1}{3}$	$\frac{16}{3}$
y_2	$-\frac{8}{3}$	-2	0	0	1	$-\frac{4}{3}$	$-\frac{2}{3}$	$-\frac{2}{3}$	1	0	$\frac{1}{3}$	$\frac{32}{3}$
y_3	$-\frac{4}{3}$	-1	0	0	1	$\frac{1}{3}$	$-\frac{7}{3}$	$-\frac{1}{3}$	0	1	$-\frac{1}{3}$	$\frac{16}{3}$
x_3	$\frac{1}{3}$	1	1	0	1	$-\frac{1}{3}$	$\frac{1}{3}$	$\frac{1}{3}$	0	0	$\frac{1}{3}$	$\frac{32}{3}$
	$\frac{2}{3}$	0	0	0	0	$\frac{13}{3}$	$\frac{11}{3}$	$\frac{5}{3}$	0	0	$-\frac{4}{3}$	$\frac{16}{3}$
	1	2	0	0	0	-3	0	0	0	0	1	16
	-2	0	0	0	0	-5	-4	-2	0	0	2	0

$$(2\text{-}5\text{-}1\text{-}8)$$

$$x^3 = (0,0,\tfrac{32}{3},\tfrac{16}{3},0,0,0)$$

construct $\overline{\Lambda}(x^3) =$
$$\begin{cases} -\lambda_1 + 2\lambda_2 \leqq \frac{2}{3} & 1. \\ 3\lambda_1 + 5\lambda_2 \leqq \frac{13}{3} & 6. \\ \lambda_1 + 2\lambda_2 \geqq \frac{4}{3} & 11. \\ \lambda_1 + \lambda_2 \leqq 1 & \\ \lambda_1, \lambda_2 \geqq 0 & \end{cases}$$

See Figure 2.5.1.1.

Notice in Figure 2.5.1.1. that we would never introduce the sixth column since the associated constraint (better, the face) does not have a point in common with Λ.

Introducing the fifth column in Tableau (2-5-1-8):

x_5	$\frac{2}{3}$	1	0	1	1	$\frac{4}{3}$	$\frac{5}{3}$	$\frac{2}{3}$	0	0	$-\frac{1}{3}$	$\frac{16}{3}$
y_2	$-\frac{10}{3}$	-3	0	-1	0	$-\frac{8}{3}$	$-\frac{7}{3}$	$-\frac{4}{3}$	1	0	$\frac{2}{3}$	$\frac{16}{3}$
y_3	-2	-2	0	-1	0	-1	-4	-1	0	1	0	0
x_3	$-\frac{1}{3}$	0	1	-1	0	$-\frac{5}{3}$	$-\frac{4}{3}$	$-\frac{1}{3}$	0	0	$\frac{2}{3}$	$\frac{16}{3}$
	$\frac{2}{3}$	0	0	0	0	$\frac{13}{3}$	$\frac{11}{3}$	$\frac{5}{3}$	0	0	$-\frac{4}{3}$	$\frac{16}{3}$
	1	2	0	0	0	-3	0	0	0	0	1	16
	-2	0	0	0	0,	-5	-4	-2	0	0	2	0

$$(2\text{-}5\text{-}1\text{-}9)$$

$$x^4 = (0,0,\tfrac{16}{3},0,\tfrac{16}{3},0,0)$$

$$\text{construct } \bar{\Lambda}(x^4) = \begin{cases} -\lambda_1 + 2\lambda_2 \overset{\leq}{=} \dfrac{2}{3} & 1. \\[2mm] 3\lambda_1 + 5\lambda_2 \overset{\leq}{=} \dfrac{13}{3} & 6. \\[2mm] \lambda_1 + 2\lambda_2 \overset{\geq}{=} \dfrac{4}{3} & 11. \\[2mm] \lambda_1 + \lambda_2 \overset{\leq}{=} 1 \\[2mm] \lambda_1, \lambda_2 \overset{\geq}{=} 0 \end{cases}$$

See Figure 2.5.1.1.

Notice $\Lambda(x^3) = \Lambda(x^4)$, $x^3 \neq x^4$. This indicates that x^3, x^4 are alternative solutions for P_λ, $\lambda \in \Lambda(x^3) = \Lambda(x^4)$.

We may use Tableau (2-5-1-7) also to demonstrate Remark 2.3.12 of section 2.3.

We construct $\Lambda(x^2)$ as:

$$\Lambda(x^2) \equiv \begin{cases} \frac{1}{2}\lambda_1 + 3\lambda_2 \geq 1 & \text{2.} \\[1em] -\frac{3}{2}\lambda_1 + 3\lambda_2 \geq 1 & \text{4.} \\[1em] -\frac{3}{2}\lambda_1 + 3\lambda_2 \geq 1 & \text{5.} \\[1em] 5\lambda_1 + \lambda_2 \leq 3 & \text{6.} \\[1em] \frac{5}{2}\lambda_1 - \lambda_2 \leq 2 & \text{7.} \\[1em] \lambda_2 \leq 1 & \text{8.} \\[1em] \frac{3}{2}\lambda_1 + \lambda_2 \geq 1 & \text{11.} \end{cases}$$

Graphically the $\Lambda(x^2)$ is represented in Figure 2.5.1.3.

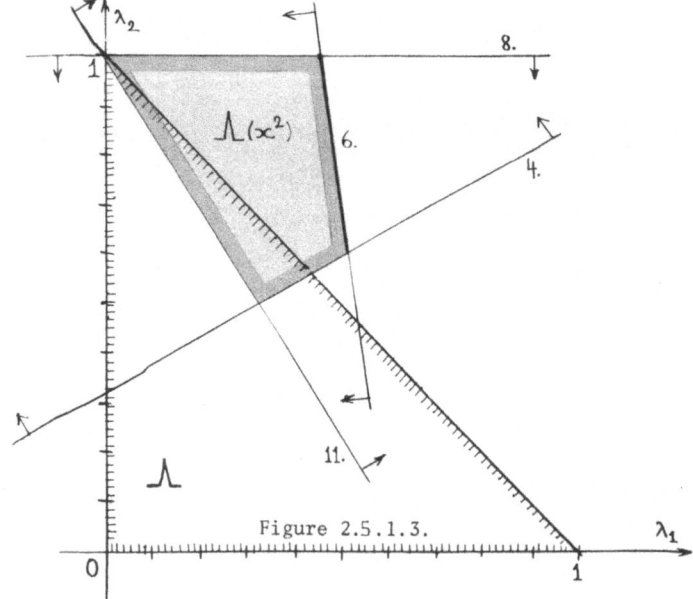

Figure 2.5.1.3.

Notice that the face corresponding to the sixth column (i.e., constraint 6.) of $\Lambda(x^2)$ satisfies

$$H_6 \cap \Lambda(x^2) \cap \overline{Int}\Lambda = \phi.$$

Using the sixth column as our pivot column we get:

x_6	$\frac{1}{2}$	$\frac{3}{4}$	0	$\frac{3}{4}$	$\frac{3}{4}$	1	$\frac{5}{4}$	$\frac{1}{2}$	0	0	$-\frac{1}{4}$	4
y_2	-2	2	0	1	2	0	1	0	1	0	0	16
y_3	$-\frac{3}{2}$	$-\frac{5}{4}$	0	$-\frac{1}{4}$	$\frac{3}{4}$	0	$\frac{11}{4}$	$-\frac{1}{2}$	0	1	$-\frac{1}{4}$	4
x_3	$\frac{1}{2}$	$\frac{5}{4}$	1	$\frac{1}{4}$	$\frac{5}{4}$	0	$\frac{3}{4}$	$\frac{1}{2}$	0	0	$\frac{1}{4}$	12
	$-\frac{3}{2}$	$-\frac{13}{4}$	0	$-\frac{13}{4}$	$\frac{13}{4}$	0	$\frac{7}{4}$	$-\frac{1}{2}$	0	0	$-\frac{1}{4}$	-12
	1	1	0	-1	-1	0	2	1	0	0	0	16
	-1	$\frac{1}{2}$	0	$\frac{1}{2}$	$\frac{1}{2}$	0	$\frac{1}{2}$	0	0	0	$\frac{1}{2}$	8

$$x^8 \in \mathcal{D}.$$

Let us return to the Tableau (2-5-1-6) and consider $\overline{\Lambda}(x^1)$ again. The constraint $-3\lambda_1 + 2\lambda_2 \overset{\geq}{=} 0$ has only one single point in common with $\overline{\Lambda}(x^1)$, specifically $\lambda_1 = 1/3$, $\lambda_2 = 1/2$. Then, of course, the adjacent polyhedron resulting from introducing the fifth column, say $\Lambda(x^5)$, will have only this one point in common with $\Lambda(x^1)$:

x_1	1	1	$\frac{1}{3}$	0	0	$\frac{1}{3}$	$\frac{1}{3}$	$\frac{1}{3}$	$-\frac{1}{3}$	0	0	0
x_5	0	$\frac{1}{2}$	$\frac{1}{3}$	$\frac{1}{2}$	1	$\frac{1}{3}$	$\frac{5}{6}$	$\frac{1}{3}$	$\frac{1}{6}$	0	0	8
y_3	0	0	$\frac{2}{3}$	-1	0	$-\frac{1}{3}$	$-\frac{10}{3}$	$-\frac{1}{3}$	$-\frac{2}{3}$	1	0	0
y_4	0	$\frac{1}{2}$	$\frac{5}{3}$	$-\frac{3}{2}$	0	$-\frac{7}{3}$	$-\frac{11}{6}$	$-\frac{1}{3}$	$-\frac{1}{6}$	0	1	8
	0	0	2	-2	0	1	1	1	0	0	0	16
	0	$\frac{1}{2}$	-2	$\frac{3}{2}$	0	-1	$\frac{3}{2}$	0	$\frac{1}{2}$	0	0	8
	0	1	$-\frac{8}{3}$	3	0	$\frac{1}{3}$	$\frac{1}{3}$	$-\frac{2}{3}$	$-\frac{1}{3}$	0	0	-16

(2-5-1-10)

$$x^5 = (0,0,0,0,8,0,0)$$

$$\text{construct } \bar{\Lambda}(x^5) = \begin{cases} 2\lambda_1 + \frac{8}{3}\lambda_2 \overset{\leq}{=} 2 & \quad 3. \\[4pt] \frac{3}{2}\lambda_1 + 3\lambda_2 \overset{\geq}{=} 2 & \quad 4. \\[4pt] \frac{1}{2}\lambda_1 - \frac{1}{3}\lambda_2 \overset{\geq}{=} 0 & \quad 9. \\[4pt] \lambda_1 + \lambda_2 \overset{\leq}{=} 1 \\[4pt] \lambda_1, \lambda_2 \overset{\geq}{=} 0 \end{cases}$$

See Figure 2.5.1.1.

Introducing the ninth column in (2-5-1-10) would lead us back to x^1. Similarly introducing the fourth column would lead to x^o. So, only the third column might be eligible for an introduction. (We would ultimately move through the series of degenerate iterations to x^3 or x^4.)

Remark 2.5.1.4. Notice that the point $\lambda_1 = \frac{1}{3}$, $\lambda_2 = \frac{1}{2}$ belongs to the boundary of all polyhedra in Figure 2.5.1.1. The space Λ is completely covered with no "holes" and still not all nondominated extreme points

may be generated as it is demonstrated by x^5 and $\overline{\Lambda}(x^5) = (\frac{1}{3},\frac{1}{2})$.

Let us review all the calculated extreme points. From x^o by

introducing the fifth column we would move directly to x^5, so this

transformation does not have to be performed. Also, from all the remain-

ing extreme points we cannot move to any yet unexplored nondominated

extreme point. The algorithm would end here.

Remark 2.5.1.5. Because of degeneracies we may have two or more different

polyhedra corresponding to the same extreme point (but two or more dif-

ferent bases). However, this can always be resolved through the series

of degenerate iterations. Consider the Tableau (2-5-1-7), introduce the

fifth column but this time choose 3 to be the pivot element. We get:

x_1	1	1	0	$\frac{1}{2}$	0	$\frac{1}{2}$	2	$\frac{1}{2}$	0	$-\frac{1}{2}$	0	0
y_2	0	$\frac{1}{3}$	0	$\frac{2}{3}$	0	-1	$\frac{13}{3}$	$\frac{1}{3}$	1	$-\frac{5}{3}$	$\frac{2}{3}$	$\frac{16}{3}$
x_5	0	$\frac{1}{3}$	0	$\frac{2}{3}$	1	1	$\frac{1}{3}$	$\frac{1}{3}$	0	$\frac{1}{3}$	$-\frac{1}{3}$	$\frac{16}{3}$
x_3	0	$\frac{1}{3}$	1	$-\frac{5}{6}$	0	$-\frac{3}{2}$	$-\frac{2}{3}$	$-\frac{1}{6}$	0	$-\frac{1}{6}$	$\frac{2}{3}$	$\frac{16}{3}$
	0	$-\frac{2}{3}$	0	$-\frac{1}{3}$	0	4	$\frac{7}{3}$	$\frac{4}{3}$	0	$\frac{1}{3}$	$-\frac{4}{3}$	$\frac{16}{3}$
	0	1	0	$-\frac{1}{2}$	0	$-\frac{7}{2}$	-2	$-\frac{1}{2}$	0	$\frac{1}{2}$	1	16
	0	2	0	1	0	-4	0	-1	0	-1	2	0

(2-5-1-11)

$$\bar{x}^4 = (0,0,\frac{16}{3},0,\frac{16}{3},0,0)$$

which is the same as x^4.

Construct $\overline{\Lambda}(x^4)$ = $\begin{cases} -\frac{1}{2}\lambda_1 + \lambda_2 \geq \frac{1}{3} & 4. \\ \frac{7}{2}\lambda_1 + 4\lambda_2 \leq 4 & 6. \\ -\frac{1}{2}\lambda_1 + \lambda_2 \leq \frac{1}{3} & 10. \\ \lambda_1 + 2\lambda_2 \geq \frac{4}{3} & 11. \\ \lambda_1 + \lambda_2 \leq 1 & \\ \lambda_1, \lambda_2 \geq 0 & \end{cases}$

See Figure 2.5.1.1.

Notice that we can move from $\bar{x}^4$ to x^4 by a series of degenerate iterations.

Considering only the calculated x^0, x^1, x^2, x^3, x^4 and x^5 we can see that

$$\overline{\Lambda}(x^0) \cup \overline{\Lambda}(x^1) \cup \overline{\Lambda}(x^2) \cup \overline{\Lambda}(x^3) \cup \overline{\Lambda}(x^4) \cup \overline{\Lambda}(x^5) = \Lambda.$$

Let us summarize the results of the calculated example. In Figure 2.5.1.1. the decomposition of Λ is represented. Notice mainly the $\overline{\Lambda}(x^5)$, $\overline{\Lambda}(\bar{x}^4)$. We list all N-points together with the values of the objective functions.

	x^0	x^1	x^2	x^3	x^4	x^5
$c^1.x$	32	0	8	21.33	21.33	24
$c^2.x$	-16	16	16	5.33	5.33	0
$c^3.x$	48	16	0	5.33	5.33	16

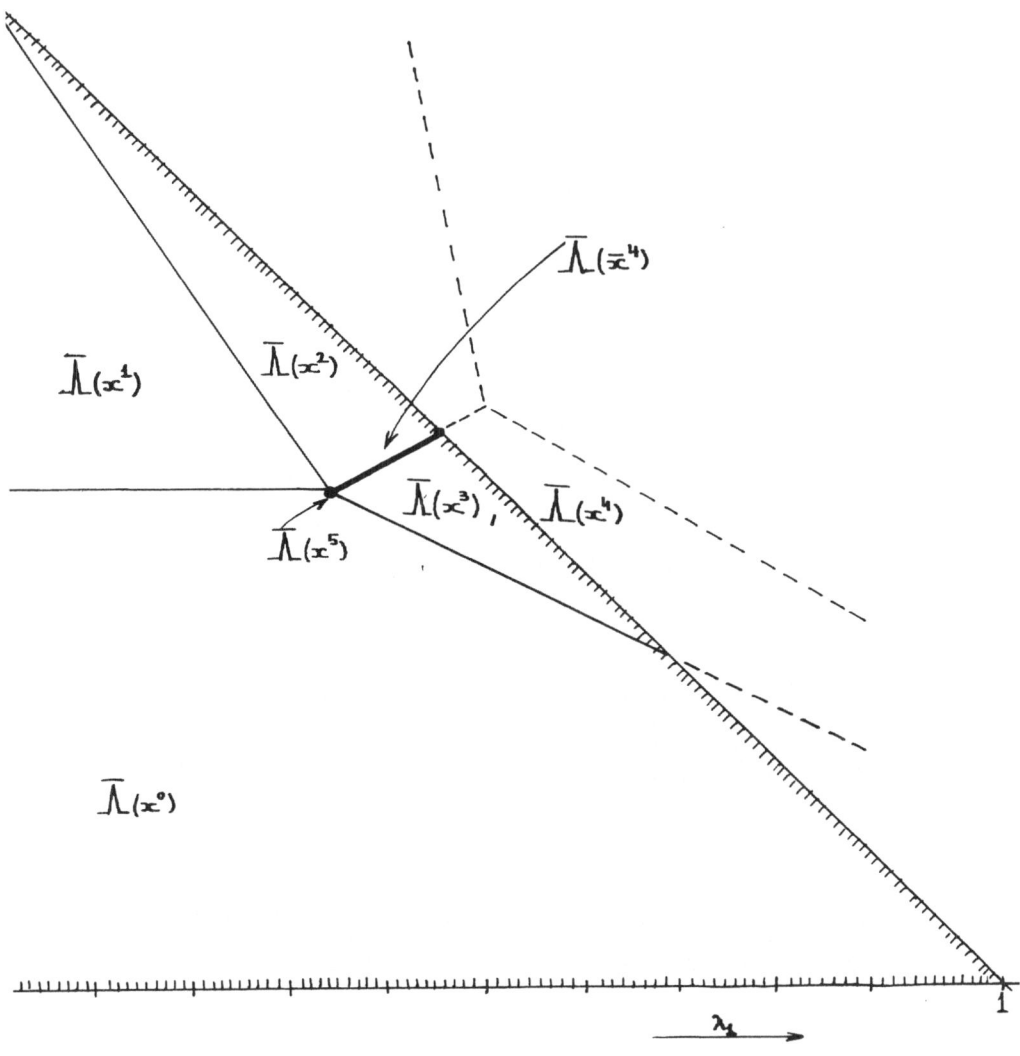

Figure 2.5.1.1.

Remark 2.5.1.6. To emphasize the ambiguity of constraint redundancy,
let us make the following remark. We have shown in Remark 2.5.1.2.
that introducing a column corresponding to a redundant constraint does
not have to lead to a meaningful decomposition. See, for example,
Figure 2.5.1.2. We cannot, however, conclude that an introduction of
a column corresponding to a redundant constraint will always lead only
to a dominated solution. The following counter example can be given:

$$\text{v-Max} \begin{cases} 4x_1 + x_2 \\ x_2 \end{cases}$$

subject to

$$2x_1 + x_2 \leq 20$$
$$\frac{5}{6}x_1 + x_2 \leq 10 \qquad '$$
$$x_1 + x_2 \geq 10 \; .$$

We get the following feasible solution, say x^o:

	1	2	3	4	5	
y_1	0	0	1	⑥	⑦	10
x_1	1	0	0	-6	-6	0
x_2	0	1	0	6	5	10
	0	0	0	-18	-19	10
	0	0	0	6	5	10

$x_1=0$, $x_2=10$, $y_1=10$, $y_2=0$, $y_3=0$

$x^o = (0,10)$

$10 \to x^o \in N$

$\Lambda(x^o)$ is given by

$$-18\lambda_1 + 6\lambda_2 \overset{\geq}{=} 0 \quad \text{redundant}$$

$$-19\lambda_1 + 5\lambda_2 \overset{\geq}{=} 0 .$$

Obviously the first constraint is redundant and is not effectively binding $\Lambda(x^o)$. Considering $\lambda_1 + \lambda_2 = 1$, i.e., $\lambda_1 = 1-\lambda_2$, we get

$$24\lambda_2 \overset{\geq}{=} 18 \quad \text{redundant}$$

$$24\lambda_2 \overset{\geq}{=} 19 .$$

Let us, however, introduce the column corresponding to the redundant constraint, i.e., the fourth column:

y_2	0	0	1,	1	$\frac{7}{6}$	$\frac{5}{3}$	
x_1	1	0	6	0	1	10	$x^1 = (10,0)$
x_2	0	1	-6	0	-2	0	
	0	0	18	0	2	40	nondominated solution
	0	0	-6	0	-2	0	

Introducing the fifth column in x^o (nonredundant) we obtain also a nondominated solution:

y_3	0	0	$\frac{1}{7}$	$\frac{6}{7}$	1	$\frac{10}{7}$	
x_1	1	0	$\frac{6}{7}$	$-\frac{6}{7}$	0	$\frac{60}{7}$	$x^2 = (\frac{60}{7},\frac{20}{7})$ which is
x_2	0	1	$-\frac{5}{7}$	$\frac{12}{7}$	0	$\frac{20}{7}$	nondominated as can be seen in Figure 2.5.1.4.
	0	0	$\frac{19}{7}$	$-\frac{12}{7}$	0	$\frac{260}{7}$	
	0	0	$-\frac{5}{7}$	$\frac{12}{7}$	0	$\frac{20}{7}$	

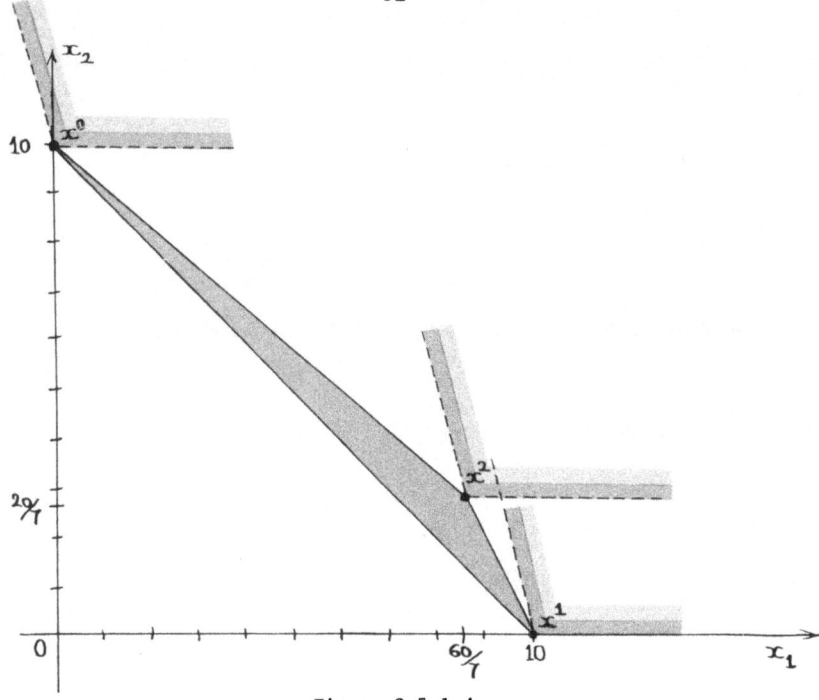

Figure 2.5.1.4.

LINEAR MULTIOBJECTIVE PROGRAMMING II.

3. Finding Nondominated Extreme Points -- A Second Approach
(Multicriteria Simplex Method)

The discussions of Section 2.5.revealed some of the difficulties which we may encounter in generating N_{ex} via the decomposition
of parametric space Λ.

In this section we shall discuss a modification of the simplex
method where the decision about nondominance of an extreme point is
not based on decomposition of Λ, though this decomposition may be a
natural byproduct, if required.

3 .1 Basic Theorems

Let the set of feasible solutions X be defined as in (2-2-3)
of Part I.   Consider the problem of maximizing a single linear
objective function, say $c^1.x$. A general simplex tableau for such
a problem may be constructed as:

				c_1^1	$\cdots$	c_m^1	c_{m+1}^1	$\cdots$	c_j^i	$\cdots$	c_n^1
r	BASIS	c^1	x^0	x_1	$\cdots$	x_m	x_{m+1}	$\cdots$	x_j	$\cdots$	x_n
1	x_1	c_1^1	y_1^0	1	$\cdots$	0	y_{1m+1}	$\cdots$	y_{1j}	$\cdots$	y_{1n}
.	.	.	.	.	.	.	.	.	.	.	.
.	.	.	.	.	.	.	.	.	.	.	.
.	.	.	.	.	.	.	.	.	.	.	.
m	x_m	c_m^1	y_m^0	0	$\cdots$	1	y_{mm+1}	$\cdots$	y_{mj}	$\cdots$	y_{mn}
			z_o^1	0	$\cdots$	0	$z_{m+1}^{(1)}$	$\cdots$	$z_j^{(1)}$	$\cdots$	$z_n^{(1)}$

Table 3.1.1.

where $z_j^{(1)} = \sum_{r=1}^{m} c_r^1 y_{rj} - c_j^1$, $j = 1,\ldots,n$ and $z_o^1 = \sum_{r=1}^{m} c_r^1 y_r^o$.

If all $z_j^{(1)} \geq 0$ for all j, then $x^o = (y_1^o, y_2^o, \ldots, y_m^o, 0, \ldots, 0)$

is a maximal feasible solution with $c^1 . x^o = z_o^1$ and $x^o \epsilon X$ is an

extreme point of X.

<u>Remark 3.1.1.</u> Notice $x^o \epsilon N_{ex}$ if x^o is unique, i.e., all

$z_j^{(1)} > 0$ for $j = m+1,\ldots,n$. In the case of alternate solutions,

we may discard those which are dominated, as discussed in Part I.

(See Lemma 2.6.)

Assume now that ℓ linear objective functions are involved, i.e.

$$c^i.x = c_1^i x_1 + c_2^i x_2 + \ldots + c_n^i x_n, \quad i = 1,\ldots,\ell.$$

With each basic solution, there are now associated ℓ criterial

rows of $z_j^{(i)}$ instead of single $z_j^{(1)}$, $i = 1,\ldots,\ell$ and $j = 1,\ldots,n$.

Notice that for all $j \epsilon J$ all $z_j^{(i)} = 0$.

Then $z_j^{(i)} = \sum_{r=1}^{m} c_r^i y_{rj} - c_j^i$ and the corresponding value of

the ith objective function is given by $z_o^i = \sum_{r=1}^{m} c_r^i y_r^o$, $i = 1,\ldots,\ell$.

Corresponding to each nonbasic column of the Table 3.1.1., there is

a column vector

$$z_j \equiv \begin{pmatrix} z_j^{(1)} \\ z_j^{(2)} \\ \cdot \\ \cdot \\ \cdot \\ z_j^{(\ell)} \end{pmatrix} \qquad\qquad (3\text{-}1\text{-}1)$$

With each basic solution (and its tableau), say x^o, there is associated a vector of values of ℓ objectives:

$$z_o \equiv \begin{pmatrix} z_o^1 \\ z_{o'}^2 \\ \cdot \\ \cdot \\ \cdot \\ z_o^\ell \end{pmatrix} \qquad\qquad (3\text{-}1\text{-}2)$$

Recall θ_j as it is defined in (2-3-23). If we introduce the jth column into the basis, we get a new basic solution, say x^1, and also a new vector $\hat{z}_o$, for which the following relation holds:

$$\hat{z}_o = z_o - \theta_j z_j ,$$

or

$$
\begin{pmatrix} \hat{z}_o^1 \\ \hat{z}_o^2 \\ \vdots \\ \hat{z}_o^\ell \end{pmatrix} = \begin{pmatrix} z_o^1 \\ z_o^2 \\ \vdots \\ z_o^\ell \end{pmatrix} - \theta_j \begin{pmatrix} z_j^{(1)} \\ z_j^{(2)} \\ \vdots \\ z_j^{(\ell)} \end{pmatrix}
\tag{3-1-3}
$$

Theorem 3.1.2. Given a basic feasible solution x^o and assuming $\theta_j > 0$ for $j \in \bar{J}$, then

    (a) if $z_j \leq 0$ (i.e. all $z_j^{(i)} \leq 0$ and at least one $z_j^{(i)} < 0$) then $x^o \notin N$.

    (b) if $z_j \geq 0$, then introducing the jth column into the basis will lead to a dominated solution.

Proof. For (a). Introducing the jth column into the basis, we get a new adjacent extreme point, say x^1, for which $\hat{z}_o \geq z_o$ because $-\theta_j z_j \geq 0$.

For (b). Introducing the jth column, we get an adjacent extreme point x^1, for which $\hat{z}_o \leq z_o$, since $-\theta_j z_j \leq 0$. Q.E.D.

Remark 3.1.3. For the discussion of degenerate case and that of $\theta_j = 0$, see Remarks 3.1.9. and 3.1.10. Notice that the jth column should never be introduced if $z_j \geq 0$ and $\theta_j > 0$ at x^o.

Theorem 3.1.4. Given a basic feasible solution x^o, if there are columns j, k such that $\theta_j z_j \leq \theta_k z_k$ (i.e., for at least one i, $\theta_j z_j^{(i)} < \theta_k z_k^{(i)}$), $j \neq k$ and $j,k \in \bar{J}$, then the solution resulting from introducing the kth column is dominated by the solution resulting from introducing the jth column.

Proof. Introducing the kth column, we get $\hat{z}_o$; and introducing the jth column, we get $\hat{\hat{z}}_o$. Then $\hat{z}_o = z_o - \theta_k z_k$ and $\hat{\hat{z}}_o = z_o - \theta_j z_j$. Since $-\theta_k z_k \leq -\theta_j z_j$ then $\hat{z}_o \geq \hat{\hat{z}}_o$.   Q.E.D.

Remark 3.1.5. Looking at criterial rows at each iteration, if $z_j^{(i)} \geq 0$ for all $j \in \bar{J}$ then the ith objective function is at its maximum and the corresponding basic solution is nondominated, provided there is no column $k \in \bar{J}$ with $z_k^{(i)} = 0$. (i.e. no alternate optimal solution).

Assume that for a basic feasible solution $\bar{x}$ there is no column with $z_j \leq 0$. Nonbasic columns with $z_j \geq 0$ and those columns $k \in \bar{J}$ for which $\theta_k z_k \geq \theta_j z_j$, $j \neq k$, cannot be considered for an introduction. Suppose also there is no row with $z_j^{(i)} \geq 0$, $j \in \bar{J}$. Then the only columns eligible for an introduction are those which are noncomparable (See notation in 1.3.) with the zero vector, i.e., $z_j \sim 0$, $j \in \bar{J}$ and among these only those which also satisfy $\theta_k z_k \sim \theta_j z_j$, $j \neq k$. We have to determine whether the corresponding

$\bar{x}$ is dominated or nondominated.

Since $\bar{x} \in X$, i.e., $\sum\limits_{j=1}^{n} a_{rj}\bar{x}_j = b_r$, $r = 1,\ldots,m$, let us

add the following constraints to X: $c^i.x \geq c^i.\bar{x}$, $i = 1,\ldots,\ell$,

where $c^i.\bar{x}$ denotes the values of $c^i.x$ at $\bar{x} \in X$. Adding the surplus

and artificial variables to these new constraints, we can write

$$c^i.x - \varepsilon_i + y_i = c^i.\bar{x}, \quad i = 1,\ldots,\ell. \qquad (3\text{-}1\text{-}4)$$

Notice that at $x = \bar{x}$, $\varepsilon_i = 0$, $y_i = 0$, for all i.

Consider the following LP problem:

$$\text{Max } v = \sum_{i=1}^{\ell} \varepsilon_i$$

subject to

$$Ax = b$$

$$c^i.x - \varepsilon_i + y_i = c^i.\bar{x}, \quad i = 1,\ldots,\ell$$

$$\varepsilon_i \geq 0, \quad x \geq 0. \qquad (3\text{-}1\text{-}5)$$

At the initial feasible solution $\bar{x} \in X$, all $\varepsilon_i = 0$

and $y_i = 0$ imply Max $v \geq 0$. Suppose that Max $v > 0$, then

at least one $\varepsilon_i > 0$.

Since $c^i.x = c^i.\bar{x} + \varepsilon_i$ we have $c^i.x > c^i.\bar{x}$ for at least one i.

Thus $cx \geq c\bar{x}$ and $\bar{x} \in D$.

If $\bar{x}$ is a maximal solution to problem (3-1-5), i.e., Max v = 0 and all ε_i = 0, then there is no feasible $x \in X$ such that $cx \geq c\bar{x}$, i.e., $\bar{x} \in N$.

The above discussion may be summarized in Theorem 3.1.6.

<u>Theorem 3.1.6.</u> Solve the following LP problem: Max v, $v = \sum_{i=1}^{\ell} \varepsilon_i$

subject to a set of constraints:

$$\tilde{X} = \{(x,\varepsilon) \mid x \in X, \ \varepsilon \geq 0, \ cx - \varepsilon \geq c\bar{x}\}.$$

Then $\bar{x} \in D$ if and only if Max v > 0 and $\bar{x} \in N$ if and only if Max v = 0.

In order to derive an efficient method for an application of Theorem 3.1.6., let us consider incorporating ℓ additional constraints of the type (3-1-4) in Table 3.1.1. We get the following general simplex tableau (Table 3.1.2.).

At $\bar{x} \in X$, $y_i = \varepsilon_i = 0$, therefore, the artificial variables $y_1, \ldots, y_\ell$ are in the basis at zero level.

Assume that for some j, $y_{rj} \neq 0$, r = m+1,...,m+ℓ, (y_{rj} can be either positive or negative). Then the corresponding artificial vector may be removed from the basis and replaced by x_j. Since the artificial variable was at a zero level, x_j will enter the basis at a zero level, and the new basic solution will stay feasible, corresponding to the same extreme point $\bar{x}$. If this

r		x_1	$\cdots$	x_m	x_{m+1}	$\cdots$	x_j	$\cdots$	x_n	ε_1	$\cdots$	ε_ℓ	y_1	$\cdots$	y_ℓ	x^o
1	x_1	1	$\cdots$	0	$y_{1(m+1)}$	$\cdots$	y_{1j}	$\cdots$	y_{1n}	0	$\cdots$	0	0	$\cdots$	0	y_1^o
$\vdots$	$\vdots$	$\vdots$		$\vdots$			$\vdots$		$\vdots$	$\vdots$		$\vdots$	$\vdots$		$\vdots$	$\vdots$
m	x_m	0	$\cdots$	1	$y_{m(m+1)}$	$\cdots$	y_{mj}	$\cdots$	y_{mn}	0	$\cdots$	0	0	$\cdots$	0	y_m^o
$m+1$	y_1	0	$\cdots$	0	$y_{(m+1)(m+1)}$	$\cdots$	$y_{(m+1)j}$	$\cdots$	$y_{(m+1)n}$	-1	$\cdots$	0	1	$\cdots$	0	0
$\vdots$	$\vdots$	$\vdots$		$\vdots$			$\vdots$		$\vdots$	$\vdots$		$\vdots$	$\vdots$		$\vdots$	$\vdots$
$m+\ell$	y_ℓ	0	$\cdots$	0	$y_{(m+\ell)(m+1)}$	$\cdots$	$y_{(m+\ell)j}$	$\cdots$	$y_{(m+\ell)n}$	0	$\cdots$	-1	0	$\cdots$	1	0
		0	$\cdots$	0	$z_{m+1}^{(1)}$	$\cdots$	$z_j^{(1)}$	$\cdots$	$z_n^{(1)}$	0	$\cdots$	0	0	$\cdots$	0	z_0^{1}
		$\vdots$		$\vdots$			$\vdots$		$\vdots$	$\vdots$		$\vdots$	$\vdots$		$\vdots$	$\vdots$
		0	$\cdots$	0	$z_{m+1}^{(\ell)}$	$\cdots$	$z_j^{(\ell)}$	$\cdots$	$z_n^{(\ell)}$	0	$\cdots$	0	0	$\cdots$	0	z_0^{ℓ}

Table 3.1.2.

process can be continued until all artificial vectors are removed,
we obtain a "degenerate" basic feasible solution:

$$\bar{x} = (y_1^o, y_2^o, \ldots, y_m^o, \underbrace{0, \ldots, 0}_{\ell})$$

where all ε_i, $i = 1,\ldots,\ell$ are outside the new basis. If we are
able to introduce at lease one ε_i into the basis at a positive
level, then

$$\sum_{i=1}^{\ell} \varepsilon_i > 0 \quad \text{and} \quad \bar{x} \in \mathcal{D}.$$

If the above procedure does not remove all artificial vectors,
we must ultimately reach a state where $y_{rj} = 0$ for all x_j and all
r corresponding to the columns containing artificial variables at a
zero level. If there are k artificial variables left in the basis
at a zero level, then k of ℓ added constraints are redundant and
do not have to be considered.

In order to simplify our analysis of Table 3.1.2., let us
define the following symbols:

$\mathcal{C}$ - $(\ell \times n)$ matrix of coefficients of ℓ linear objective functions

A - $(m \times n)$ matrix of technological coefficients of m linear constraints

$\mathcal{B}_k$ - $(m \times m)$ matrix of basic vectors at the kth iteration

$\bar{x}$ - n-dimensional vector

b - m-dimensional vector (corresponding to the right hand sides of the
constraints in X)

$\mathcal{C}_B$ - $(\ell \times m)$ matrix of coefficients corresponding to basic vectors in $\mathcal{B}_k$

1 - identity matrix (of proper order)

0 - zero matrix (of proper order)

1) The original problem (See Table 3.1.2.)

$$v - \text{Max } c_i^i x \quad i = 1,\ldots,\ell \quad \text{subject to } Ax = b, \quad x \geq 0$$

may have the associated initial simplex tableau written in the matrix

notation as follows:

Tableau 1.

$$
\begin{array}{c}
(1) \\
(2)
\end{array}
\left[
\begin{array}{c|c|c}
A & 1_{m \times m} & b \\
\hline
-c & 0_{\ell \times m} & 0_{\ell \times 1}
\end{array}
\right]
$$

Let B_k be a feasible basis corresponding to the extreme

point $\bar{x}$ and B_k^{-1}, its inverse. Then the simplex tableau associated

with B_k is given by:

Tableau 2.

$$
\begin{array}{c}
(3) \\
(4)
\end{array}
\left[
\begin{array}{c|c|c}
B_k^{-1} A & B_k^{-1} & B_k^{-1} b \\
\hline
c_B B_k^{-1} A - c & c_B B_k^{-1} & c_B B_k^{-1} b
\end{array}
\right]
$$

Notice that Row (4) = $c_B B_k^{-1}$, Row (1) + Row (2). Also, $B_k^{-1} b$ is

an m-dimensional vector constituting the first m elements of $\bar{x}$ and

$c_B B_k^{-1} b$ is an ℓ-dimensional vector of the values of objective functions

at $\bar{x}$, i.e. $c_B B_k^{-1} b = c\bar{x}$.

Let us now explore the same problem with the constraints

$$Cx \geq C\bar{x} = C_B B_k^{-1} b \quad \text{appended to the original constraints in}$$

Tableau 1:

Tableau 3.

$$
\begin{bmatrix}
(5) & A & 1_{m \times m} & 0_{m \times \ell} & 0_{m \times \ell} & b \\
(6) & C & 0_{\ell \times m} & -1_{\ell \times \ell} & 1_{\ell \times \ell} & C\bar{x} \\
(7) & -C & 0_{\ell \times m} & 0_{\ell \times \ell} & 0_{\ell \times \ell} & 0_{\ell \times 1}
\end{bmatrix}
$$

With respect to B_k, Tableau 3 could be written as:

Tableau 4.

$$
\begin{bmatrix}
(8) & B_k^{-1} A & B_k^{-1} & 0_{m \times \ell} & 0_{m \times \ell} & B_k^{-1} b \\
(9) & -C_B B_k^{-1} A + C & -C_B B_k^{-1} & -1_{\ell \times \ell} & 1_{\ell \times \ell} & 0_{\ell \times 1} \\
(10) & C_B B_k^{-1} A - C & C_B B_k^{-1} & 0_{\ell \times \ell} & 0_{\ell \times \ell} & C_B B_k^{-1} b
\end{bmatrix}
$$

Note. Row (8) $= B_k^{-1} \cdot$ Row (5)

Row (9) $=$ Row (6) $- C_B B_k^{-1} \cdot$ Row (5)

Row (10) $=$ Row (7) $+ C_B B_k^{-1} \cdot$ Row (5).

Remark 3.1.7.

    (i) Notice the right hand side of the Row (9) is $0_{\ell \times 1}$

    because $C\bar{x} = C_B B_k^{-1} b$.

    (ii) Comparing the Rows (9) and (10), notice that because

of the second column, we can write $y_{rj} = -z_j^{(r-m)}$ for

$r = m+1, \ldots, m+\ell$ and $j = m+1, \ldots, n$. (See Table 3.1.2.)

Since the values of $z_j^{(r-m)}$ are already known as the

indicators in criterial rows for the basic solution $\bar{x}$,

we can find y_{rj} directly without recalculating the

tableau.

2) The new problem, as it is formulated in (3-1-5), may be constructed

by replacing Row (10) of Tableau 4 with a new criterial Row (iii):

Tableau 5.

$$
\begin{array}{c}
\text{(i)} \\[2em]
\text{(ii)} \\[2em]
\text{(iii)}
\end{array}
\left[
\begin{array}{c:c:c:c:c}
B_k^{-1} A & B_k^{-1} & 0_{m \times \ell} & 0_{m \times \ell} & B_k^{-1} b \\
\hdashline
C - C_B B_k^{-1} A & -C_B B_k^{-1} & -1_{\ell \times \ell} & 1_{\ell \times \ell} & 0_{\ell \times 1} \\
\hdashline
0_{1 \times n} & 0_{1 \times m} & -1_{1 \times \ell} & 1_{1 \times \ell} & 0
\end{array}
\right]
$$

    Removing the artificial variables from the basis by using

the two phase method, we get:

        Row (v) $= -1_{\ell \times \ell} \cdot$ Row (ii)

    and Row (vi) $=$ Row (iii) $+ 1_{1 \times \ell} \cdot$ Row (v)

    of Tableau 6:

Tableau 6.

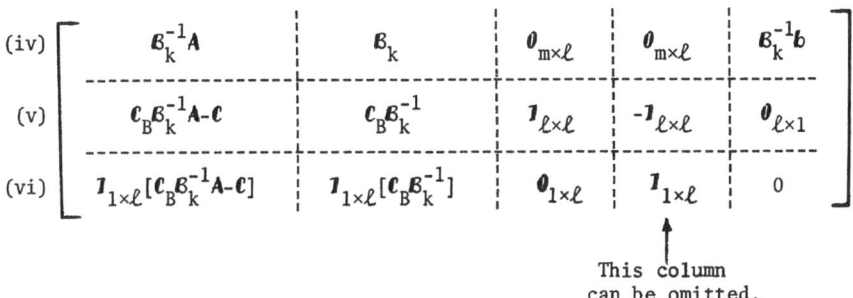

$$
\begin{array}{c}
\text{(iv)} \\
\text{(v)} \\
\text{(vi)}
\end{array}
\left[
\begin{array}{c|c|c|c|c}
\mathcal{B}_k^{-1}A & \mathcal{B}_k & \mathbf{0}_{m\times\ell} & \mathbf{0}_{m\times\ell} & \mathcal{B}_k^{-1}b \\
\hline
\mathcal{C}_B\mathcal{B}_k^{-1}A-\mathcal{C} & \mathcal{C}_B\mathcal{B}_k^{-1} & \mathbf{1}_{\ell\times\ell} & -\mathbf{1}_{\ell\times\ell} & \mathbf{0}_{\ell\times1} \\
\hline
\mathbf{1}_{1\times\ell}[\mathcal{C}_B\mathcal{B}_k^{-1}A-\mathcal{C}] & \mathbf{1}_{1\times\ell}[\mathcal{C}_B\mathcal{B}_k^{-1}] & \mathbf{0}_{1\times\ell} & \mathbf{1}_{1\times\ell} & 0
\end{array}
\right]
$$

This column
can be omitted.

Observe that Tableau 6 supplies a basic feasible solution to
our new problem. The columns corresponding to artificial variables
could be dropped from consideration.

Comparing Tableau 6 with Tableau 2, notice that the first one
may be constructed directly from the latter one. The Row (vi) represents new criterial indicators of the new problem. From this row
optimality as well as nondominance can be checked. If there is an
element of Row (vi) which is negative, say the jth, and all elements
of the jth column in Row (v) are negative, then for $\theta_j > 0$ we may
conclude that Max $v > 0$ and the corresponding basis $\bar{x}$ is dominated.
To support this conclusion, refer to Theorems 3.1.2. and 3.1.6. The
above property will be used in the subroutine for checking the nondominance. For the summary of this discussion, see Figure 3.4.1.,
giving the block diagram for nondominance subroutine.

Before we get into the details of the algorithmic procedure,
let us return to the decomposition of Λ-space.

In the multicriteria simplex method, we have appended ℓ criterial rows to the simplex tableau instead of a single one for P_λ (See Table 3.1.2.). Since we are interested in reducing the dimension of parametric space Λ, let us consider $(\ell+1)$ objectives to be appended.

Then with each $j \in \bar{J}$, there is associated a column vector (compare with (3-1-1)):

$$\mathbf{z}_j \equiv \begin{pmatrix} z_j^{(1)} \\ z_j^{(2)} \\ \cdot \\ \cdot \\ \cdot \\ z_j^{(\ell+1)} \end{pmatrix} \tag{3-1-6}$$

We would like to show that $\mathbf{z}_j$ determines $\Lambda(\bar{x})$ completely. For a definition of $\Lambda(\bar{x})$ recall Theorem 2.3.2.

Let
$$\sum_{i=1}^{\ell+1} \lambda_i z_j^{(i)} = (1 - \sum_{i=1}^{\ell} \lambda_i)\, z_j^{(\ell+1)} + \sum_{i=1}^{\ell} \lambda_i z_j^{(i)} =$$

$$= z_j^{(\ell+1)} + \sum_{i=1}^{\ell} \lambda_i [z_j^{(i)} - z_j^{(\ell+1)}]$$

From (2-3-4), we may see that $\gamma_j = z_j^{(\ell+1)}$ and $\delta_j^i = z_j^{(i)} - z_j^{(\ell+1)}$,

To demonstrate the above discussed interrelation of the two methods, let us choose some basic solution and its tableau (for example, Tableau (2-5-1-6)):

	1.	2.	3.	4.	5.	6.	7.	8.	9.	10.	11.	
x_1	1	2	1	1	2	1	2	1	0	0	0	16
y_2	0	3	2	3	6	2	5	2	1	0	0	48
y_3	0	2	2	1	4	1	0	1	0	1	0	32
y_4	0	1	2	-1	1	-2	-1	0	0	0	1	16
	0	0	2	-2	0	1	1	1	0	0	0	16
	0	-1	-1	-2	-3	-1	0	0	0	0	0	0
	0	2	0	2	2	2	3	1	0	0	0	16

We may see how we can read the constraints of $\overline{\Lambda}(x^1)$ from the last three rows of this tableau. (We consider the first row as representing the $(\ell+1)$st objective function.) We get

Nonbasic Columns j	Calculation	Constraint
2	$0 + \lambda_1(-1-0) + \lambda_2(2-0)$	$-\lambda_1 + 2\lambda_2 \geq 0$
3	$2 + \lambda_1(-1-2) + \lambda_2(0-2)$	$3\lambda_1 + 2\lambda_2 \leq 2$
4	$-2 + \lambda_1(-2+2) + \lambda_2(2+2)$	$4\lambda_2 \geq 2$
5	$0 + \lambda_1(-3-0) + \lambda_2(2-0)$	$-3\lambda_1 + 2\lambda_2 \geq 0$
6	$1 + \lambda_1(-1-1) + \lambda_2(2-1)$	$2\lambda_1 - \lambda_2 \leq 1$
7	$1 + \lambda_1(0-1) + \lambda_2(3-1)$	$\lambda_1 - 2\lambda_2 \leq 1$
8	$1 + \lambda_1(0-1) + \lambda_2(1-1)$	$\lambda_1 \leq 1$

The constraints denoted by ✓ are those of $\overline{\Lambda}(x^1)$. Graphical representation of all the constraints in two dimensions is in Figure 3.1.1.

Shaded polyhedron satisfies all the
constraints. Compare $\overline{\Lambda}(x^1)$ here with
Figure 2.5.1.1.

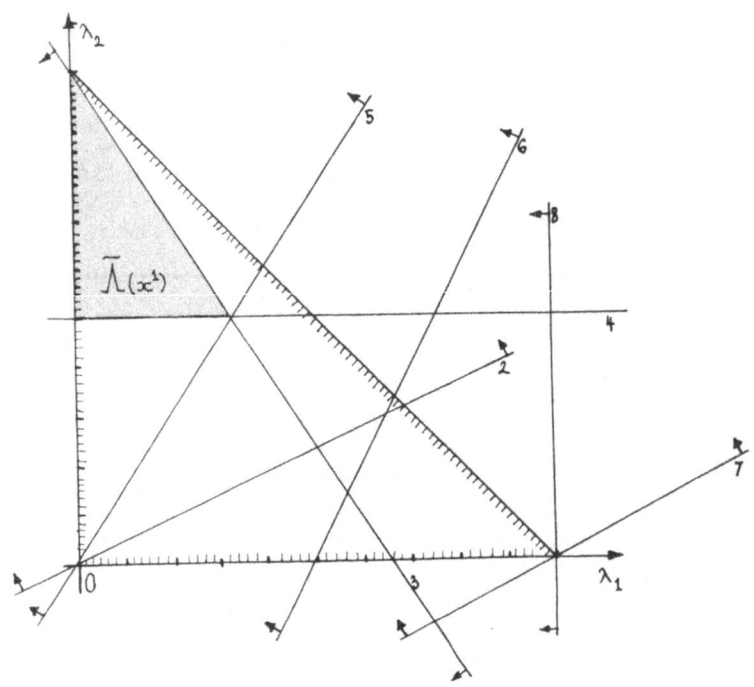

Figure 3.1.1.

Remark 3.1.8. Notice that the reduction of the dimension of parametric space might be useful to facilitate graphical representation,
but in general we can work with simpler, unreduced space. Let us
define z_j as in (3-1-1). Then for a given basic feasible solution x^o,
we may write

$$\Lambda(x^o) = \{\lambda \mid \sum_{i=1}^{\ell} \lambda_i z_j^{(i)} \geq 0; \ \lambda \in E^{\ell}; \ j \in \bar{J}\}.$$

Example. Consider the fourth column in Tableau (2-5-1-6). If we
associate λ_3 with the first row, we may write the corresponding
constraint as

$$-2\lambda_1 + 2\lambda_2 - 2\lambda_3 \geq 0$$

which gives

$$-2\lambda_1 + 2\lambda_2 - 2(1 - \lambda_1 - \lambda_2) \geq 0$$

and finally $4\lambda_2 \geq 2$ as considered previously in Figure 3.1.1.

Remark 3.1.9. It is not the degeneracy which could make the subproblem
indecisive, but rather a possibility of $\theta_j = 0$ if the jth column is
the one to be introduced. Notice that the degenerate solution itself
does not imply $\theta_j = 0$.

Remark 3.1.10. In order to keep track of corresponding values of θ_j,
we may add the coefficients of the row corresponding to a degenerate
solution to the subproblem.

3.2. Methods for Generating Adjacent Extreme Points

The next problem which has to be discussed is how to traverse
from one nondominated extreme point to another in an efficient manner.
Since a finite number of nondominated extreme points is to be generated (in general, more than one), we have to design an efficient
scheme of the order in which they will be generated.

We have shown in Theorem 2.4.2. that a set of nondominated
extreme points is a connected set, i.e., each such point can be
generated from any other by a finite series of simplex iterations.
To any connected set of extreme points (in our case N_{ex} = {set of
nondominated extreme points}) a non-directed graph $\Gamma(U,V)$ may be
adjoined, such that:

1) Set of vertices V is formed by m-tuples of unordered integers,

$$v = \{i_1, i_2, \ldots, i_m\}, \quad i_j \in J, \quad j = 1,2,\ldots,m.$$

A vertex $v \in V$ if and only if there is an extreme point in N_{ex} with a basis $\{i_1, \ldots, i_m\}$.

(Notice that two or more different v's may correspond to the same nondominated extreme point.)

2) Two vertices v_1 and v_2 have a distance $d \overset{<}{=} m$ if exactly d components of v_2 differ from components of v_1.

Two vertices v_1 and v_2 are adjacent if and only if $d = 1$. Associated with adjacent vertices is either a unique extreme point or two adjacent extreme points in N_{ex}.

3) An arc $[v_1, v_2] \in U$ if and only if v_1 and v_2 are adjacent. The graph $\Gamma(U,V)$ is always connected. Our goal is to generate the set N_{ex}. Basically, two approaches are considered; see e.g. [Hadley, 1961 or Gál, Nedoma, 1972].

A. Complete investigation of adjacent vertices,

B. Incomplete investigation of adjacent vertices.

For A. Let $\Gamma(v)$ denote a set of vertices adjacent to the vertex v, including v.

Remark 3.3.1. Let us agree that the phrase "to calculate v" means to identify the basic solution (or an extreme point) $x^k = (x_1^k, \ldots, x_n^k)$ which is associated with $v = \{i_1, i_2, \ldots, i_m\}$.

We shall construct two sequences $R_1, R_2, \ldots$ and $W_1, W_2, \ldots$, whose elements consist of vertices of Γ.

Let us assume that we have found the first nondominated extreme point $x^o \in N_{ex}$ by maximizing one of the ℓ objective functions and discarding dominated alternative solutions.

The indices of basic vectors in the simplex tableau of x^o correspond to v_o of Γ.

(i) Let $R_1 = \{v_o\}$ and $W_1 = \Gamma(v_o) - R_1$. Discard those vertices from W_1 which are dominated by using the subroutine described in section 3.1. Transform thus W_1 into $\overline{W}_1$.

(ii) Calculate all vertices from $\overline{W}_1$.

(iii) Let $R_2 = R_1 \cup \overline{W}_1$. Let v_{1i}, $i = 1,2,\ldots,r_1$ are all vertices in $\overline{W}_1$.

$$\text{Let } W_2 = \overset{r_1'}{\underset{i=1}{\cup}} \Gamma(v_{1i}) - R_2. \text{ Transform } W_2 \text{ into } \overline{W}_2.$$

(iv) Suppose we have constructed R_s and $\overline{W}_s$ for $s = 2,3,\ldots,k$. If $\overline{W}_k = \phi$, then all nondominated extreme points N_{ex} are found, i.e., $R_k = V$.

(v) If $\overline{W}_k \neq \phi$, calculate all vertices from $\overline{W}_k$ and form

$$R_{k+1} = R_k \cup \overline{W}_k$$

and

$$W_{k+1} = \overset{r_k}{\underset{i=1}{\cup}} \Gamma(v_{ki}) - R_{k+1}$$

where v_{ki} are all vertices of $\overline{W}_k$, $i = 1,...,r_k$. Transform W_{k+1} into $\overline{W}_{k+1}$ and continue until $\overline{W}_s = \phi$, $s = 2,3,...$

The above procedure is similar to Hadley's approach based on complete investigation of adjacent extreme points. For small hand computed examples, this seems to be acceptable technique because it is easy to return to previously obtained simplex tableaus.

Larger problems, requiring the use of a computer, might not be efficiently solvable by Hadley's approach. We have to store after each step k not only all vertices in R_k but also all inverse matrices from simplex tableaus corresponding to $\overline{W}_{k+1}$.

For B. The second approach has minimal requirements on computer memory at the cost of traversing some extreme points more than once. It is based on incomplete investigation of adjacent vertices.

After constructing $x^o \in N_{ex}$ and its $v_o \in V$, we continue as follows:

(i) Let $R_1 = \{v_o\}$ and $W_1 = \Gamma(v_o) - R_1$. Transform W_1 into $\overline{W}_1$.

Choose any $v_1 \in \overline{W}_1$ and calculate v_1.

(ii) Let $R_2 = R_1 \cup \{v_1\}$, $W_2 = \overline{W}_1 \cup \Gamma(v_1) - R_2$. Transform W_2 into $\overline{W}_2$.

(iii) Suppose we have constructed R_s and $\overline{W}_s$ and $\overline{W}_k \neq \phi$

for $s = 1,2,...k$.

(iv) Construct R_{k+1} and W_{k+1} as follows:

If v_{k-1} is the last vertex put in R_k, explore $\overline{W}_k$

for a vertex adjacent to v_{k-1}. If there is one, denote it

v_k and construct $R_{k+1} = R_k \cup \{v_k\}$ and $W_{k+1} = \overline{W}_k \cup \Gamma(v_k) - R_{k+1}$.

If there is no such point in $\overline{W}_k$ (having d=1 from

v_{k-1}), look for a vertex with d=2, then 3, 4, etc., until

we find the one with $1 < d \stackrel{<}{=} m$. Denote such point as v_k

and construct R_{k+1} and W_{k+1} as above. Transform

W_{k+1} into $\overline{W}_{k+1}$. Repeat the whole procedure.

After a finite number of iterations, we get $\overline{W}_k = \phi$

and $R_k = V$.

Using the above technique, we have to store only one

simplex tableau and one matrix r x m for sets R_k and $\overline{W}_k$ at any

k^{th} iteration. Both approaches are compared and summarized in

Figures 3.2.1. and 3.2.2.

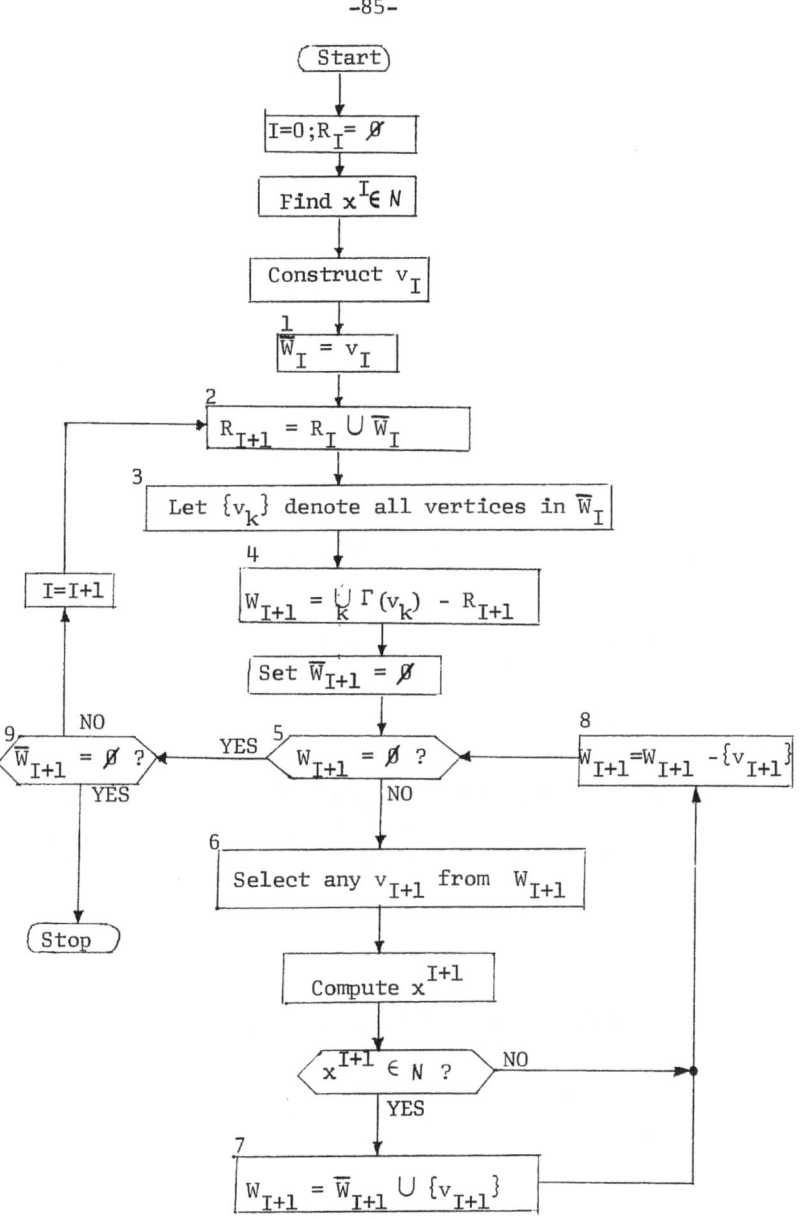

Figure 3.2.1.

Comments on Method A -- Figure 3.2.1.

(1) We calculate first N_{ex}-solution x^I and define the corresponding vertex of v_I of Γ. $\overline{W}_I$ represents all explored vertices v_I corresponding to $x^I \in N_{ex}$, whose adjacent vertices have not yet been considered.

(2) R_{I+1} collects all explored vertices v_I corresponding to $x^I \in N_{ex}$, whose adjacent vertices have been considered. So initially, $R_1 = \{v_1\}$ since $R_o = \phi$.

(3) We identify all vertices currently in $\overline{W}_I$, v_k.

(4) For each v_k, we construct $\Gamma(v_k)$ as defined, i.e. all adjacent vertices to each v_k. So, $\underset{k}{\cup}\Gamma(v_k)$ represents all vertices (explored or unexplored) which are directly reachable from all vertices in $\overline{W}_I$. We construct W_{I+1} which collects only those which were not yet explored.

(5) Obviously, if $W_{I+1} = \phi$ then $\overline{W}_{I+1} = \phi$, and we stop.

(6) If $W_{I+1} \neq \phi$, there might be vertices corresponding to dominated or nondominated solutions. We check all $v_{I+1} \in W_{I+1}$ for nondominance sequentially.

(7) If $x^{I+1} \in N$, then transfer v_{I+1} into $\overline{W}_{I+1}$.

(8) Remove the decided vertex from W_{I+1} and check (5) again. After all $v_{I+1} \in W_{I+1}$ are decided, then $W_{I+1} = \phi$. However, $\overline{W}_{I+1}$ may or may not be empty.

⑨ If $\overline{W}_{I+1} = \phi$, we stop. All nondominated solutions have been found.

If $\overline{W}_{I+1} \neq \phi$, we add $\overline{W}_{I+1}$ to our current R_{I+1} formed in ② and continue with ③ .

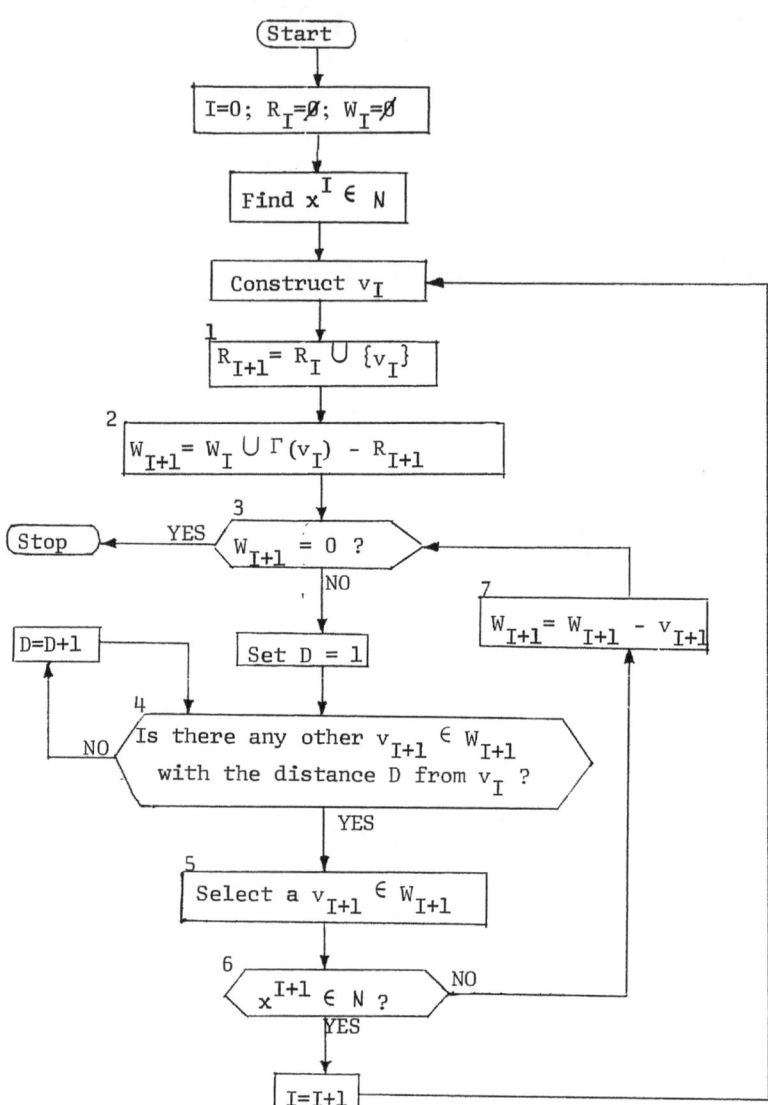

Figure 3.2.2.

Comments on Method B -- Figure 3.2.2.

(1) The main difference from Method A is in this block. Instead of adding to R_{I+1} <u>all</u> adjacent vertices $\overline{W}_I$, we add only one which was found nondominated in (6). So, initially $R_1 = \{v_1\}$ because $R_0 = \phi$.

(2) We find $\Gamma(v_I)$ only for the vertex last added to R_{I+1}. W_{I+1} now contains all unexplored vertices. So, initially $W_1 = \Gamma(v_1) - \{v_1\}$ since $R_1 = v_1$ and $W_0 = \phi$.

(3) If $W_{I+1} = \phi$ there are no unexplored vertices and we stop.

(4) If $W_{I+1} \neq \phi$ we choose some vertex v_{I+1} adjacent to the v_I last added to R_{I+1}. If there is none, we look for the "next closest," i.e. with the distance D+1. There is always at least one vertex v_{I+1} with the distance $1 \stackrel{<}{=} D \stackrel{<}{=} m$ (m is the number of basic columns) because $W_{I+1} \neq \phi$.

(5) We select v_{I+1} which is closest to v_I.

(6) Check the nondominance of corresponding x^{I+1}. If $x^{I+1} \in N$, we add v_{I+1} to our current R_{I+1} formed in (1) and continue with (2).

(7) If $x^{I+1} \notin N$, we subtract v_{I+1} from the current W_{I+1} and continue with (3).

Notice that transformation of W_I into $\overline{W}_I$ described in the text for method B is replaced by block 6 of this routine.

Instead of lengthy numerical examples, let us demonstrate the differences between the two techniques on a simple connected set of extreme points and its associated graph Γ.   See Figure 3.2.3.

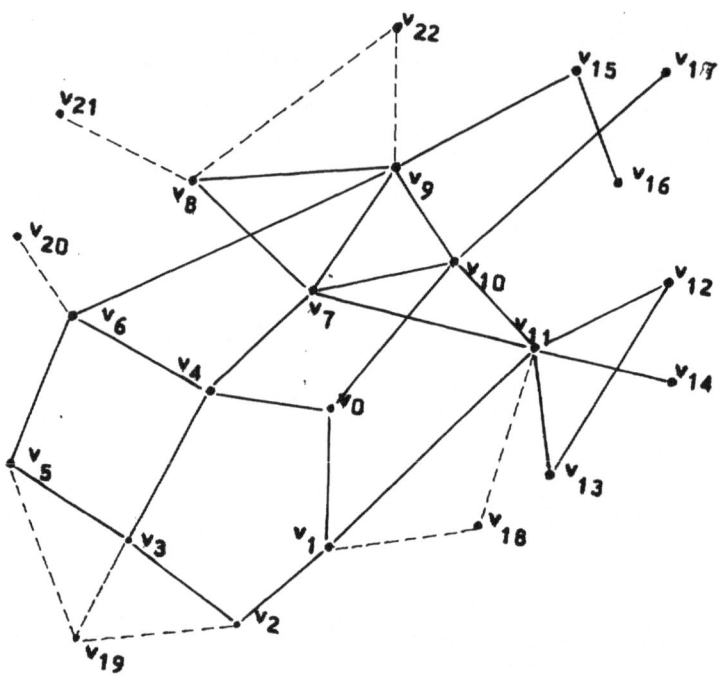

v_o - v_{17} are vertices corresponding to N_{ex}.

v_{18} - v_{22} are vertices corresponding to dominated extreme points.

Figure 3.2.3.

Method A.

a) $R_1 = \{v_o\}$ $W_1 = \{v_1, v_4, v_{10}\}$ $\overline{W}_1 = W_1$

b) $R_2 = \{v_o, v_1, v_4, v_{10}\}$ $W_2 = \{v_{11}, v_{18}, v_2, v_3, v_6, v_7, v_9, v_{17}\}$

$\overline{W}_2 = \{v_{11}, v_2, v_3, v_6, v_7, v_9, v_{17}\}$

c) $R_3 = \{v_o, v_1, v_2, v_3, v_4, v_6, v_7, v_9, v_{10}, v_{11}, v_{17}\}$

$W_3 = \{v_5, v_8, v_{12}, v_{13}, v_{14}, v_{15}, v_{18}, v_{19}, v_{20}, v_{22}\}$

$\overline{W}_3 = \{v_5, v_8, v_{12}, v_{13}, v_{14}, v_{15}\}$

d) $R_4 = \{v_o, v_1, v_2, v_3, v_4, v_5, v_6, v_7, v_8, v_9, v_{10}, v_{11}, v_{12}, v_{13},$

$v_{14}, v_{15}, v_{17}\}$

$W_4 = \{v_{16}, v_{19}, v_{22}\}$ $\overline{W}_4 = \{v_{16}\}$

e) $R_5 = \{v_o, v_1, v_2, v_3, v_4, v_5, v_6, v_7, v_8, v_9, v_{10}, v_{11}, v_{12}, v_{13},$

$v_{14}, v_{15}, v_{16}, v_{17}\}$

$W_4 = \phi$ $\overline{W}_4 = \phi$ STOP.

Method B.

1) $R_1 = \{v_o\}$ $W_1 = \{v_1, v_4, v_{10}\}$ $\overline{W}_1 \equiv W_1$

2) $R_2 = \{v_o, v_1\}$ $W_2 = \{v_4, v_2, v_{10}, v_{11}, v_{18}\}$

$\overline{W}_2 = \{v_4, v_2, v_{10}, v_{11}\}$

3) $R_3 = \{v_0, v_1, v_2\}$ $W_3 = \{v_3, v_4, v_{10}, v_{11}, v_{19}\}$

$\overline{W}_3 = \{v_3, v_4, v_{10}, v_{11}\}$

4) $R_4 = \{v_0, v_1, v_2, v_3\}$ $W_4 = \{v_4, v_5, v_{10}, v_{11}, v_{19}\}$

$\overline{W}_4 = \{v_4, v_5, v_{10}, v_{11}\}$

5) $R_5 = \{v_0, v_1, v_2, v_3, v_4\}$ $W_5 = \{v_5, v_6, v_7, v_{10}, v_{11}\} \equiv \overline{W}_5$

6) $R_6 = \{v_0, v_1, v_2, v_3, v_4, v_6\}$

$\overline{W}_6 = \{v_5, v_7, v_9, v_{10}, v_{11}\}$

7) $R_7 = \{v_0, v_1, v_2, v_3, v_4, v_6, v_5\}$

$\overline{W}_7 = \{v_7, v_9, v_{10}, v_{11}\}$

8) $R_8 = \{v_0, v_1, v_2, v_3, v_4, v_6, v_5, v_9\}$

$\overline{W}_8 = \{v_7, v_8, v_{10}, v_{11}, v_{15}\}$

9) $R_9 = \{v_0, v_1, v_2, v_3, v_4, v_6, v_5, v_9, v_7\}$

$\overline{W}_9 = \{v_8, v_{10}, v_{11}, v_{15}\}$

10) $R_{10} = \{v_0, v_1, v_2, v_3, v_4, v_6, v_5, v_9, v_7, v_8\}$

$\overline{W}_{10} = \{v_{10}, v_{11}, v_{15}\}$

11) $R_{11} = R_{10} \cup v_{15}$ $\overline{W}_{11} = \{v_{10}, v_{11}, v_{16}\}$

12) $R_{12} = R_{11} \cup v_{16}$ $\overline{W}_{12} = \{v_{10}, v_{11}\}$

13) $R_{13} = R_{12} \cup v_{10}$ $\qquad$ $\overline{W}_{13} = \{v_{11}, v_{17}\}$

14) $R_{14} = R_{13} \cup v_{17}$ $\qquad$ $\overline{W}_{14} = \{v_{11}\}$

15) $R_{15} = R_{14} \cup v_{11}$ $\qquad$ $\overline{W}_{15} = \{v_{12}, v_{13}, v_{14}\}$

16) $R_{16} = R_{15} \cup v_{12}$ $\qquad$ $\overline{W}_{16} = \{v_{13}, v_{14}\}$

17) $R_{17} = R_{16} \cup v_{13}$ $\qquad$ $\overline{W}_{17} = \{v_{14}\}$

18) $R_{18} = R_{17} \cup v_{14}$ $\qquad$ $\overline{W}_{18} = \phi$ $\qquad$ STOP.

3.3. Computerized Procedure -- An Example.

The multicriteria simplex method, as it has been discussed in previous paragraphs, is still not fully suitable for computerization. Some of the computational details and additions are discussed and demonstrated on fairly complicated example. Later on we introduce a basic block diagram from which the computer program has been developed.

We shall use an additional (composite) objective function to facilitate some of the computations. This composite function is obtained as a simple sum $\qquad$ $\sum\limits_{i=1}^{\ell} c^i . x$ $\qquad$ (See Tableau 6 of section 3.1.).

A general simplex tableau can now be sketched as follows:

B	x_1	$\cdots$	x_m	x_{m+1}	$\cdots$	x_n	
x_1	1	$\cdots$	0	$y_{1(m+1)}$	$\cdots$	y_{1n}	y_1^o
$\cdot$	$\cdot$		$\cdot$	$\cdot$		$\cdot$	$\cdot$
$\cdot$	$\cdot$		$\cdot$	$\cdot$		$\cdot$	$\cdot$
$\cdot$	$\cdot$		$\cdot$	$\cdot$		$\cdot$	$\cdot$
x_m	0	$\cdots$	1	$y_{m(m+1)}$	$\cdots$	y_{mn}	y_m^o
	0	$\cdots$	0	$z_{m+1}^{(1)}$	$\cdots$	$z_n^{(1)}$	z_o^1
	$\cdot$		$\cdot$	$\cdot$		$\cdot$	$\cdot$
	$\cdot$		$\cdot$	$\cdot$		$\cdot$	$\cdot$
	$\cdot$		$\cdot$	$\cdot$		$\cdot$	$\cdot$
	0	$\cdots$	0	$z_{m+1}^{(\ell)}$	$\cdots$	$z_n^{(\ell)}$	z_o^ℓ
$\sum$	0	$\cdots$	0	$z_{m+1}^{(\ell+1)}$	$\cdots$	$z_n^{(\ell+1)}$	$z_o^{\ell+1}$	Composite Function

$$(3-3-1)$$

After obtaining a basic solution which is nondominated, we consider only nonbasic vectors leading to noncomparable adjacent extreme points as eligible for pivot columns. At some basic solution, no objective function will be at its maximum and only noncomparable adjacent basic solutions will be reachable. Then a subroutine must be employed to establish nondominance.

The subroutine may be summarized as follows (See also Figure 3.3.1.):

(1) Check the $(\ell+1)$st row of the simplex tableau and find the largest negative coefficient. If there is none -- PRINT since

$$x^o = (y_1^o, \ldots, y_m^o) \text{ is nondominated.}$$

(2) In the column chosen at (1), say the jth, we may find two cases:

(i) All coefficients of the criterial part of the simplex tableau (framed in Tableau (3-3-1)) are nonpositive. If the corresponding $\theta_j > 0$ then $x^o \in \mathcal{D}$.

(ii) There is at least one positive coefficient in the column j of the criterial part of the simplex table. Perform simplex iteration with the largest positive coefficient to be the pivot element. Go back to (1).

Remark 3.3.1. The situation described in (2i) can occur, however, only at later stages of the subroutine since we have assumed that only $z_j \sim 0$ or $z_j \geq 0$, $j \in \bar{J}$ is true for nonbasic columns.

If $\theta_j = 0$ in (2i), we perform the iteration in view of Remark 3.1.10.

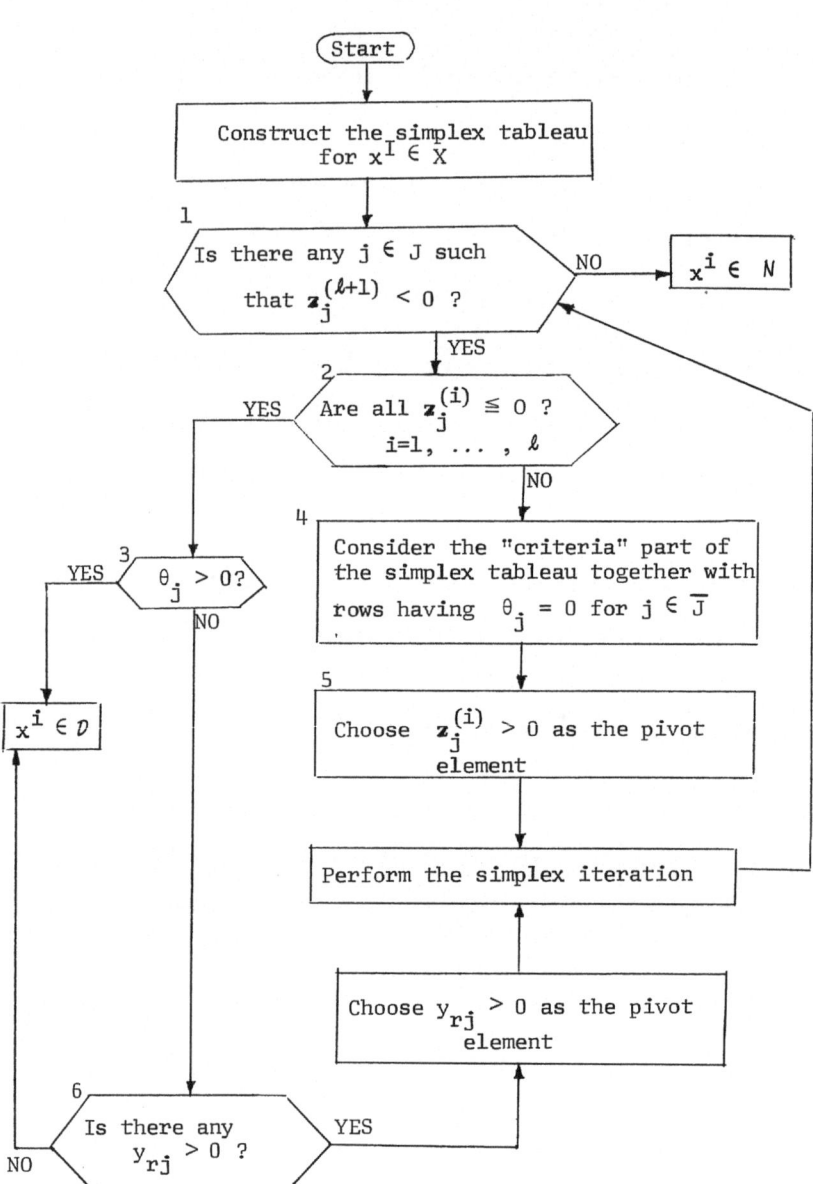

Figure 3.3.1.

Comments on Nondominance Subroutine -- Figure 3.3.1.

(1) First, we check the composite, i.e. $(\ell+1)$st criterial row. If there is no negative element, then Max $v = 0$ and $x^i \in N$. (See Theorem 3.1.6.)

(2) If there is at least one element in (1) which is negative, say $z_j^{(\ell+1)}$, and if all $z_j^{(i)} \leq 0$ (Notice that $z_j \leq 0$ since $z_j^{(\ell+1)} < 0$) then go to (3). If there is at least one $z_j^{(i)} > 0$ go to (4).

(3) If $\theta_j > 0$, obviously by introducing the jth column, we get Max $v > 0$ and $x^i \in \mathcal{D}$. If $\theta_j = 0$, go to (6).

(4) Form the problem by using only "criterial" parts of the simplex tableau as it is framed in (3-3-2). If $\theta_j > 0$, we go directly to (5) since it will stay positive for the iteration. If $\theta_j = 0$, for $j \in \bar{J}$ we add the corresponding row(s) to the problem to keep track of any change in θ_j. (See Remark 3.1.10.).

(5) Perform the simplex iteration on $z_j^{(i)} > 0$ from (2) and go back to (1).

(6) If we added the rows giving $\theta_j = 0$ in (4) then we may explore them after each step for any $y_{rj} > 0$. If there is none, then actual $\theta_j > 0$ since we assume bounded solution exists. If there is $y_{rj} > 0$, then $\theta_j = 0$ and we perform the next iteration around y_{rj}.

The framed part of Tableau (3-3-2) describes the subroutine

situation. Notice that only the framed part of the tableau is considered in the case of nondegenerate solution.

	x_1	$\cdots$	x_m	x_{m+1}	$\cdots$	x_n	y_1	$\cdots$	y_ℓ	
x_1	1	$\cdots$	0	$y_{1(m+1)}$	$\cdots$	y_{1n}	0	$\cdots$	0	y_1^o
$\vdots$	$\vdots$		$\vdots$	$\vdots$		$\vdots$	$\vdots$		$\vdots$	$\vdots$
x_m	0	$\cdots$	1	$y_{m(m+1)}$	$\cdots$	y_{mn}	0	$\cdots$	0	y_m^o
y_1	0	$\cdots$	0	$z_{m+1}^{(1)}$	$\cdots$	$z_n^{(1)}$	1	$\cdots$	0	0
$\vdots$	$\vdots$		$\vdots$	$\vdots$		$\vdots$	$\vdots$		$\vdots$	$\vdots$
y_ℓ	0	$\cdots$	0	$z_{m+1}^{(\ell)}$	$\cdots$	$z_n^{(\ell)}$	0	$\cdots$	1	0
	0	$\cdots$	0	$z_{m+1}^{(\ell+1)}$	$\cdots$	$z_n^{(\ell+1)}$	0	$\cdots$	0	0

$$(3\text{-}3\text{-}2)$$

Now we are ready to construct a basic block diagram describing some of the main features of the algorithm. This is just a logical scheme which had to be expanded in much more detail for actual program construction. See Figure 3.3.2.

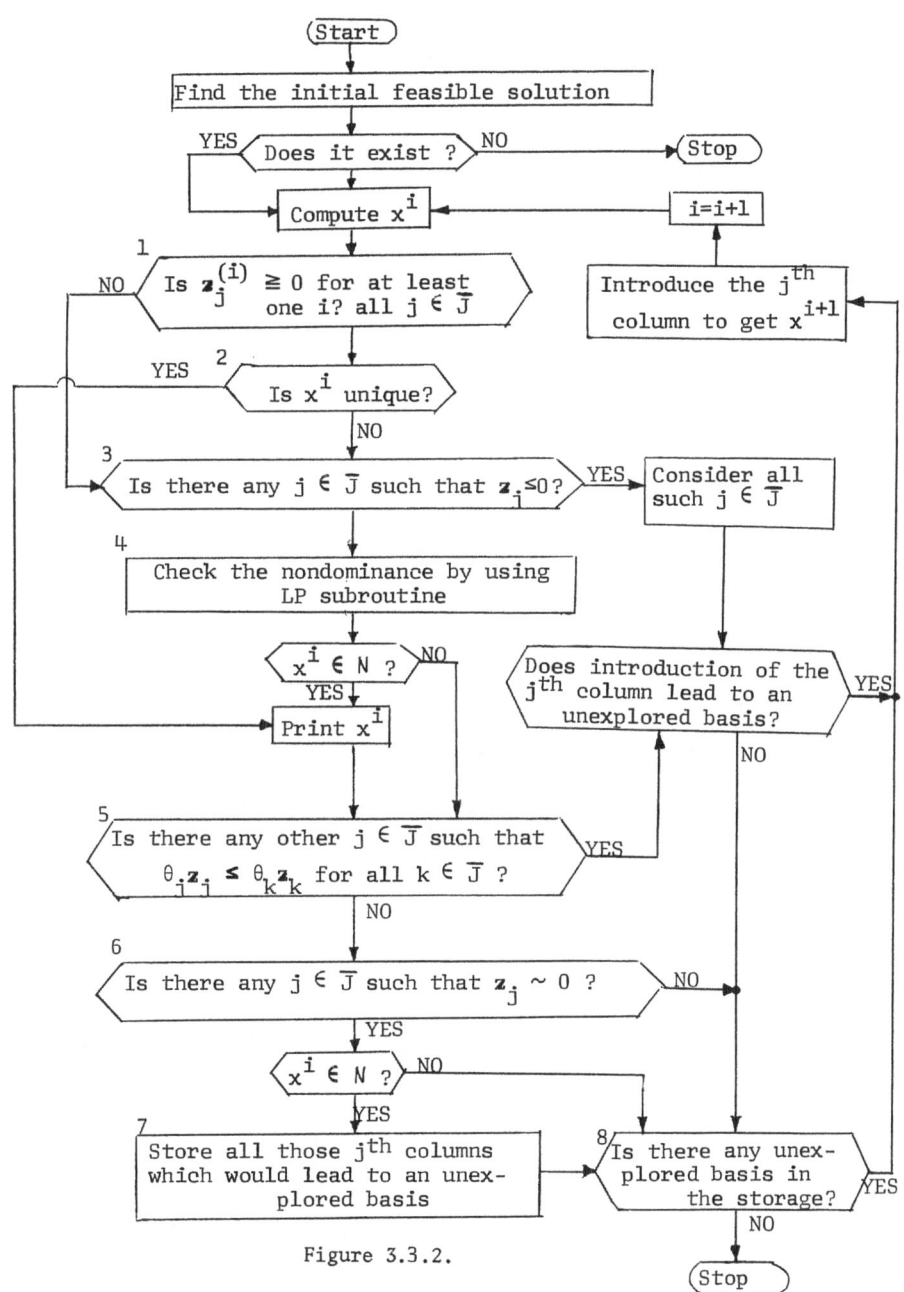

Figure 3.3.2.

Comments on Multicriteria Simplex Method -- Figure 3.3.2.

(1) For some basic solution $x^i \in X$, we first check whether any of the objective function is maximized at this point. This assures that x^i or some alternative solution will be nondominated.

(2) If x^i uniquely maximizes at least one objective function, then $x^i \in N$ and we print x^i.

(3) We use Theorem 3.1.2.(a) here. If $z_j \leq 0$ exists for at least one $j \in \bar{J}$, then $x^i \in D$ if $\theta_j > 0$. If the corresponding j^{th} column leads to an unexplored basis, we make the transformation and go back to (1). Otherwise, go to (8).

(4) Use the nondominance subroutine as described in Figure 3.4.1.

(5) We look for a column which would give us a solution dominating all other points reachable from x^i. If there is one yet unexplored, we make the transformation. Otherwise, go to (8).

(6) Here we look for columns which would lead us to solutions "noncomparable" to x^i. If there are none, go to (8). If there are some, but $x^i \in D$, go to (8).

(7) Select and store those j^{th} columns (and their bases) which would lead to an unexplored solution. These are bases which might potentially be nondominated.

(8) Whenever storage (7) is empty, we stop. (Compare with W_{I+1} in Figure 32.2.

To demonstrate the procedure, we shall analyze a larger example step by step.

$$V\text{-Max} \begin{cases} c^1.x = x_1 + 2x_2 - x_3 + 3x_4 + 2x_5 + x_7 \\ c^2.x = x_2 + x_3 + 2x_4 + 3x_5 + x_6 \\ c^3.x = x_1 + x_3 - x_4 - x_6 - x_7 \end{cases}$$

subject to

$$x_1 + 2x_2 + x_3 + x_4 + 2x_5 + x_6 + 2x_7 \leqq 16$$

$$-2x_1 - x_2 + x_4 + 2x_5 + x_7 \leqq 16$$

$$- x_1 + x_3 + 2x_5 - 2x_7 \leqq 16$$

$$x_2 + 2x_3 - x_4 + x_5 - 2x_6 - x_7 \leqq 16$$

$$x_i \geqq 0, \quad i = 1,2,\ldots,7.$$

The composite function, denoted $\sum$ is calculated as:

$$\sum = 2x_1 + 3x_2 + x_3 + 4x_4 + 5x_5.$$

Now we may construct the initial simplex tableau:

$$x^1 = (0,0,0,0,0,0,0) \qquad (3\text{-}3\text{-}3)$$

y_1	1	2	1	1	②	1	2	1	0	0	0	16
y_2	-2	-1	0	1	2	0	1	0	1	0	0	16
y_3	-1	0	1	0	2	0	-2	0	0	1	0	16
y_4	0	1	2	-1	1	-2	-1	0	0	0	1	16
	-1	-2	1	-3	-2	0	-1	0	0	0	0	0
	0	-1	-1	-2	-3	-1	0	0	0	0	0	0
	-1	0	-1	1	0	1	1	0	0	0	0	0
$\sum$	-2	-3	-1	-4	-5	0	0	0	0	0	0	0

We can see that $x^1 \in \mathcal{D}$ by looking at the fifth column and recalling Theorem 3.1.2.

Replace y_1 by x_5:

x_5	$\frac{1}{2}$	1	$\frac{1}{2}$	$\frac{1}{2}$	1	$\frac{1}{2}$	1	$\frac{1}{2}$	0	0	0	8
y_2	-3	-3	-1	0	0	-1	-1	-1	1	0	0	0
y_3	-2	-2	0	-1	0	-1	-4	-1	0	1	0	0
y_4	$-\frac{1}{2}$	0	$\frac{3}{2}$	$-\frac{3}{2}$	0	$-\frac{5}{2}$	-2	$-\frac{1}{2}$	0	0	1	8
	0	0	2	-2	0	1	1	1	0	0	0	16
	$\frac{3}{2}$	2	$\frac{1}{2}$	$-\frac{1}{2}$	0	$\frac{1}{2}$	3	$\frac{3}{2}$	0	0	0	24
	-1	0	-1	0	0	1	1	0	0	0	0	0
Σ	$\frac{1}{2}$	2	$\frac{3}{2}$	$-\frac{3}{2}$	0	$\frac{5}{2}$	5	$\frac{5}{2}$	0	0	0	40

$$(3\text{-}3\text{-}4)$$

No objective is at its maximum at $x^2 = (0,0,0,0,8,0,0)$. Use the subroutine to establish nondominance:

0	0	2	-2	1	1	1	1	0	0		0
$\frac{3}{2}$	2	$\frac{1}{2}$	$-\frac{1}{2}$	$\frac{1}{2}$	3	$\frac{3}{2}$	0	1	0		0
-1	0	-1	(1)	1	1	0	0	0	1		0
$\frac{1}{2}$	2	$\frac{3}{2}$	$-\frac{3}{2}$	$\frac{5}{2}$	5	$\frac{5}{2}$	0	0	0		0

-2	0	0	0	3	3	1	1	0	2		0
(1)	2	0	0	1	$\frac{7}{2}$	$\frac{3}{2}$	0	1	$\frac{1}{2}$		0
-1	0	-1	1	1	1	0	0	0	1		0
-1	2	0	0	4	$\frac{13}{2}$	$\frac{5}{2}$	0	0	$\frac{3}{2}$		0

0	4	0	0	5	10	4	1	2	-3		0
1	2	0	0	1	$\frac{7}{2}$	$\frac{3}{2}$	0	1	$\frac{1}{2}$		0
0	2	-1	1	2	$\frac{9}{2}$	$\frac{3}{2}$	0	1	$\frac{3}{2}$		0
0	4	0	0	5	10	4	0	1	2		0

PRINT

$x^2 \in N_{ex}$

$\Rightarrow$ Max $v = 0$

For the next step, replace x_5 by x_4:

x_4	①	2	1	1	2	1	2	1	0	0	0	16
y_2	-3	-3	-1	0	0	-1	-1	-1	1	0	0	0
y_3	-1	0	1	0	2	0	-2	0	0	1	0	16
y_4	1	3	3	0	3	-1	1	1	0	0	1	32
	2	4	4	0	4	3	5	3	0	0	0	48
	2	3	1	0	1	1	4	2	0	0	0	32
	-2	-2	-2	0	-2	0	-1	-1	0	0	0	-16
$\sum$	2	5	3	0	3	4	8	4	0	0	0	64

$$(3\text{-}3\text{-}5)$$

This point $x^3 = (0,0,0,16,0,0,0)$ is nondominated because, for example, the first and the second objective functions are at their maximum here (unique). PRINT x^3. (Similarly, the auxiliary objective function is at its unique maximum.)

Next introduce the first column. (The other choice might be the third column.)

x_1	1	2	1	1	2	1	2	1	0	0	0	16
y_2	0	3	2	3	6	2	5	2	1	0	0	48
y_3	0	2	2	1	4	1	0	1	0	1	0	32
y_4	0	1	②	-1	1	-2	-1	0	0	0	1	16
	0	0	2	-2	0	1	1	1	0	0	0	16
	0	-1	-1	-2	-3	-1	0	0	0	0	0	0
	0	2	0	2	2	2	3	1	0	0	0	16
$\sum$	0	1	1	-2	-1	2	4	2	0	0	0	32

$$(3\text{-}3\text{-}6)$$

Again, PRINT x^4 = (16,0,0,0,0,0,0) since the third objective function
is at its maximum here. The alternate solution resulting from introducing the third column gives us a vector of values of objective
functions:

$$\begin{pmatrix} 0 \\ 8 \\ 16 \\ \hline 24 \end{pmatrix} \sim \begin{pmatrix} 16 \\ 0 \\ 16 \\ \hline 32 \end{pmatrix}.$$

Introduce the third column next:

x_1	1	$\frac{3}{2}$	0	$\left(\frac{3}{2}\right)$	$\frac{3}{2}$	2	$\frac{5}{2}$	1	0	0	$-\frac{1}{2}$	8
y_2	0	2	0	4	5	4	6	2	1	0	-1	32
y_3	0	1	0	2	3	3	1	1	0	1	-1	16
x_3	0	$\frac{1}{2}$	1	$-\frac{1}{2}$	$\frac{1}{2}$	-1	$-\frac{1}{2}$	0	0	0	$\frac{1}{2}$	8
	0	-1	0	-1	-1	3	2	1	0	0	-1	0
	0	$-\frac{1}{2}$	0	$-\frac{5}{2}$	$-\frac{5}{2}$	-2	$-\frac{1}{2}$	0	0	0	$\frac{1}{2}$	8
	0	2	0	2	2	2	3	1	0	0	0	16
Σ	0	$\frac{1}{2}$	0	$-\frac{3}{2}$	$-\frac{3}{2}$	3	$\frac{9}{2}$	2	0	0	$-\frac{1}{2}$	24

$$(3\text{-}3\text{-}7)$$

PRINT $x^5 = (8,0,8,0,0,0,0)$ since the third objective function is at its maximum and the two alternate solutions x^4 and x^5 are noncomparable.

Introduce the fourth column:

x_4	$\frac{2}{3}$	1	0	1	(1)	$\frac{4}{3}$	$\frac{5}{3}$	$\frac{2}{3}$	0	0	$-\frac{1}{3}$	$\frac{16}{3}$
y_2	$-\frac{8}{3}$	-2	0	0	1	$-\frac{4}{3}$	$-\frac{2}{3}$	$-\frac{2}{3}$	1	0	$\frac{1}{3}$	$\frac{32}{3}$
y_3	$-\frac{4}{3}$	-1	0	0	1	$\frac{1}{3}$	$-\frac{7}{3}$	$-\frac{1}{3}$	0	1	$-\frac{1}{3}$	$\frac{16}{3}$
x_3	$\frac{1}{3}$	1	1	0	1	$-\frac{1}{3}$	$\frac{1}{3}$	$\frac{1}{3}$	0	0	$\frac{1}{3}$	$\frac{32}{3}$
	$\frac{2}{3}$	0	0	0	0	$\frac{13}{3}$	$\frac{11}{3}$	$\frac{5}{3}$	0	0	$-\frac{4}{3}$	$\frac{16}{3}$
	$\frac{5}{3}$	2	0	0	0	$\frac{4}{3}$	$\frac{11}{3}$	$\frac{5}{3}$	0	0	$-\frac{1}{3}$	$\frac{64}{3}$
	$-\frac{4}{3}$	0	0	0	0	$-\frac{2}{3}$	$-\frac{1}{3}$	$-\frac{1}{3}$	0	0	$\frac{2}{3}$	$\frac{16}{3}$
$\sum$	1	2	0	0	0	5	7	3	0	0	-1	32

$$(3\text{-}3\text{-}8)$$

Here $x^6 = (0,0,\frac{32}{3},\frac{16}{3},0,0,0)$ and since no objective function

is at its maximum, we have to use the subroutine for nondominance:

$\frac{2}{3}$	0	$\frac{13}{3}$	$\frac{11}{3}$	$\frac{5}{3}$	$-\frac{4}{3}$	1	0	0	0
$\frac{5}{3}$	2	$\frac{4}{3}$	$\frac{11}{3}$	$\frac{5}{3}$	$\frac{1}{3}$	0	1	0	0
$-\frac{4}{3}$	0	$-\frac{2}{3}$	$\frac{1}{3}$	$\frac{1}{3}$	$\left(\frac{2}{3}\right)$	0	0	1	0
1	2	5	7	3	-1	0	0	0	0

-2	0	3	3	1	0	1	0	2	0
(1)	2	1	$\frac{21}{6}$	$\frac{3}{2}$	0	0	1	$\frac{1}{2}$	0
-2	0	-1	$-\frac{1}{2}$	$-\frac{1}{2}$	1	0	0	$\frac{3}{2}$	0
-1	2	4	$\frac{13}{2}$	$\frac{5}{2}$	0	0	0	$\frac{3}{2}$	0

0	4	5	10	4	0	1	2	3	0
1	2	1	$\frac{21}{6}$	$\frac{3}{2}$	0	0	1	$\frac{1}{2}$	0
0	4	1	$\frac{13}{2}$	$\frac{5}{2}$	1	0	2	$\frac{5}{2}$	0
0	4	5	10	4	0	0	1	2	0

PRINT x^6. Next introduce the fifth column in the simplex tableau for x^6 -- it will give us the same values for all objective functions, i.e., we can PRINT x^7 without further analysis (x^6 and x^7, though different, both have identical image in the value space.) We get:

x_5	$\frac{2}{3}$	1	0	1	1	$\boxed{\frac{4}{3}}$	$\frac{5}{3}$	$\frac{2}{3}$	0	0	$-\frac{1}{3}$	$\frac{16}{3}$
y_2	$-\frac{10}{3}$	-3	0	-1	0	$\frac{8}{3}$	$\frac{7}{3}$	$-\frac{4}{3}$	1	0	$\frac{2}{3}$	$\frac{16}{3}$
y_3	-2	-2	0	-1	0	-1	-4	-1	0	1	0	0
x_3	$-\frac{1}{3}$	0	1	-1	0	$-\frac{5}{3}$	$\frac{4}{3}$	$-\frac{1}{3}$	0	0	$\frac{2}{3}$	$\frac{16}{3}$
	$\frac{2}{3}$	0	0	0	0	$\frac{13}{3}$	$\frac{11}{3}$	$\frac{5}{3}$	0	0	$-\frac{4}{3}$	$\frac{16}{3}$
	$\frac{5}{3}$	2	0	0	0	$\frac{4}{3}$	$\frac{11}{3}$	$\frac{5}{3}$	0	0	$-\frac{1}{3}$	$\frac{64}{3}$
	$-\frac{4}{3}$	0	0	0	0	$-\frac{2}{3}$	$\frac{1}{3}$	$-\frac{1}{3}$	0	0	$\frac{2}{3}$	$\frac{16}{3}$
Σ	1	2	0	0	0	5	7	3	0	0	-1	32

(3-3-9)

PRINT $x^7 = (0,0,\frac{16}{3},0,\frac{16}{3},0,0)$.

We may introduce the sixth or seventh column. Introducing the sixth column, we get the following:

x_6	$\frac{1}{2}$	$\frac{3}{4}$	0	$\frac{3}{4}$	$\frac{3}{4}$	1	$\left(\frac{5}{4}\right)$	$\frac{1}{2}$	0	0	$-\frac{1}{4}$	4
y_2	-2	2	0	1	2	0	1	0	1	0	0	16
y_3	$-\frac{3}{2}$	$-\frac{5}{4}$	0	$-\frac{1}{4}$	$\frac{3}{4}$	0	$\frac{11}{4}$	$-\frac{1}{2}$	0	1	$-\frac{1}{4}$	4
x_3	$\frac{1}{2}$	$\frac{5}{4}$	1	$\frac{1}{4}$	$\frac{5}{4}$	0	$\frac{3}{4}$	$\frac{1}{2}$	0	0	$\frac{1}{4}$	12
	$-\frac{3}{2}$	$-\frac{13}{4}$	0	$-\frac{13}{4}$	$-\frac{13}{4}$	0	$-\frac{7}{4}$	$-\frac{1}{2}$	0	0	$\frac{1}{4}$	-12
	1	1	0	-1	-1	0	2	1	0	0	0	16
	-1	$\frac{1}{2}$	0	$\frac{1}{2}$	$\frac{1}{2}$	0	$\frac{1}{2}$	0	0	0	$\frac{1}{2}$	8
Σ	$-\frac{3}{2}$	$-\frac{7}{4}$	0	$-\frac{15}{4}$	$-\frac{15}{4}$	0	$\frac{3}{4}$	$\frac{1}{2}$	0	0	$\frac{1}{4}$	12

(3-3-10)

So, $x^8 = (0,0,12,0,0,4,0)$. To check the nondominance of x^8, we must use the subroutine:

$-\frac{3}{2}$	$\frac{13}{4}$	$\frac{13}{4}$	$\frac{13}{4}$	$\frac{7}{4}$	$\frac{1}{2}$	$\frac{1}{4}$	1	0	0	0
1	1	-1	-1	2	1	0	0	1	0	0
-1	$\frac{1}{2}$	$\left(\frac{1}{2}\right)$	$\frac{1}{2}$	$\frac{1}{2}$	0	$\frac{1}{2}$	0	0	1	0
$-\frac{3}{2}$	$\frac{7}{4}$	$\frac{15}{4}$	$\frac{15}{4}$	$\frac{3}{4}$	$\frac{1}{2}$	$\frac{1}{4}$	0	0	0	0

-8	0	0	0	$\frac{3}{2}$	$-\frac{1}{2}$	3	1	0	$\frac{13}{2}$	0
-1	2	0	0	3	1	1	0	1	2	0
-2	1	1	1	1	0	1	0	0	2	0
-9	2	0	0	$\frac{9}{2}$	$\frac{1}{2}$	4	0	0	$\frac{15}{2}$	0

↑

Because of the first column and $\theta_1 > 0$, $x^8 \in \mathcal{D}$. Let us now

introduce the seventh column:

(3-3-11)

x_7	$\frac{2}{5}$	$\frac{3}{5}$	0	$\frac{3}{5}$	$\frac{3}{5}$	$\frac{4}{5}$	1	$\frac{2}{5}$	0	0	$-\frac{1}{5}$	$\frac{16}{5}$
y_2	$-\frac{12}{5}$	$\frac{7}{5}$	0	$\frac{2}{5}$	$\frac{7}{5}$	$\frac{4}{5}$	0	$-\frac{2}{5}$	1	0	$\frac{1}{5}$	$\frac{64}{5}$
y_3	$-\frac{2}{5}$	$\frac{2}{5}$	0	$\frac{7}{5}$	$\frac{12}{5}$	$\frac{11}{5}$	0	$\frac{3}{5}$	0	1	$\frac{4}{5}$	$\frac{64}{5}$
x_3	$\frac{1}{5}$	$\frac{4}{5}$	1	$-\frac{1}{5}$	$\frac{4}{5}$	$-\frac{3}{5}$	0	$\frac{1}{5}$	0	0	$\frac{2}{5}$	$\frac{48}{5}$
	$-\frac{4}{5}$	$-\frac{11}{5}$	0	$\frac{11}{5}$	$-\frac{11}{5}$	$\frac{7}{5}$	0	$\frac{1}{5}$	0	0	$-\frac{3}{5}$	$-\frac{32}{5}$
	$\frac{1}{5}$	$-\frac{1}{5}$	0	$-\frac{11}{5}$	$-\frac{11}{5}$	$\frac{8}{5}$	0	$\frac{1}{5}$	0	0	$\frac{2}{5}$	$\frac{48}{5}$
	$-\frac{6}{5}$	$\frac{1}{5}$	0	$\frac{1}{5}$	$\frac{1}{5}$	$-\frac{2}{5}$	0	$-\frac{1}{5}$	0	0	$\frac{3}{5}$	$\frac{32}{5}$
Σ	$\frac{9}{5}$	$-\frac{11}{5}$	0	$-\frac{21}{5}$	$-\frac{21}{5}$	$-\frac{3}{5}$	0	$\frac{1}{5}$	0	0	$\frac{2}{5}$	$\frac{48}{5}$

So, $x^9 = (0,0,\frac{48}{5}, 0,0,0,\frac{16}{5})$. To check the nondominance, use the subroutine:

$-\frac{4}{5}$	$-\frac{11}{5}$	$-\frac{11}{5}$	$-\frac{11}{5}$	$\frac{7}{5}$	$\frac{1}{5}$	$-\frac{3}{5}$	1	0	0	0
$\frac{1}{5}$	$-\frac{1}{5}$	$-\frac{11}{5}$	$-\frac{11}{5}$	$\frac{8}{5}$	$\frac{1}{5}$	$\frac{2}{5}$	0	1	0	0
$-\frac{6}{5}$	$\frac{1}{5}$	$\left(\frac{1}{5}\right)$	$\frac{1}{5}$	$\frac{2}{5}$	$-\frac{1}{5}$	$\frac{3}{5}$	0	0	1	0
$-\frac{9}{5}$	$-\frac{11}{5}$	$-\frac{21}{5}$	$-\frac{21}{5}$	$\frac{3}{5}$	$\frac{1}{5}$	$\frac{2}{5}$	0	0	0	0

-14	0	0	0	-3	-2	6	1	0	11	0
-13	2	0	0	-6	-2	7	0	1	11	0
- 6	1	1	1	-2	-1	3	0	0	5	0
-27	2	0	0	-9	-4	13	0	0	$\frac{107}{5}$	0

We see that x^9 is obviously dominated because of the first column and $\theta_1 > 0$.

To summarize the results, we have explored the following noncomparable extreme points and established their dominance $\mathcal{D}$

or nondominance N:

	x^2	x^3	x^4	x^5	x^6	x^7	x^8	x^9
$c^1.x$	16	48	16	0	5.33	5.33	-12	-6.4
$c^2.x$	24	32	0	8	21.33	21.33	16	9.6
$c^3.x$	0	-16	16	16	5.33	5.33	8	6.4
	N	N	N	N	N	N	D	D

$$(3\text{-}3\text{-}12)$$

Notice that though all the extreme points are noncomparable with each other, x^8 and x^9 are dominated. We can see that for example: x^8 is dominated by $\frac{1}{2} x^2 + \frac{1}{2} x^5$, i.e.

$$\frac{1}{2}\begin{pmatrix} 16 \\ 24 \\ 0 \end{pmatrix} + \frac{1}{2}\begin{pmatrix} 0 \\ 8 \\ 16 \end{pmatrix} = \begin{pmatrix} 8 \\ 16 \\ 8 \end{pmatrix} \geq \begin{pmatrix} -12 \\ 16 \\ 8 \end{pmatrix}$$

Also, x^9 is dominated by the same point, i.e.,

$$\begin{pmatrix} 8 \\ 16 \\ 8 \end{pmatrix} \geq \begin{pmatrix} -6.4 \\ 9.6 \\ 6.4 \end{pmatrix}$$

3. 4. Computer Analysis.

The block diagram in Figure 3.3.2. can be expanded into more detailed form, suitable for computer analysis. Most computations were performed on IBM 7040 and thus the computing times should be only of a relative value.

The program has been coded in Fortran and the entire code is presented in App'x A3 together with all subroutines. The program is currently limited to eight constraints, forty variables and eight objective functions. This can, however, be easily expanded, actually a problem with 20 variables, 12 constraints and 5 objectives has also been computed. No claim is made with regard to professional efficiency of the code since the author is not a computer programmer by profession.

Some difficulties, additional to the traditional simplex method, are introduced by the fact that many different bases must be explored and many of their adjacent bases stored. The problem of how to traverse all eligible bases efficiently, i.e. without repetition, has been resolved.

One other problem comes from the fact that the problem is usually sufficiently lengthy and complex so that round-off errors may accumulate to the point where they obscure the actual result. Especially using the inflexible definition of N-points as we do the round-off errors may lead us to declare a point as nondominated when it actually is dominated and vice versa. This problem is hard to resolve though double precision arithmetic might be used to improve the accuracy.

Careful analysis of print-outs is, however, always necessary to eliminate the round-off errors.

Three example problems have been constructed to check the speed, efficiency of the search, subroutines, storage and other aspects of the program.

(1) The first example computed is the problem of section 3.3. whose initial simplex tableau is given in (3-3-3). This is by no means a trivial example since degeneracies as well as alternate solutions appear. We can compare computer results with hand calculations as they are summarized in (3-3-12). From printouts on pages 197 - 199 of Appendix A2 we get:

	x^2	x^4	x^5	x^6	x^3	x^7
$c^1.x$	16	16	0	5.33	(48)	5.33
$c^2.x$	24	0	7.99	21.33	(32)	21.33
$c^3.x$	0	(16)	(16)	5.33	-16	5.33
Σ	40	32	24	32	64	32

These results correspond exactly to those obtained from hand analysis. Total time has been 2.881 minutes.

(2) The second problem is constructed especially to demonstrate the speed and the efficiency of the program. The problem contains eight constraints, eight variables and three objective functions.

$$\text{v-Max} \begin{cases} 2x_1 + 5x_2 + x_3 - x_4 + 6x_5 + 8x_6 + 3x_7 - 2x_8 \\ 5x_1 - 2x_2 + 5x_3 \quad + 6x_5 + 7x_6 + 2x_7 + 6x_8 \\ x_1 + x_2 + x_3 + x_4 + x_5 + x_6 + x_7 + x_8 \end{cases}$$

subject to:

$$x_1 + 3x_2 - 4x_3 + x_4 - x_5 + x_6 + x_7 + x_8 \leq 40$$

$$5x_1 + 2x_2 + 4x_3 - x_4 + 3x_5 + 7x_6 + 2x_7 + 7x_8 \leq 84$$

$$4x_2 - x_3 - x_4 - 3x_5 \quad + x_8 \leq 18$$

$$-3x_1 - 4x_2 + 8x_3 + 2x_4 + 3x_5 - 4x_6 + 5x_7 - x_8 \leq 100$$

$$12x_1 + 8x_2 - x_3 + 4x_4 \quad + x_6 + x_7 \leq 40$$

$$x_1 + x_2 + x_3 + x_4 + x_5 + x_6 + x_7 + x_8 \geq 12$$

$$8x_1 - 12x_2 - 3x_3 + 4x_4 - x_5 \leq 30$$

$$-5x_1 - 6x_2 + 12x_3 + x_4 \quad - x_7 + x_8 \leq 100$$

$$x_i \geq 0; \quad i = 1,\ldots,8$$

The problem is intentionally complicated. For example, the third objective appears also as the sixth constraint with $\geq$. Also notice that for example, the third constraint equals the second constraint minus the second objective function. From printouts on page 201 of Appendix A2 :

	x^1	x^2	x^3
$c^1.x$	$173.3\dot{3}$	$176.8\dot{3}3$	170.55319
$c^2.x$	$178.6\dot{6}$	$176.3\dot{3}$	179.06383
$c^3.x$	$35.1\dot{1}$	$38.61\dot{1}$	39.34751
$\sum$	$387.1\dot{1}$	$391.7\dot{7}$	388.96453

Though the problem may have up to 12870 extreme points, the actual number of N_{ex} is only three for this example. The program handled the situation quite effectively as it is reflected in total time of 0.814 minutes. The next problem has been also done on IBM 360/91.

(3) This problem is specifically constructed to contain very large number of nondominated bases. It contains eight constraints, eight variables and five objective functions. Some dependencies to introduce degeneracies and alternate solutions are also present.

$$
\text{v-Max}
\begin{cases}
3x_1 - 7x_2 + 4x_3 + x_4 \quad\quad\quad - x_6 - x_7 + 8x_8 \\
2x_1 + 5x_2 + x_3 - x_4 + 6x_5 + 8x_6 + 3x_7 - 2x_8 \\
5x_1 - 2x_2 + 5x_3 \quad\quad + 6x_5 + 7x_6 + 2x_7 + 6x_8 \\
\quad\quad 4x_2 - x_3 - x_4 - 3x_5 \quad\quad\quad\quad x_8 \\
x_1 + x_2 + x_3 + x_4 + x_5 + x_6 + x_7 + x_8
\end{cases}
$$

subject to:

$$x_1 + 3x_2 - 4x_3 + x_4 - x_5 + x_6 + 2x_7 + 4x_8 \leq 40$$

$$5x_1 + 2x_2 + 4x_3 - x_4 - 3x_5 + 7x_6 + 2x_7 + 7x_8 \leq 84$$

$$4x_2 - x_3 - x_4 - 3x_5 + x_8 \leq 18$$

$$-3x_1 - 4x_2 + 8x_3 + 2x_4 + 3x_5 - 4x_6 + 5x_7 - x_8 \leq 100$$

$$12x_1 + 8x_2 - x_3 + 4x_4 + x_6 + x_7 \leq 40$$

$$x_1 + x_2 + x_3 + x_4 + x_5 + x_6 + x_7 + x_8 \geq 12$$

$$8x_1 - 12x_2 - 3x_3 + 4x_4 - x_5 \leq 30$$

$$-5x_1 - 6x_2 + 12x_3 + x_4 - x_7 + x_8 \leq 100$$

$$x_i \geq 0, \quad i = 1,\ldots,8,$$

In this problem, the round-off errors accumulated enough to obscure some of the results. However, after some analysis of printouts for Problem (3), we may form the following table of results:

	$c^1.x$	$c^2.x$	$c^3.x$	$c^4.x$	$c^5.x$
1	115.93	-28.75	87.18	-3.18	26.13
2	116.08	-29.07	87.00	-3.00	25.55
3	64.39	16.74	81.13	2.87	17.65

cont.

	$c^1.x$	$c^2.x$	$c^3.x$	$c^4.x$	$c^5.x$
4	37.20	49.33	86.54	-2.54	22.46
5	110.84	-22.72	88.12	-4.12	27.12
6	82.72	28.52	111.24	-27.24	28.99
7	(117.25)	-27.75	89.50	-5.50	27.00
8	-17.73	106.18	88.45	-4.45	26.64
9	-37.52	111.59	74.07	9.92	22.63
10	-29.00	106.55	77.55	6.45	29.44
11	-12.09	102.56	90.46	-6.47	31.66
12	-19.09	125.21	106.13	-22.13	33.43
13	-37.72	135.90	98.17	-14.17	31.78
14	-36.53	159.20	122.66	-38.66	33.24
15	-35.00	173.00	138.00	-54.00	29.66
16	-2.78	86.78	84.00	0.00	12.70
17	-36.37	105.85	69.48	14.52	14.59
18	8.51	170.55	(179.06)	-95.06	(39.35)
19	10.00	168.94	178.94	-94.94	37.49
20	-0.50	(176.83)	176.33	-92.33	38.61
21	5.33	173.33	178.66	-94.66	35.11
22	24.00	150.00	174.00	-90.00	39.00
23	85.84	38.35	124.18	-40.18	33.56
24	95.40	-1.38	94.01	-10.01	31.08
25	31.75	51.42	83.17	0.83	26.22
26	7.05	63.63	70.68	13.31	28.11
27	77.84	12.10	89.94	-5.94	31.30

cont.

	$c^1.x$	$c^2.x$	$c^3.x$	$c^4.x$	$c^5.x$
28	35.74	82.51	118.25	-34.25	34.60
29	9.31	93.48	102.80	-18.80	29.03
30	86.73	-11.89	74.84	9.16	13.08
31	66.34	-0.34	66.00	18.00	15.00
32	66.56	-0.56	66.00	18.00	19.84
33	72.00	-6.00	66.00	18.00	14.62
34	30.40	35.60	66.00	18.00	14.00
35	33.12	32.88	66.00	18.00	14.35
36	15.89	50.11	66.00	18.00	16.30
37	-17.73	83.73	66.00	18.00	14.80
38	29.34	36.65	66.00	18.00	21.37
39	30.43	35.57	66.00	18.00	21.36
40	30.62	35.38	66.00	18.00	21.42
41	29.72	36.28	66.00	18.00	21.50
42	56.30	-4.70	51.61	18.00	12.00
43	48.85	-0.77	49.63	18.00	12.00
44	40.80	12.20	53.00	18.00	12.00
45	47.13	2.71	49.84	18.00	12.00
46	72.00	2.67	74.67	9.33	12.00
47	95.27	-21.27	74.00	10.00	12.55
48	19.55	46.46	66.00	18.00	24.44
49	-9.06	75.06	66.00	18.00	17.88
50	117.19	-24.95	92.24	-8.24	28.09
51	-13.34	99.19	85.85	-1.85	28.22

cont.

	$c^1.x$	$c^2.x$	$c^3.x$	$c^4.x$	$c^5.x$
52	-19.18	118.22	99.00	-15.04	29.75
53	49.25	35.93	85.18	-1.18	21.20
54	84.66	-8.00	76.60	7.33	13.30
55	-18.00	102.00	84.00	0.00	24.00
56	86.80	15.60	102.40	-18.40	24.80
57	91.60	-7.50	84.00	0.00	15.30
58	15.88	55.14	71.03	12.96	25.57
59	36.34	101.60	138.00	-54.00	34.34
60	27.40	73.40	100.80	-16.80	31.13
61	23.13	69.95	93.00	-9.07	22.24
62	31.75	100.21	131.90	-47.96	23.12
63	16.00	140.00	156.00	-72.00	26.66
64	49.28	77.60	126.80	-42.80	22.50
65	-20.72	121.58	100.86	-16.86	31.80
66	47.80	46.12	93.94	-9.94	17.36
67	-0.17	71.74	71.57	12.42	21.00
68	-12.00	96.00	84.00	0.00	12.00
69	81.37	-6.40	75.00	9.00	12.94
70	26.00	66.23	92.33	-8.33	15.57

It is seen that we have identified 70 different N_{ex}-points. Individual maxima of all objectives are encircled to simplify the review of data.

LINEAR MULTIOBJECTIVE PROGRAMMING   III.

4. A Method for Generating All Nondominated Solutions of X

We have described some techniques for calculating all nondominated extreme points of X, N_{ex}. The problem which remains to be solved is concerned with generating a complete set N from N_{ex}.

Though this might seem to be superfluous work, we may well imagine situations where a non-extreme nondominated solution might be preferred to any extreme nondominated solution.

4.1. Some basic theorems on properties of N

<u>Lemma 4.1.1.</u> Let $x^1, x^2 \in X$. Then

(a) If $x^1, x^2 \in \mathcal{D}$, then $[x^1, x^2] \subset \mathcal{D}$.

(b) If $x^1 \in N$, $x^2 \in \mathcal{D}$, then $(x^1, x^2] \subset \mathcal{D}$.

(c) If $x \in (x^1, x^2)$ and $x \in N$, then $[x^1, x^2] \subset N$.

(d) If $x \in (x^1, x^2)$ and $x \in \mathcal{D}$, then $(x^1, x^2) \subset \mathcal{D}$.

<u>Proof.</u>

(a) Since $x^1, x^2 \in \mathcal{D}$, there exist some $\bar{x}^1, \bar{x}^2 \in X$ such that $c\bar{x}^1 \geq cx^1$ and $c\bar{x}^2 \geq cx^2$. Let $x = \lambda x^1 + (1-\lambda)x^2$. Notice, $\lambda\bar{x}^1 + (1-\lambda)\bar{x}^2 \in X$. Then $\lambda c\bar{x}^1 + (1-\lambda)c\bar{x}^2 \geq \lambda cx^1 + (1-\lambda)cx^2 = cx$.

(b) For $0 \leq \lambda < 1$ let $x = x^2 + \lambda(x^1 - x^2)$, i.e., $x \in (x^1, x^2]$. Notice that $\bar{x} = \bar{x}^2 + \lambda(x^1 - \bar{x}^2) \in X$, and $c\bar{x} = c\bar{x}^2 + \lambda cx^1 - \lambda c\bar{x}^2 =$

$= (1-\lambda)c\bar{x}^2 + \lambda cx^1 \geq (1-\lambda)cx^2 + \lambda cx^1 = cx$.

(c) Notice $x^1, x^2 \in \mathcal{D}$ implies $x \in \mathcal{D}$, i.e., contradiction. If $x^1 \in \mathcal{D}$, $x^2 \in N$ or $x^1 \in N$, $x^2 \in \mathcal{D}$, this implies $x \in \mathcal{D}$ and we have a contradiction again. So $x \in N$ must imply $x^1, x^2 \in N$. In order to see that $[x^1, x^2] \subset N$, suppose there is some $\bar{x} \in (x^1, x^2)$ such that $\bar{x} \in \mathcal{D}$. Then $x \in (x^1, \bar{x})$ or $x \in (\bar{x}, x^2)$. According to part (b) of this lemma, $(x^1, \bar{x}] \subset \mathcal{D}$, and $[\bar{x}, x^2) \subset \mathcal{D}$ which imply $x \in \mathcal{D}$.

    (d) Proof is similar to that for part (c) since this is a partial converse of (c). Q.E.D.

    Let us state a generalization of Lemma 4.1.1. We shall denote $C[x^1, \ldots, x^k]$ to be a convex hull of the set of points $\{x^1, \ldots, x^k\}$. Also recall from our notational agreement in section 1.4. the relative interior of X is denoted X^I as opposed to Int X.

Theorem 4.1.2. Let $H = C[x^1, \ldots, x^k]$ be the convex hull of the set of points $\{x^1, \ldots, x^k\}$. Then

    (i) If there is $x \in H^I$ such that $x \in N$, then $H \subset N$;

    (ii) If there is $x \in H^I$ such that $x \in \mathcal{D}$, then $H^I \subset \mathcal{D}$.

Proof.

    (i) If at least one $x^i \in \mathcal{D}$, $x^i \in \{x^1, \ldots, x^k\}$ then there is some $\bar{x} \in H$ such that $x \in (\bar{x}, x^i)$. Then $x^i \in \mathcal{D}$ implies $x \in \mathcal{D}$. Assume that there is some $\bar{x} \in H$ such that $\bar{x} \in \mathcal{D}$. Then there exists at least one point $\hat{x} \in H$ such that $x \in (\bar{x}, \hat{x})$. It follows from Lemma 4.1.1. (a) and (b) that $x \in \mathcal{D}$, a contradiction.

    (ii) If $\bar{x} \in H^I$ and $\bar{x} \in N$, then $H \subset N$. This implies $H^I \subset N$ and $x \in N$ which contradicts the original assumption $x \in \mathcal{D}$. Q.E.D.

    Let the feasible set X be defined:

$$X = \{x | x \in E^n; \ A_r x \overset{\leq}{=} b_r\}, \tag{4-1-1}$$

where A_r is the rth row of matrix A, $r = 1, \ldots, m+n$. Notice that this definition of X differs from that in (2-2-3). Also, the nonnegativity constraints are incorporated in general inequality constraints.

Let $R = \{1, \ldots, m+n\}$. For $x \in X$ define:

$$R(x) = \{r | r \in R; \ A_r x = b_r\}. \tag{4-1-2}$$

Notice if $x \in \partial X$ then $R(x) \neq \phi$.

Let $N_{ex} = \{x^i\}$, $i \in K = \{1, \ldots, k\}$. Since any such extreme point of X is also a boundary point of X, then $R(x^i) \neq \phi$, $i \in K$. Each $x^i \in N$ divides the components $A_r x^i \overset{\leq}{=} b_r$, $r \in R$ into two subsets:

(a) active constraints satisfying $A_r x^i = b_r$

and (b) inactive constraints satisfying $A_r x^i < b_r$.

The above defined set $R(x^i)$ identifies the active constraints. Let $\bar{R}(x^i)$ be the complement of $R(x^i)$, then $R(x^i) \cup \bar{R}(x^i) = R$, $i \in K$.

For a particular $r \in R$, define

$$I(r) = \{i | i \in K; \ A_r x^i = b_r\} \tag{4-1-3}$$

as a set of indices $i \in K$ such that their corresponding $x^i \in N$ make the rth constraint active, i.e., $A_r x^i = b_r$ for all $i \in I(r)$.

Let $\bar{I}(r) = K - I(r)$. Given $r \in R$ define

$$H_r = \{x | x \in E^n; \ A_r x = b_r\} \tag{4-1-4}$$

as a (n-1) dimensional hyperplane in E^n.

Let $P_r = C[x^i | i \in I(r)]$, i.e., P_r is a convex hull of all points

x^i, $i \in K$, belonging to H_r. Note, $P_r \subset H_r$.

As a corollary to Theorem 4.1.2., we have

Corollary 4.1.3. The following statement holds:

  (i) if there is $x \in P_r^I$ such that $x \in N$, then $P_r \subset N$.

  (ii) if there is $x \in P_r^I$ such that $x \in D$, then $P_r^I \subset D$.

Remark 4.1.4. Two extreme points of a closed polyhedron are called adjacent if the line connecting them is an edge of the polyhedron. If by performing a single simplex transformation we can from one of the two points reach the other point, then both points are the endpoints of an edge of X.

Given a family of subsets of R

$$J_t = \{I_r^{(t)} | r=1, \ldots, K_t, \text{ card } I_r^{(t)} = t\}, \tag{4-1-5}$$

where r is the index of subsets, $t = 1, \ldots, m+n$, we can define

$$X_t(r) = \{x \in X | A_r^{(t)} x = 0\} \tag{4-1-6}$$

and

$$X_t^*(r) = N_{ex} \cap X_t(r). \tag{4-1-7}$$

Note $X_t(r)$ is the rth hyperplane defined by t linear equalities and $X_t^*(r)$ is the set of N_{ex}-points contained in $X_t(r)$.

Recalling definition (2-1-5) we may write

$$G[X_t(r)] = \{h | h = \mu_r^{(t)} \cdot A_r^{(t)}, \mu_r^{(t)} \gtreqless 0\}. \tag{4-1-8}$$

Remark 4.1.5. Notice that $G[X_t(r)]$ is independent of x in $X_t(r)$. That is, it depends only on t, r. Thus we will denote it by $G_r^{(t)}$. Also, notice $\mu_r^{(t)}$ is the rth t-dimensional vector, independent of r, so we may use $\mu^{(t)}$. We can see $X_t^*(r) \subset X_t(r)$.

According to Theorem 2.1.5. and Corollary 4.1.3. we can prove the following:

Theorem 4.1.6.

  (a) If $H^> \cap G_r^{(t)} \neq \phi$, then $C[X_t^*(r)] \subset N$

  (b) If $H^\geq \cap G_r^{(t)} = \phi$, then $C[X_t^*(r)]^I \cap N = \phi$.

Proof. Recall the definition of G(x) in (2-1-5).

  (a) Observe that for each $x \in X_t(r) \cap X$, $G_r^{(t)} \subset G(x)$ by definition. By assumption

$$H^> \cap G(x) \neq \phi \text{ for all } x \in X_t(r).$$

In view of Theorems 2.1.1. and 2.1.5. the assertion of (a) clearly follows.

  (b) Observe that $G(x) = G_r^{(t)}$ for each $x \in C[X_t^*(r)]^I$. The conclusion (b) follows immediately from Theorems 2.1.1. and 2.1.5. Q.E.D.

Corollary 4.1.7.

  If $C[X_t^*(r)] \subset N$ and $X_t^*(r_1) \subset X_t^*(r)$, then $C[X_t^*(r_1)] \subset N$.

4.2. An algorithm for generating N from known N_{ex}.

Our goal is to generate all nondominated faces of X given N_{ex}. In the following discussion we shall use t to indicate a number of active constraints, $i \in K$ the index of N_{ex}-points, and $\mathbf{r}$ the index of subsets of R having exactly t elements (recall definition of J_t in (4-1-5)).

We shall recursively define a sequence of matrices $N^{(t)}$:

$$N^{(t)} = \left[n_{ir}^{(t)}\right], \qquad t = 1,2,\ldots,m+n \qquad\qquad (4\text{-}2\text{-}1)$$

$$\mathbf{r} = 1,2,\ldots,K_t.$$

which associates N_{ex}-points with the K_t subsets of the set J_t, which has exactly t active constraints.

Let, for example, $t = 1$, i.e., all constraints are considered individually. Then $K_1 = m+n$ and $N^{(1)} = \left[n_{ir}^{(1)}\right]$ may be written as follows:

	1	2	$\ldots$	m	m+1	$\ldots$	m+n
x^1	$n_{11}^{(1)}$	$n_{12}^{(1)}$	$\ldots$	$n_{1m}^{(1)}$	$n_{1(m+1)}^{(1)}$	$\ldots$	$n_{1(m+n)}^{(1)}$
x^2	$n_{21}^{(1)}$	$n_{22}^{(1)}$	$\ldots$	$n_{2m}^{(1)}$	$n_{2(m+1)}^{(1)}$	$\ldots$	$n_{1(m+n)}^{(1)}$
.	.	.	.	.	.	.	.
.	.	.	.	.	.	.	.
.	.	.	.	.	.	.	.
x^k	$n_{k1}^{(1)}$	$n_{k2}^{(1)}$	$\ldots$	$n_{km}^{(1)}$	$n_{k(m+1)}^{(1)}$	$\ldots$	$n_{k(m+n)}^{(1)}$
	$n_1^{(1)}$	$n_2^{(1)}$	$\ldots$	$n_m^{(1)}$	$n_{m+1}^{(1)}$	$\ldots$	$n_{m+n}^{(1)}$

where $\quad n_{ir}^{(1)} = \begin{cases} 1 & \text{if } x^i \text{ makes the } \mathbf{r}^{th} \text{ constraint of } J_1 \text{ active} \\ 0 & \text{otherwise} \end{cases}$

$$(4\text{-}2\text{-}2)$$

and $\quad n_{\mathbf{r}}^{(1)} = \sum_{i=1}^{k} n_{i\mathbf{r}}^{(1)}, \quad \mathbf{r} = 1,2,\ldots,K_1.$

The $n_r^{(1)}$ indicates the number of points x^i, $i \in K$ which make the rth constraint active. Notice that $0 \leq n_r^{(1)} \leq k$, $r = 1, \ldots, K_1$.

Observe, if the rth column of $N^{(1)}$ contains only one or less non-zero elements, then $n_r^{(1)} = 0$ or $n_r^{(1)} = 1$. If $n_r^{(1)} = 0$, then the hyperplane $X_1(r)$ (see (4-1-6)) contains no N_{ex}-point, i.e., the rth constraint is not active for any $x^i \in N_{ex}$. Since any N-point is a convex combination of N_{ex}-points, then all $x \in X_1(r)$ must be dominated. Therefore, the rth column may be deleted from $N^{(1)}$ and from further consideration.

Similarly, if $n_r^{(1)} = 1$, then $X_1(r)$ contains exactly one N_{ex}-point. Then all other points $x \in X_1(r)$ will be dominated and the rth column may be deleted from $N^{(1)}$. (See, Theorem 4-1-2).

In general, a matrix $N^{(t)}$ may be written as:

	1	2	$\cdots$	K_t
x^1	$n_{11}^{(t)}$	$n_{12}^{(t)}$	$\cdots$	$n_{1K_t}^{(t)}$
x^2	$n_{21}^{(t)}$	$n_{22}^{(t)}$	$\cdots$	$n_{2K_t}^{(t)}$
$\vdots$	$\vdots$	$\vdots$	$\vdots$	$\vdots$
x^k	$n_{k1}^{(t)}$	$n_{k2}^{(t)}$	$\cdots$	$n_{kK_t}^{(t)}$
	$n_1^{(t)}$	$n_2^{(t)}$	$\cdots$	$n_{K_t}^{(t)}$

where
$$n_{ir}^{(t)} = \begin{cases} 1 & \text{if } x^i \text{ makes the } r^{th} \text{ subset of } t \text{ constraints in } J_t \text{ active} \\ 0 & \text{otherwise} \end{cases}$$

(4-2-3)

and $\qquad n_r^{(t)} = \sum_{i=1}^{k} n_{ir}^{(t)}, \quad r = 1,2,\ldots,K_t.$

Notice that $n_r^{(t)}$ indicates the number of points x^i, $i \in K$ which make the rth t-tuple of constraints active.

Remark 4.2.1.

(a) Suppose the rth column of $N^{(t)}$ contains no non-zero element $(n_r^{(t)} = 0)$. Then $X_t^*(r) = \phi$. (See (4-1-7)). If $n_r^{(t)} = 1$, then $X_t(r)$ (and $X_t^*(r)$) contains exactly one N_{ex}-point. Then $C[X_t^*(r)] \subset N$ by assumption. In both cases we may delete the rth column from $N^{(t)}$.

(b) Notice $X_t(r)$ is an $(n-t)$ dimensional subset of X (assuming nonredundant constraints only). $X_t(r)$ contains nondominated subset $C[X_t^*(r)]$ only if there is at least n-t of N_{ex}-points in $X_t(r)$. Then the rth constraint cannot be deleted. We may delete the rth column from $N^{(t)}$ only if $X_t(r)$ contains less than n-t of N_{ex}-points. If $C[X_t^*(r)] \subset N$, then all of its boundary, which is the intersection of $X_t^*(r)$ with other hyperplanes, is also nondominated. We may then delete the rth column from $N^{(t)}$. To check whether $C[X_t^*(r)] \subset N$, use Theorem 4.1.6. For simplicity, let us denote $N_{ex} \equiv X^*$.

Remark 4.2.2. Each column of $N^{(t)}$ corresponds to a face of $(n-t)^{th}$ dimension of the polyhedron $X \subset E^n$.

To restate our problem we want to find all subsets of X^* such that their convex combination belongs to N.

Let us define a subset of X^* as follows: (See 4-1-7)

$$X_t^*(r) = \{x^i \in X^* | n_{ir}^{(t)} = 1\} \qquad (4\text{-}2\text{-}4)$$

The set X^* of k elements is to be decomposed into subsets $X_t^*(r)$ such that $C[X_t^*(r)]^I \subset N$. (Recall that $C[X_t^*(r)]$ is a convex combination of all $x^i \in X_t^*(r)$.)

Let us start with the matrix $N^{(1)}$. All columns must contain at least two 1's, since we have deleted those with $n_r^{(1)} = 0$ and $n_r^{(1)} = 1$. The number of such columns is K_1, i.e., $r = 1,2,\ldots,K_1$. We shall investigate all columns successively in the order of decreasing $n_r^{(1)}$, i.e., $n_r^{(1)} \geq n_{r+1}^{(1)}$. Choose the column with Max $n_r^{(1)}$ first. In the case of a tie let the choice be arbitrary.

The investigation of columns now proceeds naturally from 1 to K_1.

Step 1.   Let $n_1^{(1)} = \text{Max } n_r^{(1)}$, $r = 1,\ldots,K_1$. Two cases may be distinguished:

(A) $C[X_1^*(1)]^I \subset N$

(B) $C[X_1^*(1)]^I \not\subset N$.

Case (A).   In this case the $X_1^*(1)$ is a part of the resulting decomposition (solution to our problem). All possible convex combinations of all $x^i \in X_1^*(1)$ belong to N, i.e., $C[X_1^*(1)] \subset N$. Now we may delete the first column from $N^{(1)}$. Similarly, we delete all columns r such that $X_1^*(r) \subset X_1^*(1)$, $r = 2,3,\ldots,K_1$. This follows from Corollary 4.1.7. That is, if the column $N_r^{(1)}$ of $N^{(1)}$ is such that

$$N_1^{(1)} - N_r^{(1)} \geq 0, \quad r = 2,3,\ldots,K_1 \ ,$$

then $N_r^{(1)}$ will be deleted.

<u>Case (B)</u>. In this case $X_1^*(1)$ is not part of the solution since $C[X_1^*(1)]^I \notin N$ and not all possible combinations of all $x^i \in X_1^*(1)$ belong to N. The corresponding $N_1^{(1)}$ may not be deleted from $N^{(1)}$.

We repeat this step for all $r = 1, 2, \ldots, K_1$, i.e., until all $X_1^*(r)$ are investigated.

Let us define a <u>reduced matrix</u> $\overline{N}(t)$ of $N^{(t)}$:

<u>Definition 4.2.3.</u> The reduced matrix $\overline{N}^{(t)}$ is such a matrix $N^{(t)}$ in which all columns r with $C[X_t^*(r)]^I \subset N$ have been eliminated. The number of columns K_t of $N^{(t)}$ is reduced to $\overline{K}_t$ of $\overline{N}^{(t)}$. Notice that $\overline{K}_t \overset{\leq}{=} K_t$.

We see now that Step 1 leads to the reduction of $N^{(1)}$ to $\overline{N}^{(1)}$. This reduced $\overline{N}^{(1)}$ with $\overline{K}_1$ columns corresponding to $X_1^*(r)$, $r = 1, \ldots, \overline{K}_1$, such that $C[X_1^*(r)]^I \notin N_1$, will be the starting point for the next step.

<u>Step 2.</u> From $\overline{N}^{(1)}$ with $\overline{K}_1$ columns let us construct $N^{(2)}$ with K_2 columns in the following way:

$$N^{(2)} = \left[n_{ir}^{(2)} \right], \quad n_{ir}^{(2)} = \begin{cases} 1 & \text{if } x^i \text{ makes the } r^{th} \text{ subset of } J_2 \text{ active} \\ 0 & \text{otherwise} \end{cases}$$

(a) Let $\overline{N}_z^{(1)}$ and $\overline{N}_w^{(1)}$ be two different columns of $\overline{N}^{(1)}$. A column $N_r^{(2)}$ of $N^{(2)}$ could be derived as follows:

If $I_r^{(2)} = I_z^{(1)} \cup I_w^{(1)}$, we define

$$N_r^{(2)} = \overline{N}_z^{(1)} \odot \overline{N}_w^{(1)}, \qquad (4\text{-}2\text{-}5)$$

where $\odot$ indicates elementwise multiplication of vectors $\overline{N}_z^{(1)}$ and $\overline{N}_w^{(1)}$.

More precisely,

$$N_r^{(2)} = \begin{pmatrix} n_{1z}^{(1)} & \cdot & n_{1w}^{(1)} \\ & \cdot & \\ & \cdot & \\ & \cdot & \\ n_{\overline{K},z}^{(1)} & \cdot & n_{\overline{K},w}^{(1)} \end{pmatrix} .$$

Remark 4.2.4. Now $n_{ir}^{(2)} = 1$ implies that x^i makes the zth and the wth constraints active. Notice that r is the index for the set $\{z,w\}$. Also, $I_r^{(2)}$ contains exactly one more element than $I_z^{(1)}$. For generalization of (4-2-5) see Step 3.

So we generate $N^{(2)}$ with columns $N_r^{(2)}$, where $r = 1,2,\ldots,K_2$

(b) K_2 columns of $N^{(2)}$ may be again reordered so that $n_1^{(2)} \geq n_2^{(2)} \geq \ldots \geq n_{K_2}^{(2)}$; The reduction procedure (Step 1) is now applied sequentially for $r = 1,2,\ldots,K_2$ and all $X_2^*(r)$ are investigated. We delete the columns with $C[X_2^*(r)]^I \subset N$ and those with $X_2^*(k) \subset X_2^*(r)$, $k \neq r$, from $N^{(2)}$ (see Corollary 4.1.7.). The result will be a reduced matrix $\overline{N}^{(2)}$ with $\overline{K}_2$ columns.

Step 3. In general, $\overline{N}^{(t)}$ is transformed into $N^{(t+1)}$ using the following rule:

$$N_r^{(t+1)} = \overline{N}_z^{(t)} \odot \overline{N}_w^{(1)}, \quad r = 1,\ldots,K_{t+1} \tag{4-2-6}$$

where $\overline{N}_z^{(t)}$ and $\overline{N}_w^{(1)}$ are columns of $\overline{N}^{(t)}$ and of $\overline{N}^{(1)}$ respectively, and $I_r^{(t+1)} = I_z^{(t)} \cup I_w^{(1)}$.

The K_{t+1} columns of $N^{(t+1)}$ are reordered in such a way that

$n_1^{(t+1)} \geq n_2^{(t+1)} \geq \ldots \geq n_{K_{t+1}}^{(t+1)}$. The reduction procedure is then applied

as in the previous steps sequentially for $\mathbf{r} = 1,2,\ldots,K_{t+1}$.

All $X_{t+1}^*(\mathbf{r})$ are then investigated. Columns with $C[X_{t+1}^*(\mathbf{r})]^I \subset N$

and those with $X_{t+1}^*(k) \subset X_{t+1}^*(\mathbf{r})$, $k \neq \mathbf{r}$, $\mathbf{r} = 1,\ldots,K_{t+1}$ are deleted.

Resulting is $\overline{N}^{(t+1)}$ with $\overline{K}_{t+1}$ columns.

The whole routine goes through the sequence of transformations:

$$N^{(1)} \to \overline{N}^{(1)} \to N^{(2)} \to \overline{N}^{(2)} \to \ldots \to N^{(t)} \to \overline{N}^{(t)} \to \ldots \to N^{(n)} \to \overline{N}^{(n)},$$

i.e., for $t = 1,2,\ldots,m+n$. The routine ends whenever some $\overline{N}^{(t)}$ becomes

a vacuous matrix. For summary see Figure 4.2.1.

Remark 4.2.5. As a matter of fact, the routine ends always before reaching $N^{(n)}$ because all $n_{\mathbf{r}}^{(n)} < 2$, $\mathbf{r} = 1,2,\ldots,K_n$.

Remark 4.2.6. The advantage of investigating the columns of $N^{(t)}$ in the

order of decreasing $n_{\mathbf{r}}^{(t)}$ is due to a simple way of identification of all

subsets of $X_t^*(\mathbf{r})$ in the case that $C[X_t^*(\mathbf{r})]^I \subset N$.

In the next section, we will demonstrate the described procedure

on simple examples.

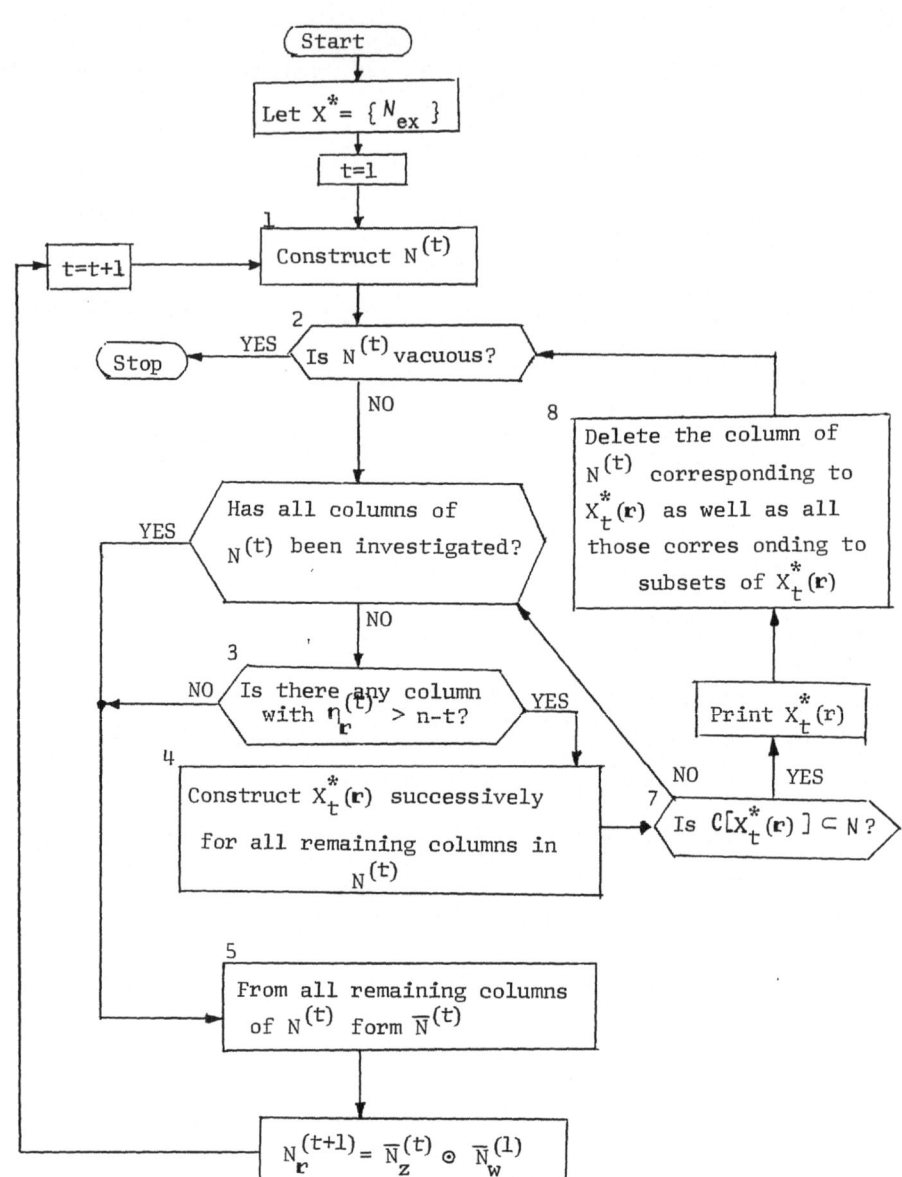

Figure 4.2.1.

Comments on matrix reduction - Figure 4.2.1.

1. Construct the matrix $N^{(t)}$ as defined in (4-2-3). Initially $N^{(1)}$ as in (4-2-2).

2. Calculate $n_r^{(t)}$ for all columns of $N^{(t)}$, $r = 1, \ldots, K_t$. Delete all those with $n_r^{(t)} \leq n-t$ in view of Remark 4.2.1.

3. If $N^{(t)}$ is vacuous, stop. Also consider Remark 4.2.5. Otherwise go to 4.

4. Construct all $X_t^*(r)$ and go to 7.

5. All columns for which $C[X_t^*(r)] \not\subset N$ are retained. All such columns form reduced matrix $\bar{N}^{(t)}$.

6. Calculate $N^{(t+1)}$ from $\bar{N}^{(t)}$ using the prescription (4-2-6). Go back to 1.

7. Check whether $C[X_t^*(r)] \subset N$ by using Theorem 4.1.6. If YES we can print all $x^i \in X_t^*(r)$ since all their convex combinations are non-dominated.

8. Delete all columns corresponding to $X_t^*(r)$ and its subsets in view of Corollary 4.1.7. Go to 3.

4.3. Numerical examples

For simplicity we shall demonstrate the matrix reduction procedure and the nondominance subroutine separately.

4.3.1. An example of matrix reduction

We shall consider a simple 3-dimensional case mainly because it is instructive to have a graphical representation for a reference. Consider the 3-dimensional convex polyhedron in Figure 4.3.1. with the set of non-dominated extreme points $\{x^1, x^2, x^3, x^4, x^5, x^6\}$. Let us assume that only the shaded combinations (faces) are nondominated. Our goal is to identify them by using the matrix reduction method. We do not assume any exact form of objective functions, we just want to show how the matrix reduction method identifies the shaded areas.

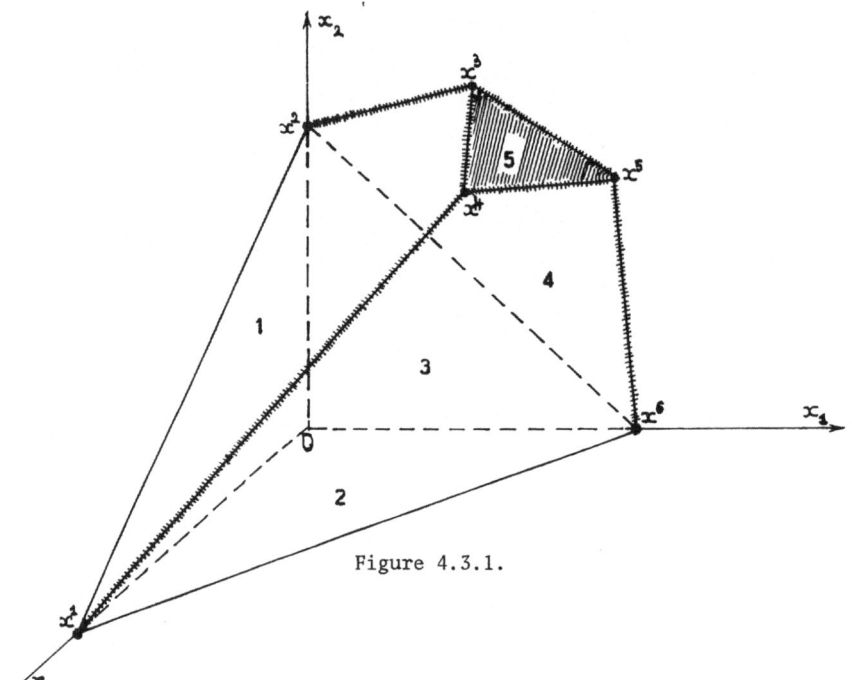

Figure 4.3.1.

The polyhedron in Figure 4.3.1. is defined by five linear constraints plus the nonnegativity conditions which are, however, redundant in this particular example. They define five faces of the highest dimension (i.e., two) which are denoted as:

1. $C[x^1, x^2, x^3, x^4]$

2. $C[x^1, x^4, x^5, x^6]$

3. $C[x^1, x^2, x^6]$

4. $C[x^2, x^3, x^5, x^6]$

5. $C[x^3, x^4, x^5]$

Let $X^* = \{x^1, x^2, x^3, x^4, x^5, x^6\} \subset N$.

First we shall construct the matrix $N^{(1)} = \left[n_{ir}^{(1)} \right]$, where $r = 1, 2, 3, 4, 5$,

i.e., $K_1 = 5$.

r renumbered columns	1	2	3	4	⑤	Nonnegativity conditions		
$I_r^{(1)}$	$\{1\}$	$\{2\}$	$\{3\}$	$\{4\}$	$\{5\}$	x_1	x_2	x_3
x^1	1	1	1			1	1	
x^2	1		1	1		1		1
x^3	1			1	1			1
x^4	1	1			1			
x^5		1		1	1			1
x^6		1	1	1			1	1
Σ	4	4	3	4	3	may be omitted because of their redundancy.		

Notice that all $n_r^{(1)} > 2$ and $\text{Max } n_r^{(1)} = 4$. We can recognize that the subsets $X_1^*(r)$ are as follows:

$$X_1^*(1) = \{x^1, x^2, x^3, x^4\}$$

$$X_1^*(2) = \{x^1, x^4, x^5, x^6\}$$

$$X_1^*(3) = \{x^1, x^2, x^6\}$$

$$X_1^*(4) = \{x^2, x^3, x^5, x^6\}$$

$$X_1^*(5) = \{x^3, x^4, x^5\}$$

Using the nondominance subroutine we would check now $C[X_1^*(\mathbf{r})]^I$ for non-dominance. From Figure 4.3.1. we see that $C[X_1^*(5)]^I \subset N \Rightarrow C[X_1^*(5)] \subset N$. Then $C[x^3, x^4, x^5] \subset N$ is a part of the resulting decomposition and the fifth column may be deleted. No further columns may be deleted. Thus the reduced matrix $\overline{N}^{(1)}$ has been obtained with the number of columns $\overline{K}_1 = 4$.

The next step is to construct the matrix $N^{(2)} = \left[n_{i\mathbf{r}}^{(2)} \right]$, $\mathbf{r} = 1, \ldots, K_2$. The $\mathbf{r}^{th}$ column of $N^{(2)}$ is obtained by (see (4-2-5)):

$$N_{\mathbf{r}}^{(2)} = \overline{N}_z^{(1)} \odot \overline{N}_w^{(1)}.$$

Repeating this for all possible pairs z and w we obtain all columns of $N^{(2)}$. We shall consider only those columns $\mathbf{r}$ with $n_{\mathbf{r}}^{(2)} \geq 2$ and get $N^{(2)}$:

r renumbered columns	①	②	③	④	⑤	⑥
$I_r^{(2)}$	{1,2}	{1,3}	{1,4}	{2,3}	{2,4}	{3,4}
x^1	1	1		1		
x^2		1	1			1
x^3			1			
x^4	1					
x^5					1	
x^6				1	1	1
Σ	2	2	2	2	2	2

Notice $r = 1,2,\ldots,6$, i.e., $K_2 = 6$. Now we can identify the subsets:

$$X_2^*(1) = \{x^1,x^4\}, \; X_2^*(2) = \{x^1,x^2\}, \; X_2^*(3) = \{x^2,x^3\},$$

$$X_2^*(4) = \{x^1,x^6\}, \; X_2^*(5) = \{x^5,x^6\}, \; X_2^*(6) = \{x^2,x^6\}.$$

Checking $C[X_2^*(r)]^I$ for nondominance we can see from Figure 4.3.1. that only $C[X_2^*(1)]$, $C[X_2^*(3)]$ and $C[X_2^*(5)]$ are part of N, so the first, third and fifth columns may be deleted in $N^{(2)}$. Then $C[x^1,x^4]$, $C[x^2,x^3]$, and $C[x^5,x^6]$ are part of the resulting decomposition.

We have obtained the reduced matrix $\overline{N}^{(2)}$ with the number of columns $\overline{K}_2 = 3$. To demonstrate that the algorithm ends before reaching $N^{(3)}$ because all $n_r^{(3)} = 1$, $r = 1,\ldots,K_3$, we shall perform the next step:

From $\overline{N}^{(2)}$ we construct $N^{(3)}$.

Remark 4.3.1. Notice also that at each step we may check the rows of $\overline{N}^{(t)}$ and delete those which have all zero elements, e.g., we may delete rows for x^3, x^4 and x^5 in $\overline{N}^{(2)}$ of our example.

To get the new columns for $N^{(3)}$ we multiply the columns $\overline{N}_r^{(2)} \odot \overline{N}_w^{(1)}$. Notice that only $\overline{N}_2^{(2)} \odot \overline{N}_2^{(1)}$, $\overline{N}_2^{(2)} \odot \overline{N}_3^{(1)}$, and $\overline{N}_4^{(2)} \odot \overline{N}_3^{(1)}$ are sufficient since all remaining combinations are identical. We obtain:

r renumbered columns	1	2	3	
$I_r^{(3)}$	{1,2,3}	{1,3,4}	{2,3,4}	
x^1	1			$X_3^*(1) = \{x^1\}$
x^2		1		$X_3^*(2) = \{x^2\}$
x^3			1	$X_3^*(3) = \{x^6\}$
$\sum$	1	1	1	

But x^1, x^2, and x^6 are nondominated by definition so the entire step is unnecessary.

The final decomposition may be sketched as follows:

$$X^* = \{x^1, x^2, x^3, x^4, x^5, x^6\} \begin{cases} \{x^3, x^4, x^5\} \\ \{x^1, x^4\} \\ \{x^2, x^3\} \\ \{x^5, x^6\} \end{cases}$$

meaning that $C[x^3, x^4, x^5]$, $C[x^1, x^4]$, $C[x^2, x^3]$ and $C[x^5, x^6] \subset N$.

4.3.2. An example of nondominance subroutine.

Consider the following problem:

$$
\text{V-Max} \begin{cases} c^1.x = 4x_1 + x_2 + 2x_3 \\ c^2.x = x_1 + 3x_2 - x_3 \\ c^3.x = -x_1 + x_2 + 4x_3 \end{cases}
$$

subject to

$$
X = \begin{cases} x_1 + x_2 + x_3 \leq 3 & 1. \\ 2x_1 + 2x_2 + x_3 \leq 4 & 2. \\ x_1 - x_2 \leq 0 & 3. \\ x_1 \geq 0 & 4. \\ x_2 \geq 0 & 5. \\ x_3 \geq 0 & 6. \end{cases}
$$

Solving this problem we get the following set of nondominated extreme points:

$x^1 = (0,0,3,0,1,0)$

$x^2 = (0,1,2,0,0,1)$

$x^3 = (\frac{1}{2},\frac{1}{2},2,0,0,0)$

$x^4 = (0,2,0,1,0,2)$

$x^5 = (1,1,0,1,0,0)$

	x^1	x^2	x^3	x^4	x^5
$c^1.x$	6	5	6.5	2	5
$c^2.x$	-3	1	0	6	4
$c^3.x$	12	9	8	2	0

We would like to decompose $X^* = \{x^1,x^2,x^3,x^4,x^5\}$ into all subsets whose convex combinations are nondominated. First construct $N^{(1)} = \left[n_{ir}^{(1)} \right]$.

r renumbered columns	①	②	3	4	5	⑥
$I_r^{(1)}$	{1}	{2}	{3}	{4}	{5}	{6}
x^1	1		1	1	1	
x^2	1	1		1		
x^3	1	1	1			
x^4		1		1		1
x^5		1	1			1
$\sum$	3	4	3	3	1 X	2

Excluding the fifth column, all $n_r^{(1)} \geq 2$, $r = 1,\ldots,6$.

First establish $H^{>}$ and $H^{\geq}$:

$$H^{>} = \{\lambda_1(1,3,-1) + \lambda_2(4,1,2) + \lambda_3(-1,1,4) \,|\, (\lambda_1,\lambda_2,\lambda_3) > 0\}$$

$$= \{(\lambda_1+4\lambda_2-\lambda_3, \ 3\lambda_1+\lambda_2+\lambda_3, \ -\lambda_1+2\lambda_2+4\lambda_3) \,|\, (\lambda_1,\lambda_2,\lambda_3) > 0\}$$

$$H^{\geq} = \{(\lambda_1+4\lambda_2-\lambda_3, \ 3\lambda_1+\lambda_2+\lambda_3, \ -\lambda_1+2\lambda_2+4\lambda_3) \,|\, (\lambda_1,\lambda_2,\lambda_3) \geq 0\}.$$

Since Max $n_r^{(1)} = n_2^{(1)}$, start with

$$X_1(2) = \{x \in X \,|\, 2x_1 + 2x_2 + x_3 = 4\}; \text{ then}$$

$G_2^{(1)} = \{\mu(2,2,1) \,|\, \mu \geq 0\}$. We may set up the following system:

$$2\mu = \lambda_1 + 4\lambda_2 - \lambda_3$$
$$2\mu = 3\lambda_1 + \lambda_2 + \lambda_3$$
$$\mu = -\lambda_1 + 2\lambda_2 + 4\lambda_3 \qquad \lambda_1,\lambda_2,\lambda_3 > 0, \ \mu \geq 0.$$

This may be rewritten as the system of homogeneous equations and investigated for the existence of a nontrivial solution:

$$
\left.\begin{array}{l}
3\lambda_1 \qquad\quad - 9\lambda_3 = 0 \\
-2\lambda_1 + 3\lambda_2 - 2\lambda_3 = 0 \\
5\lambda_1 - 3\lambda_2 + 7\lambda_3 = 0
\end{array}\right\} \rightarrow
\left.\begin{array}{l}
\lambda_1 \qquad\quad - 3\lambda_3 = 0 \\
3\lambda_2 - 8\lambda_3 = 0 \\
- 3\lambda_2 + 8\lambda_3 = 0
\end{array}\right\} \rightarrow
\left.\begin{array}{l}
\lambda_1 \qquad\quad - 3\lambda_3 = 0 \\
\lambda_2 - \tfrac{8}{3}\lambda_3 = 0 \\
0 \qquad = 0
\end{array}\right\}
$$

The last system has a nontrivial solution, e.g., $\lambda_1 = 9$, $\lambda_2 = 8$, $\lambda_3 = 3$.
Therefore

$$
H^{>} \cap G_2^{(1)} \neq \phi \implies C[x_1^{*}(2)] \subset N.
$$

We conclude $C[x^2, x^3, x^4, x^5] \subset N$ and the second column of $N^{(1)}$ may be deleted as well as the sixth column, since $x_1^{*}(6) \subset x_1^{*}(2)$, i.e.,
$C[x^4, x^5] \subset N$.

Next construct $G_1^{(1)} = \{\mu(1,1,1) \,|\, \mu \overset{\geq}{=} 0\}$. We obtain the following system:

$$
\left.\begin{array}{l}
\mu = \lambda_1 + 4\lambda_2 \quad \lambda_3 \\
\mu = 3\lambda_1 + \lambda_2 + \lambda_3 \\
\mu = -\lambda_1 + 2\lambda_2 + 4\lambda_3
\end{array}\right\} \rightarrow
\left.\begin{array}{l}
2\lambda_1 + 2\lambda_2 - 5\lambda_3 = 0 \\
-2\lambda_1 + 3\lambda_2 - 2\lambda_3 = 0 \\
4\lambda_1 - \lambda_2 - 3\lambda_3 = 0
\end{array}\right\} \rightarrow
$$

$$
\left.\begin{array}{l}
\lambda_1 + \lambda_2 - \tfrac{5}{2}\lambda_3 = 0 \\
5\lambda_2 + 7\lambda_3 = 0 \\
-5\lambda_2 + 7\lambda_3 = 0
\end{array}\right\} \rightarrow
\left.\begin{array}{l}
\lambda_1 + \lambda_2 - \tfrac{5}{2}\lambda_3 = 0 \\
\lambda_2 - \tfrac{7}{5}\lambda_3 = 0 \\
0 \qquad = 0
\end{array}\right\}
$$

So the last system has a nontrivial solution, e.g., $\lambda_1 = 5.5$, $\lambda_2 = 7$,

$\lambda_3 = 5$. Therefore

$$H^> \cap G_1^{(1)} \neq \phi \Rightarrow C[x_1^*(1)] \subset N,$$

i.e.,

$$C[x^1, x^2, x^3] \subset N.$$

We may delete the first column from $N^{(1)}$.

Next construct $G_3^{(1)} = \{\mu(1, -1, 0) \mid \mu \stackrel{>}{=} 0\}$. Obtain the following system:

$$
\left.
\begin{aligned}
\mu &= \lambda_1 + 4\lambda_2 - \lambda_3 \\
-\mu &= 3\lambda_1 + \lambda_2 + \lambda_3 \\
0 &= -\lambda_1 + 2\lambda_2 + 4\lambda_3
\end{aligned}
\right\}
\rightarrow
\left.
\begin{aligned}
4\lambda_1 + 5\lambda_2 &= 0 \\
-\lambda_1 + 2\lambda_2 + 4\lambda_3 &= 0 \\
5\lambda_1 + 3\lambda_2 - 4\lambda_3 &= 0
\end{aligned}
\right\}
$$

From the first equation of the last system we see that the solution does not exist for $\lambda_1 > 0$, $\lambda_2 > 0$. Therefore, the third column of $N^{(1)}$ may not be deleted.

Construct $G_4^{(1)} = \{\mu(-1, 0, 0) \mid \mu \stackrel{>}{=} 0\}$. Then we have:

$$
\begin{aligned}
-\mu &= \lambda_1 + 4\lambda_2 - \lambda_3 \\
0 &= 3\lambda_1 + \lambda_2 + \lambda_3 \\
0 &= -\lambda_1 + 2\lambda_2 + 4\lambda_3
\end{aligned}
$$

where from the second equation it is seen that the system is not satisfied for $\lambda_1 > 0$, $\lambda_2 > 0$, $\lambda_3 > 0$. The fourth column cannot be deleted. We end up with the reduced matrix $\overline{N}^{(1)}$ with columns 3 and 4 left. Construct $N^{(2)}$:

$\mathbf{r}$ renumbered columns	1
$I_{\mathbf{r}}^{(2)}$	$\{3,4\}$
x^1	1
x^2	0
x^3	0
x^4	0
x^5	0
$\sum$	1

Since $n_1^{(2)} = 1$, we would delete the first column and end up with a vacuous matrix. The x^1 is assumed to be non-dominated. The algorithm ends.

The final partition:

$$X^* = \{x^1, x^2, x^3, x^4, x^5\} \begin{array}{c} \nearrow \{x^2, x^3, x^4, x^5\} \\ \searrow \{x^1, x^2, x^3\}, \end{array}$$

meaning that $C[x^2, x^3, x^4, x^5]$ and $C[x^1, x^2, x^3] \subset N$.

5. Additional Topics and Extensions.

5.1. Alternative Approach to Finding N_{ex}.

In search for the most efficient computation of nondominated extreme points some other possible approaches may be suggested.

In the multicriteria simplex method described earlier, we were checking the nondominance using linear programming subroutine for each basic solution which was found to be noncomparable to some other non-dominated extreme point. We can find the first nondominated solution by maximizing any one of our ℓ objectives and by discarding all domin-ated alternative solutions. Then we introduce only those columns which are noncomparable with zero vector, i.e., $z_j \sim 0$, $j = m+1, \ldots, n$ and among these only those which also satisfy $\theta_k z_k \sim \theta_j z_j$, $j \neq k$ for all j, $k = m+1, \ldots, n$. Recall that

$$z_j \equiv \begin{pmatrix} z_j^{(1)} \\ z_j^{(2)} \\ \cdot \\ \cdot \\ \cdot \\ z_j^{(\ell)} \end{pmatrix} \quad \text{and} \quad \theta_j = \underset{r}{\text{Min}} \left\{ \frac{y_r^0}{y_{rj}} ; \ y_{rj} > 0 \right\}$$

from (3-1-1) and (2-3-23) respectively.

It is obvious that computing all points which are noncomparable to the first nondominated extreme point and also noncomparable with each other is much faster and more efficient than solving LP subroutine at each iteration.

This set of all noncomparable extreme points is in general larger

than N_{ex} but all points of N_{ex} are included in it. The problem remains
of how do we screen out the points which are dominated.

Let us demonstrate the concept using a simple graphical example.
Let us assume that $\theta[X] = Y \subset E^2$, according to general notation introduced at the beginning of Section 2, and that the situation is described
in Figure 5.1.1.

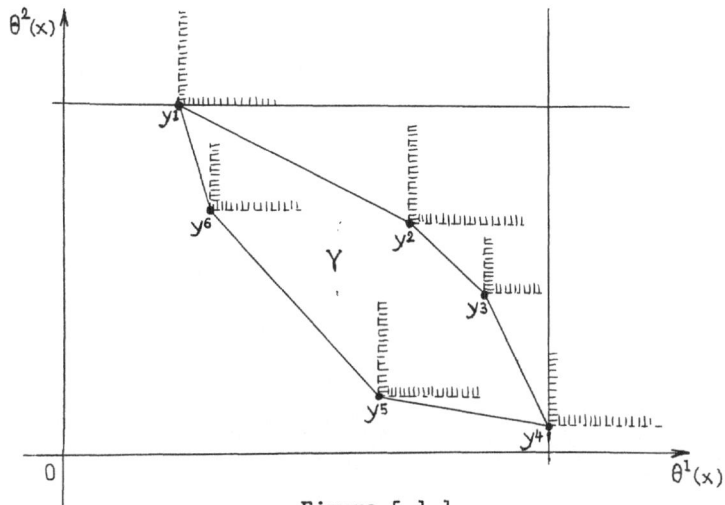

Figure 5.1.1.

Observe in Figure 5.1.1. that y^1, y^2, y^3 and y^4 are all nondominated extreme points of the $\theta[X]$. By multicriteria simplex
method we would start, say, at y^1 then move to y^6 and find it to be
dominated. We would discard y^6 and move from y^1 to y^2. Doing this
we generate only y^1, y^2, y^3 and y^4.

The alternative approach concentrates first on finding all noncomparable points. So we would start at y^1 and establish its nondominance.

Then we would find adjacent noncomparable points, y^6 and y^2. From these we would find again adjacent noncomparable, i.e., y^5 and y^3. Because y^5 is clearly dominated by y^2 and y^3 we may delete y^5 at this stage. Adjacent noncomparable to y^3 is y^4. So we would end with the set $\{y^1, y^2, y^3, y^4, y^6\}$ which contains $N_{ex} = \{y^1, y^2, y^3, y^4\}$. Notice that y^6 cannot be discarded by direct comparison of extreme points since it is dominated only by some convex combination of y^1 and y^2. So the problem is how to discard the points of the type y^6, i.e., those which are noncomparable with others but dominated only by some convex combination of others.

There are some properties of $\theta[X]$ for linear case which allow us to work with $\theta[X]$ or the image instead of with X directly. For example, an extreme point of $\theta[X]$ is the image of one or more extreme points in X. Also, if X has k extreme points, then $\theta[X]$ can have at most k extreme points. For proofs see e.g. [Charnes, Cooper, 1961].

Let us assume that we have generated k extreme points $\{x^1, x^2, \ldots, x^k\}$ of X which have the property that they are all noncomparable with each other and also with some nondominated extreme point (and therefore with all nondominated extreme points). We can construct the following matrix:

	$\theta^1(x)$	$\theta^2(x)$		$\theta^\ell(x)$
x^1	$\theta^1(x^1)$	$\theta^2(x^1)$	$\ldots$	$\theta^\ell(x^1)$
x^2	$\theta^1(x^2)$	$\theta^2(x^2)$	$\ldots$	$\theta^\ell(x^2)$
.	.	.	.	.
.	.	.	.	.
.	.	.	.	.
x^k	$\theta^1(x^k)$	$\theta^2(x^k)$	$\ldots$	$\theta^\ell(x^k)$

For example, let us assume the following numerical values:

	$\theta^1(x)$	$\theta^2(x)$	$\theta^3(x)$	$\theta^4(x)$
x^1	6	3	4	8
x^2	6	8	4	6
x^3	8	2	6	4
x^4	7	2	5	6
x^5	6	7	5	6

It is obvious that x^1, x^2 and x^3 are nondominated since each function reaches its unique maximum at one of these points. Points x^4 and x^5 are not dominated by any of these points. But they can still be dominated or nondominated. Like, for example, x^4 is dominated by a convex combination of x^1 and x^3 with $\lambda = \frac{1}{2}$, i.e.,

$$x^* = \frac{1}{2}x^1 + \frac{1}{2}x^3 \Rightarrow \theta(x^*) = \frac{1}{2}\theta(x^1) + \frac{1}{2}\theta(x^3)$$

$$= \frac{1}{2}(6, 3, 4, 8) + \frac{1}{2}(8, 2, 6, 4) = (7, 2.5, 5, 6)$$

and $(7, 2.5, 5, 6) \geq (7, 2, 5, 6)$.

On the other hand, x^5 is not dominated by any convex combination of these points. Therefore, x^5 is nondominated.

The following are some concepts designed to resolve the above problem.

5.1.1. The concept of cutting hyperplane.

If we are dealing with just two objective functions, the resolution of the discussed problem is simple. We may actually resolve it graphically since the image $\theta[X] \subset E^2$. So we can plot all non-comparable vectors $(\theta^1(x), \theta^2(x))$ for all noncomparable extreme points $\{x^1, x^2, \ldots, x^k\}$ and delete those which are dominated, by simple inspection.

If we want to avoid graphical plotting we may develop a so-called cutting hyperplane.

Let $\theta^1(x) = c_.^1 x$, $\theta^2(x) = c_.^2 x$, where

$$c_.^i x = c_1^i x_1 + \ldots + c_n^i x_n, \quad i = 1, 2.$$

We can use the following lemma:

Lemma 5.1.1.

Let (x_1, y_1) and (x_2, y_2) be two distinct points in E^2. Then

$$L = \left\{ (x,y) \,|\, y - \left(\frac{y_2 - y_1}{x_2 - x_1}\right)x = y_1 - \left(\frac{y_2 - y_1}{x_2 - x_1}\right)x_1 \right\} \tag{5-1-1}$$

is the straight line connecting (x_1, y_1) and (x_2, y_2).

Note,

$$\nabla\left(y - \left(\frac{y_2 - y_1}{x_2 - x_1}\right)x\right) = \left(-\frac{y_2 - y_1}{x_2 - x_1},\ 1\right) \geq (0,\ 0).$$

See Figure 5.1.2.:

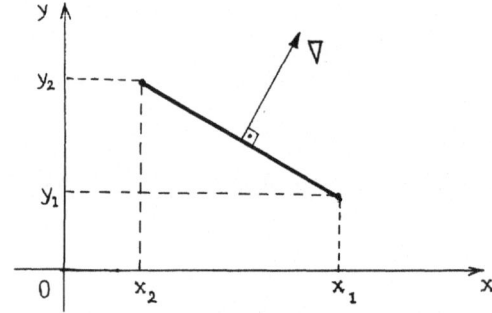

Figure 5.1.2.

Since we consider only two objectives we may further simplify our notation. Let for any $x \in X$, $\mu = \theta^1(x)$, $\upsilon = \theta^2(x)$.

Let x^1, $x^2 \in X$ be unique (i.e. nondominated) maxima of $\theta^1(x)$ and $\theta^2(x)$ respectively.

Denote $(\mu_1, \upsilon_1) = (\theta^1(x^1), \theta^2(x^1))$ and

$$(\mu_2, \upsilon_2) = (\theta^1(x^2), \theta^2(x^2)),$$

as it is represented in Figure 5.1.3.:

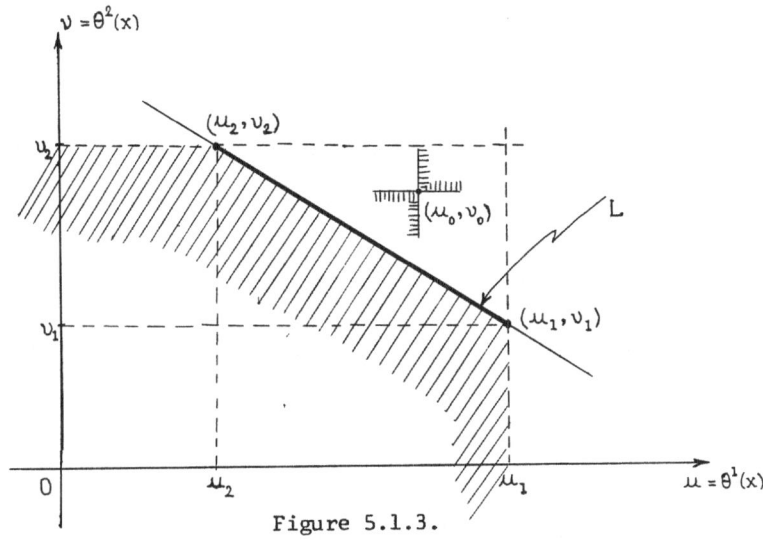

Figure 5.1.3.

Definition 5.1.2. The cutting hyperplane is defined as

$$L = \left\{ (\mu,\upsilon) \,\middle|\, \upsilon - \left(\frac{\upsilon_2-\upsilon_1}{\mu_2-\mu_1}\right)\mu = \upsilon_1 - \left(\frac{\upsilon_2-\upsilon_1}{\mu_2-\mu_1}\right)\mu_1 \right\}. \qquad (5\text{-}1\text{-}2)$$

Define,

$$L^{\geq} = \left\{ (\mu,\upsilon) \,\middle|\, \upsilon - \left(\frac{\upsilon_2-\upsilon_1}{\mu_2-\mu_1}\right)\mu \geq \upsilon_1 - \left(\frac{\upsilon_2-\upsilon_1}{\mu_2-\mu_1}\right)\mu_1 \right\}, \qquad (5\text{-}1\text{-}3)$$

and

$L^{<}$ its complement.

Define,

$$\theta[X] = \left\{ (\mu, \upsilon) \mid \mu = \theta^1(x), \ \upsilon = \theta^2(x); \ x \in X \right\}$$

and

$$\hat{\theta}[X] = \left\{ (\mu, \upsilon) \mid \mu \leqq \mu_1, \ \upsilon \leqq \upsilon_2 \right\}. \tag{5-1-4}$$

Theorem 5.1.3. Let x^0 be a basic feasible solution of X. Then $x^0 \in N_{ex}$ if and only if, for $\mu_0 = \theta^1(x^0)$ and $\upsilon_0 = \theta^2(x^0)$, $(\mu_0, \upsilon_0) \in L^{\geqq}$.

Proof. The proof can be made simply by graphical analysis, looking at Figure 5.1.3.

a) $\theta[X] \subseteq \hat{\theta}[X]$

b) Any $(\mu, \upsilon) \in L^{<}$ is dominated by some $(\mu, \upsilon) \in L$.

Any $(\mu, \upsilon) \in L^{<} \cap \hat{\theta}[X]$ is dominated by some $(\mu, \upsilon) \in \left[(\mu_1, \upsilon_1), (\mu_2, \upsilon_2) \right]$ i.e. closed line segment connecting (μ_1, υ_1) and (μ_2, υ_2). Because of a) the necessary condition is proven.

c) Let x^0 is an extreme point of X and let $(\mu_0, \upsilon_0) \in L^{\geqq}$. To prove the sufficient condition we have to show that $x^0 \in N_{ex}$. Suppose $x^0 \notin N_{ex}$, i.e. some $x \in X$ exists such that $(\mu, \upsilon) \geqq (\mu_0, \upsilon_0)$. Then of course (μ_0, υ_0) can be expressed as a convex combination of some $(\mu, \upsilon) \geqq (\mu_0, \upsilon_0)$ and of some $(\mu, \upsilon) \in L$ which contradicts the assumption that x^0 is an extreme point. Q.E.D.

Example 5.1.4. Suppose $\theta^1(x) = 2x_1 + 3x_2$, $\theta^2(x) = 4x_1 + x_2$ and let $x^1 = (4, 6)$ and $x^2 = (8, 3)$. Then $\mu_1 = \theta^1(x^1) = 26$, $\upsilon_1 = \theta^2(x^1) = 22$, $\mu_2 = \theta^1(x^2) = 25$, and $\upsilon_2 = \theta^2(x^2) = 35$.

Then L can be written as

$$\upsilon - \frac{35-22}{25-26} \cdot \mu = 22 - \frac{35-22}{25-26} \cdot 26$$

i.e. $\upsilon + 13\mu = 360$

Substituting for $\upsilon = \theta^2(x)$ and $\mu = \theta^1(x)$ we can actually express the cutting hyperplane directly for $X \subseteq E^n$:

$$4x_1 + x_2 + 13(2x_1 + 3x_2) = 360$$
$$30x_1 + 40x_2 = 360.$$

Substituting x^1 and x^2 we see that the conditions of the definition of cutting hyperplane are satisfied. Graph see in Figure 5.1.3.

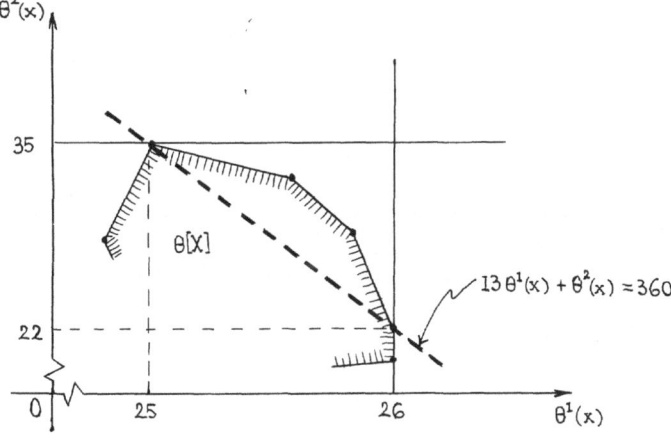

Figure 5.1.3.

This looks like a very plausible concept to be generalized. Some effort has been expanded toward this problem. The conclusions are that though the concept of the cutting hyperplane may be generalized to higher dimensions, there is no guarantee that such a structure always exists.

The above theory can be used safely only in two dimensions, i.e., for two objective functions. In higher dimensions the problems of uniqueness and degeneracy of the cutting hyperplane make its use questionable at this point. A couple of graphical examples should clarify the difficulties.

Example 5.1.5. In this example we have a case of degenerate lower dimensional image $\theta[X]$. Here the $\theta[X]$ is just 2-dimensional polyhedron in three dimensional space.

	$\theta^1(x)$	$\theta^2(x)$	$\theta^3(x)$
x^1	16.6	3.3	6.6
x^2	40	0	10
x^3	37	2.85	11.4
x^4	10	10	10

Respective maxima are:
x^2, x^4, x^3

Notice that x^1 is dominated by $\frac{1}{2}x^3 + \frac{1}{2}x^4 = (23.5, 6.425, 10.7)$. To construct the cutting hyperplane we use the graphical analysis in Figure 5.1.4. Actually only x^2 and x^4 are to be used to construct the cutting hyperplane. The cutting hyperplane is:

$$\theta^1(x) + 3\theta^2(x) = 40$$

Substituting x^3:

$$37 + 3.(2.85) = 45.55 \Rightarrow x^3 \in N_{ex}$$

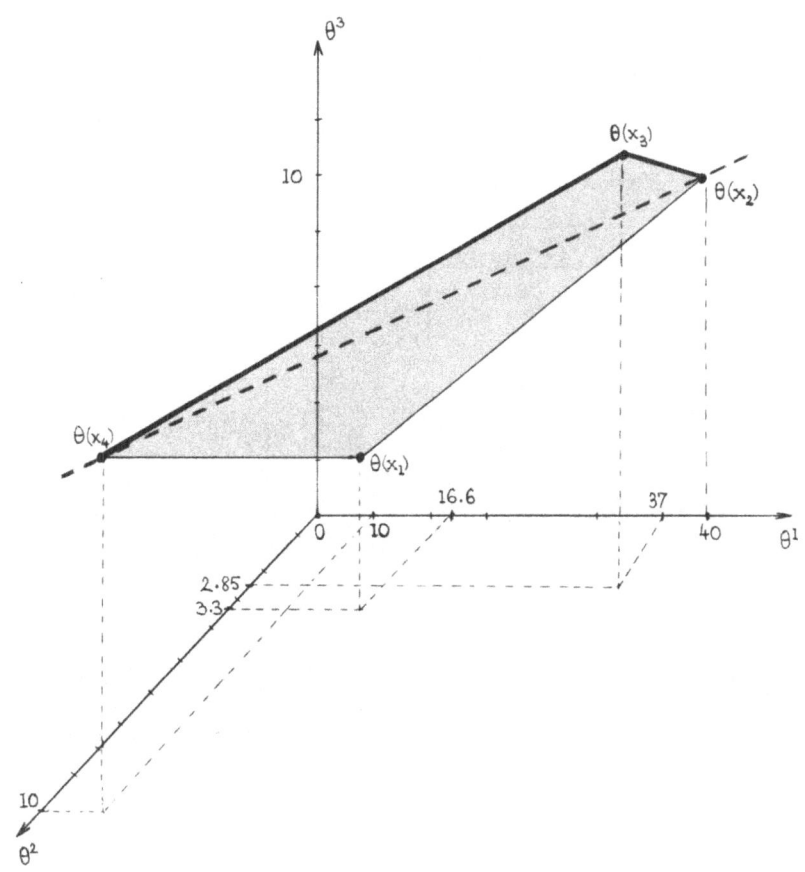

Figure 5.1.4.

Substituting x^1:

$16.6 + 3.(3.3) = 26.5 \Rightarrow x^1 \notin N_{ex}.$

Example 5.1.6. In this example we are facing a problem of multiple cutting hyperplanes. Let

	$\theta^1(x)$	$\theta^2(x)$	$\theta^3(x)$
x^1	9	8	8
x^2	8	9	8
x^3	8	8	9
x^4	0	8.8	8.8

Maxima: x^1, x^2, x^3

Minima: x^4, x^1, x^2, x^3

See Figure 5.1.5.

For example, using x^1, x^2, x^3 to construct the hyperplane, we get

$\theta^1(x) + \theta^2(x) + \theta^3(x) = 25$

Substituting x^4 we get

$8.8 + 8.8 = 17.6$

which would indicate that x^4 is dominated when it is actually non-dominated. Using x^3, x^1, x^2 and x^4 we find that the cutting hyper-plane does not exist. This is the case of multiple cutting hyper-planes, constructed with x^1, x^4, x^2 and with x^1, x^4, x^3:

$\frac{4}{49}\theta^1(x) + \frac{4}{49}\theta^2(x) + \frac{41}{49}\theta^3(x) = 396$

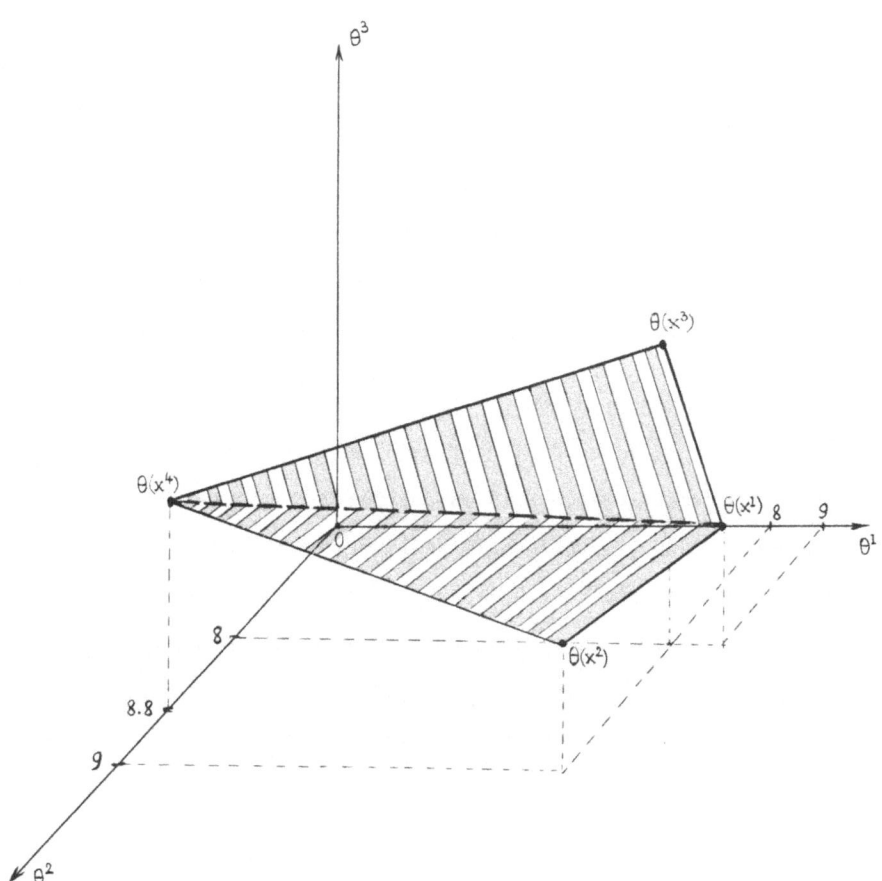

Figure 5.1.5.

and

$$\frac{4}{49}\theta^1(x) + \frac{41}{49}\theta^2(x) + \frac{4}{49}\theta^3(x) = 396.$$

A nondominated point must produce values larger or equal to 396 in both hyperplanes. For example, point (8.4, 8.5, 7) gives us value 410.1 for the second cutting hyperplane. But since it gives us only 354.6 for the first one, it must be dominated; for instance, by $\frac{1}{2}x^1 + \frac{1}{2}x^2 = (8.5, 8.5, 8)$.

5.1.2. Nondominance in lower dimensions.

Following is a short discussion of another interesting property of nondominated solutions. In connection with the two dimensional theory of cutting hyperplane, it will help us to determine non-dominance of many noncomparable extreme points.

Let $\theta(x) = (\theta^1(x), \ldots, \theta^\ell(x))$, where $\theta^i(x)$, $\theta^j(x)$ are any two objectives with $i \neq j$, i, j = 1, $\ldots$, ℓ.

From the definition of nondominance we know that $x^* \epsilon X$ is nondominated if and only if $\theta(x) \geq \theta(x^*) \Rightarrow \theta(x) = \theta(x^*)$ for all $x \epsilon X$.

Definition 5.1.7. $x^* \epsilon X$ is nondominated in (i, j) if and only if $(\theta^i(x), \theta^j(x)) \geq (\theta^i(x^*), \theta^j(x^*)) \Rightarrow (\theta^i(x), \theta^j(x)) = (\theta^i(x^*), \theta^j(x^*))$. In other words, there is no $x \epsilon X$ such that $(\theta^i(x), \theta^j(x)) \geq (\theta^i(x^*), \theta^j(x^*))$ and $(\theta^i(x), \theta^j(x)) \neq (\theta^i(x^*), \theta^j(x^*))$.

Definition 5.1.8. x*εX is strictly nondominated in (i, j) if there is no point xεX such that

$$(\theta^i(x), \theta^j(x)) \gneqq (\theta^i(x^*), \theta^j(x^*)).$$

Theorem 5.1.9. x*εX is nondominated if it is strictly nondominated in at least one pair (i, j), i, j = 1, ..., ℓ.

Proof. Let x*εX is strictly nondominated in at least one (i, j), i, j = 1, ..., ℓ. Let there exist some xεX such that $\theta(x) \geq \theta(x^*)$. This implies that also $\theta^i(x) \gneqq \theta^i(x^*)$ and $\theta^j(x) \gneqq \theta^j(x^*)$. We have a contradiction. Q.E.D.

Remark 5.1.10. Theorem 5.1.9. is a generalization of one dimen_sional domination (i.e. x* uniquely maximizes $\theta^i(x)$ then x*εN). It could be generalized into k-pair strict nondominance, $1 \lneqq k \lneqq \ell$.

Though a strict nondominance in (i, j) is a sufficient condition for nondominance, it is not a necessary condition. For example, consider:

	$\theta^1(x)$	$\theta^2(x)$	$\theta^3(x)$	$\theta^4(x)$
x^1	2	2	2	2
x^2	3	3	0	0
x^3	0	0	3	3
x^4	0	3	3	0
x^5	0	3	0	3
x^6	3	0	3	0
x^7	3	0	0	3

x^1 is strictly nondominated in no pair (i,j) but it is still a non-dominated point.

Remark 5.1.11. The previously discussed concepts may be used for identification of N_{ex} from some generally larger set of extreme points which are noncomparable with each other and also with some nondominated extreme points. If we have k of such points, notice that if

$$\lambda_1 \theta^1(x^r) + \lambda_2 \theta^2(x^r) + \ldots + \lambda^{\ell} \theta^{\ell}(x^r),$$

$\lambda_i \geq 0$, $\sum_{i=1}^{\ell} \lambda_i = 1$ exists such that

$$\sum_{i=1}^{\ell} \lambda_i \theta^i(x^r) \geq \sum_{i=1}^{\ell} \lambda_i \theta^i(x^j), \quad j=1, \ldots, k; \ j \neq r$$
$$r=1, \ldots, k$$

then x^r is nondominated solution. In other words, we would check whether a feasible solution exists to the system:

$$\sum_{i=1}^{\ell} \lambda_i \theta^i(x^r) \geq \sum_{i=1}^{\ell} \lambda_i \theta^i(x^j), \quad j = 1, \ldots, k$$

$$\sum_{i=1}^{\ell} \lambda_i = 1, \ \lambda_i \geq 0, \ i = 1, \ldots, \ell.$$

If the solution exists then x^r would be nondominated point.

An alternative procedure might be as follows:

$$\sum_{j=1}^{k} \lambda_j \theta^i(x^j) \geq \theta^i(x^r), \quad i = 1, \ldots, \ell$$

$$\sum_{j=1}^{k} \lambda_j = 1, \ \lambda_j \geq 0, \ j = 1, \ldots, k \ .$$

If the solution to the above system exists, then x^r is dominated

extreme point. Any of the above approaches may be used after other,

heuristic ways of screening have been used and some of the points

still stay undetermined with respect to nondominance.

To demonstrate, let us return to the example in Section 3.3.

on Multicriteria Simplex Method. Suppose that we did not use the

nondominance subroutine and ended with all the noncomparable extreme

points:

	$\theta^1(x)$	$\theta^2(x)$	$\theta^3(x)$
x^2	16	24	0
x^3	(48)	(32)	-16
x^4	16	0	(16)
x^5	0	8	(16)
x^6	5.33	21.33	5.33
x^7	5.33	21.33	5.33
x^8	-12	16	8
x^9	- 6.4	9.6	6.4

We do not know whether these points are dominated or nondominated.

None of these points is dominated by some other--they are all non-

comparable. First of all, points containing maximal element in any

particular column (circled) i.e., x^3, x^4, $x^5 \epsilon N_{ex}$. Taking the sum of

all pairs of columns, point x^6 produces maximum for the last two

columns 21.33+5.33 = 26.66 and therefore x^6, $x^7 \epsilon N_{ex}$. Looking at

the last two columns, notice that x^2 is strictly nondominated in

(2,3) and therefore $x^2 \epsilon N_{ex}$. So we have established nondominance of
all points except x^8 and x^9. The dominance of these two points may
be established by solving one of the above mentioned linear programming
problems.

5.2. Some Notes on Nonlinearity.

The methods introduced in this study are applicable only when the
assumption that the image $\theta[X]$ of X is a convex set can be satisfied.
Otherwise we are facing so-called "gap problem" which will be clari-
fied in the following simple graphical analysis.

Consider a simple two dimensional case with $\theta(x) = (\theta^1(x), \theta^2(x))$,
$X \subseteq E^n$ and assume that $\theta[X] \subseteq E^2$ is not a convex set but exhibits a
"gap" as indicated in the following Figure 5.2.1.

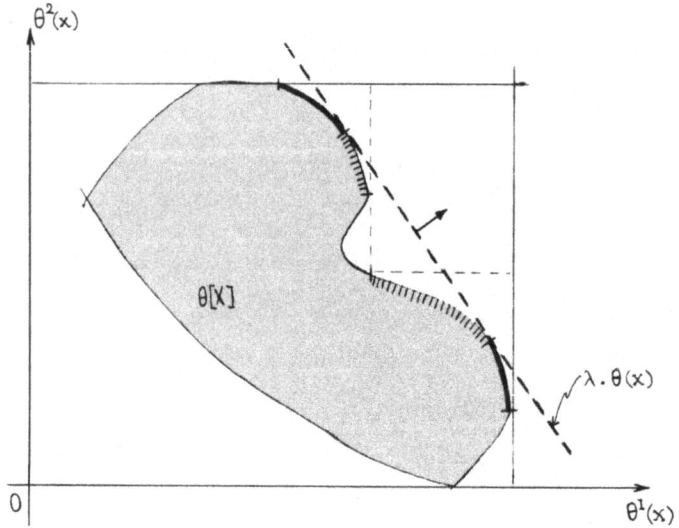

Figure 5.2.1.

The convex linear combination of $\theta^1(x)$ and $\theta^2(x)$, denoted

$\lambda \cdot \theta(x)$ represented by ---. We can see that maximization of

$\lambda \cdot \theta(x)$ for all λ the part of N designated by ▄▄▄ on the boundary

of $\theta[X]$ while the part of N designated by ⅏⅏⅏⅏ remains undetected.

We will show that we can locate the set N even without strong

assumptions on θ and X. The "gap resolution" will be based on maxi-

mizing one objective function while treating all the others as con-

straints varying within a set of parameters.

First, we shall illustrate the concept graphically. Consider

$\theta(x) = (\theta^1(x), \theta^2(x))$ and let $\theta[X]$ be nonconvex with a "gap" as in

Figure 5.2.2.

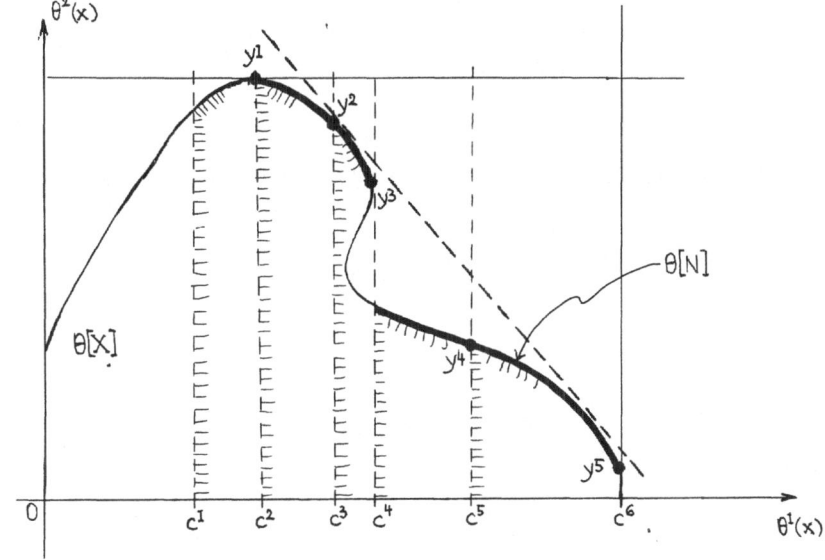

Figure 5.2.2.

Fix $\theta^1(x) = c^1$ and solve Max $\theta^2(x)$ subject to $\theta^1(x) \doteq c^1$ and $\theta[X]$.

The solution is denoted as y^1. Next solve Max $\theta^2(x)$ subject to $\theta^1(x)$ $\doteq c^2$, getting y^1 again. Solving the same problem consecutively for c^3, c^4, c^5 and c^6 we get y^2, y^3, y^4 and y^5. Notice that by solving for all $c\epsilon[c^1, c^6]$ we may compute the whole set N while simultaneously resolving the gap.

We will show that by this technique the whole set N may be obtained even under general nonlinearity conditions.

Let us define general vector maximization problem (VMP) as follows:

Definition 5.2.1. Let $\theta:E^n \rightarrow E^\ell$, $g:E^n \rightarrow E^m$, $h:E^n \rightarrow E^k$, $x^o \subseteq E^n$. Then VMP is to find an x^*, if it exists, such that

$$\theta(x) \geq \theta(x^*) \Rightarrow \theta(x) = \theta(x^*),$$
$$x^* \epsilon X = \left\{x \mid x\epsilon X^o, \ g(x) \leqq 0, \ h(x) = 0\right\},$$

where X is a feasible set, x^* is a nondominated solution, $X^o \subseteq E^n$, and $\theta(x^*)$ is a vector maximum.

We will need the following notational agreement:

If $\theta(x) = (\theta^1(x), \ \ldots, \ \theta^i(x), \ \ldots, \ \theta^\ell(x))$ is an ℓ-dimensional vector function, then we can define $\tilde{\theta}^{(i)}(x) = (\theta^1(x), \ \ldots, \ \theta^{i-1}(x), \ \theta^{i+1}(x), \ \ldots, \ \theta^\ell(x))$ which is derived from $\theta(x)$ by deleting its ith component $\theta^i(x)$. $\tilde{\theta}^{(i)}(x):E^n \rightarrow E^{\ell-1}$.

Let us define the following scalar maximization problem (MP):

$$\theta^i(x^*) = \underset{x\epsilon X^{(i)}}{\text{Max}} \ \theta^i(x), \ x^*\epsilon X^{(i)} = \left\{x \mid x\epsilon X^o, \ \tilde{\theta}^{(i)}(x) \doteq \tilde{c}^{(i)}, \ x\epsilon X\right\}$$

where $\tilde{c}^{(i)} = (c^1, \ldots, c^{i-1}, c^{i+1}, \ldots, c^{\ell})$

and $\tilde{c}^{(i)} \epsilon C = \left\{ \tilde{c}^{(i)} \mid \tilde{c}^{(i)} \epsilon E^{\ell-1}, -\infty < c^i < \infty \right\}$. Using Fritz John stationary

point necessary optimality theorem [see Mangasarian, 1969] we can state

the following necessary conditions for $x^* \epsilon X$ to be nondominated.

Theorem 5.2.2. Let X^o be an open set in E^n. Let $\theta : E^n \to E^{\ell}$, $g : E^n \to E^m$,

$h : E^n \to E^k$, all defined on X^o. Let x^* be a solution to VMP:

$\theta(x) \geq \theta(x^*) \Rightarrow \theta(x) = \theta(x^*)$

$x, x^* \epsilon X = \left\{ x \mid x \epsilon X^o, g(x) \leqq 0, h(x), = 0 \right\}$.

Let θ and g be differentiable at x^*, and let h have continuous

first partial derivatives at x^*. Then there exists $\lambda_i^* \epsilon E$, $\lambda^* \epsilon E^{\ell-1}$,

$r^* \epsilon E^m$, $s^* \epsilon E^k$ and $\tilde{c} \epsilon E^{\ell-1}$ such that the following conditions are

satisfied:

$$\lambda_i^* \nabla \theta^i(x^*) + \lambda^* \nabla (\tilde{\theta}^{(i)}(x^*) - \tilde{c}^{(i)}) + r^* \nabla g(x^*) + s^* \nabla h(x^*) = 0$$

$$\lambda^* \tilde{\theta}^{(i)}(x^*) - \lambda^* \tilde{c}^{(i)} + rg(x^*) = 0$$

$$(\lambda_i^*, \lambda^*, r^*) \geqq 0$$

$$(\lambda_i^*, \lambda^*, r^*, s^*) \neq 0.$$

Proof. (i) Observe, if $x^* \epsilon N$, then x^* is the solution of

$\text{Max } \theta^i(x) \text{ s.t. } x \epsilon X^{(i)} = \left\{ x \epsilon X \mid \tilde{\theta}^{(i)}_{(x)} \geqq \tilde{\theta}^{(i)}(x^*) \right\}$

for each $i = 1, \ldots, \ell$. Otherwise $x^* \notin N$.

(ii) By replacing $\tilde{\theta}^{(i)}_{(x^*)}$ by $\tilde{c}^{(i)}$ we get MP.

(iii) Applying Fritz John's theorem we get the desired

results. Q.E.D.

Given $c \epsilon C$, denote as MP(c) the problem of finding a point $x* \epsilon X$ such that $\theta^i(x*) \geq \theta^i(x)$ for all $x \epsilon X$ and $\tilde{\theta}^{(i)}(x) \geq c$; i.e., MP(c) is defined as

$$\theta^i(x*) = \underset{x \epsilon X*}{\text{Max}} \ \theta^i(x), \ x* \epsilon X* = \left\{ x | x \epsilon X^0, \ \tilde{\theta}^{(i)}(x) \geq c, \ x \epsilon X \right\}.$$

Let us define the following:

$$N = \left\{ x | x \epsilon X, \ x \text{ solves VMP} \right\}$$

$$C = \left\{ x | x \epsilon X, \ x \text{ solves MP(c)}, \ c \epsilon C \right\}.$$

Then we can state the following:

Theorem 5.2.3. $N \subseteq C$.

Proof. Suppose $x* \epsilon N$ and $x* \notin C$. Then there exists some $x^1 \epsilon X*$ such that for any c, $\theta^i(x^1) > \theta^i(x*)$ and $\tilde{\theta}^{(i)}(x^1) \geq c$. We can, however, make

$$c^1 = c(x*) \geq c.$$

Then, of course, MP(c^1) not having a solution means

$$\theta^i(x) > \theta^i(x*) \text{ and } \tilde{\theta}^{(i)}(x^1) \geq c^1 = c(x*) = \tilde{\theta}^{(i)}(x*) \geq c$$

which contradicts $x* \epsilon N$.

5.3. A Selection of the final solution.

We have suggested some algorithms which would allow us to compute all nondominated solutions of the set X of all feasible solutions. If the decision maker's utility (preference, trade-off) function is unknown or too complex to be reliably constructed, then the set of all nondominated solutions assures that such a function would reach its maximum somewhere in this set.

This knowledge of N might be quite helpful and sufficient to reach an acceptable decision if the actual number of nondominated solutions is small. For example, in Problem (2) of section 3.4. the nondominated extreme points were only three out of a possible 12870 extreme point solutions. On the other hand, the number of nondominated solutions might be too large as it is illustrated in Problem (3) of section 3.4. In this case the final decision might still be hard to achieve.

Ultimately the decision maker must choose a single nondominated solution as the solution of a given problem. Many existing approaches might be helpful to achieve this. At the end of section 3.1. we discuss the relationship between the multicriteria simplex method and the decomposition of Λ-space. It is concluded that for each $x^i \in N_{ex}$ the corresponding $\Lambda(x^i)$ is obtained as a by-product of this method. This $\Lambda(x^i)$ represents a set of optimal weights for x^i. So, we have a very useful additional information which associates each x^i with the set of weights $\lambda \in \Lambda(x^i)$ such that $\lambda.cx$ is maximized at x^i.

Obviously, the decision maker might arrive at the same $x^i \in N$

by estimating the proper set of weights $\lambda \varepsilon \Lambda(x^i)$. These weights measure the relative importance (or attention levels) of individual objectives.

The set of all N-solutions corresponds to the complete decomposition of the parametric space Λ. Each objective is allowed to be weighted from 0 to 1 in all possible combinations. Observe that if there is complete uncertainty as what the actual weights should be, i.e. all $\lambda \varepsilon \Lambda$ are considered equally plausible, then the entire set N is the result. If the decision maker could limit the choice of weights, the set N could be correspondingly reduced.

Let us consider some subset of Λ, say Λ^1, and assume that $\Lambda^1 \subseteq \Lambda$, i.e. Λ^1 is contained in Λ. By maximizing $\lambda \cdot \theta(x)$ for all $\lambda \varepsilon \Lambda^1$ we obtain <u>reduced set of nondominated solutions</u>, say N^1. Obviously $N^1 \subseteq N$. Let $\Lambda = \Lambda^0$ and $N = N^0$. Then we can recursively define Λ^n and calculate corresponding N^n for $n = 0, 1, 2, \ldots$, such that $\Lambda^{n+1} \subseteq \Lambda^n$ and $N^{n+1} \subseteq N^n$. We shall call any subset of N a <u>set of compromise solutions</u>. Any reduction of N, which is not completely random or arbitrary, reflects particular utilization of an additional information the decision maker has provided. If the decision maker can express reliably his preference between say x^j, $x^k \varepsilon N$, then if x^j is preferred to x^k we can remove x^j from further consideration and thus reduce N. The resulting set of compromise solutions is then further analyzed. Such ability to express strict preference is decreasing rapidly as the number of applicable criteria gets larger than one. More often the <u>decision maker cannot compare, does not want to compare or does not know how to compare</u> any two alternatives with multiple criteria consequences.

5.3.1. <u>Direct Assessment of Weights</u>.

In section 2 we have shown that if an appropriate set of
weights λ could be assigned to $\theta(x)$ reliably, the corresponding
nondominated solution (s) could be safely located. It is conceivable
that even though the decision maker could not probably pinpoint
λ exactly, he might be able to determine at least intervals for
its components. By recursive and interactive reduction of Λ the
necessary reduction of N can be achieved. In this section we
discuss some points <u>against</u> such an approach.

I. <u>Human ability to arrive at an overall evaluation by weighting</u>
<u>and combining diverse attributes is not very impressive.</u>
Recent psychological studies [19] clearly indicate that such
weighting process is unstable, suboptimal, and often arbitrary.
It has been our conceit that ·the subtle weighting and combining
of attributes can be accomplished only by the mysterious intuitive
deliberations of human intelligence.

II. <u>The task of a multiattribute weighting is complicated by a</u>
<u>fuzzy logic employed by the decision maker when facing a not fully</u>
<u>comprehensible problem.</u>
It is ambitious, for example, to expect the decision maker to state
that "λ_i = .42", or that ".45 < λ_i < .5". More likely he would
express himself in such terms as: "λ_i should be substantially
larger than .5", or "λ_i should be in the vicinity of .4 but
rather larger", or some similar fuzzy statement. The newly de-
veloping theory of fuzzy set is intended to formalize such
language [27].

III. <u>The total number of all possible (and identifiable) criteria</u>
<u>or attributes is usually very large.</u> Obviously we cannot expect
any human being to assign priority weights to the thousands of
attributes with any reliability. Yet the selection of the "most
relevant" attributes is usually achieved by applying some weighting
structure to the complete identifiable set of attributes and then
by disregarding those which have received their weight below some
predetermined threshold level.

IV. <u>To any set of priority weights, even if "correctly" estimated,</u>
<u>there might still correspond a large number (possibly infinite)</u>
<u>of equally plausible solutions.</u> The solution maximizing implicit
utility function, x*, does not have to be an N_{ex} solution in linear
cases, i.e. it might belong to the relative interior of some
face of polyhedron X. Then there is no set of weights which
could do anything more than to identify the face containing x*.
V. <u>Alterations of weights reflect the fact that they are de-</u>
<u>pendent on a particular set of feasible alternatives considered.</u>
So the changes in X would impute different λ to $\theta(x)$ even if U
is considered fixed. As discussion and examples in [30] suggest,
any particular weighting structure must be learned, it is not in the
independent possession of the decision maker and cannot be simply
"extracted". Priority weights should be a result of the analysis
rather than its input.

<u>EXAMPLE.</u> We refer to decomposition of Λ in Figure 2.5.1.1. We could
reduce the original N_{ex} by recursive reduction of Λ as it is indicated
in Figure 5.3.1.

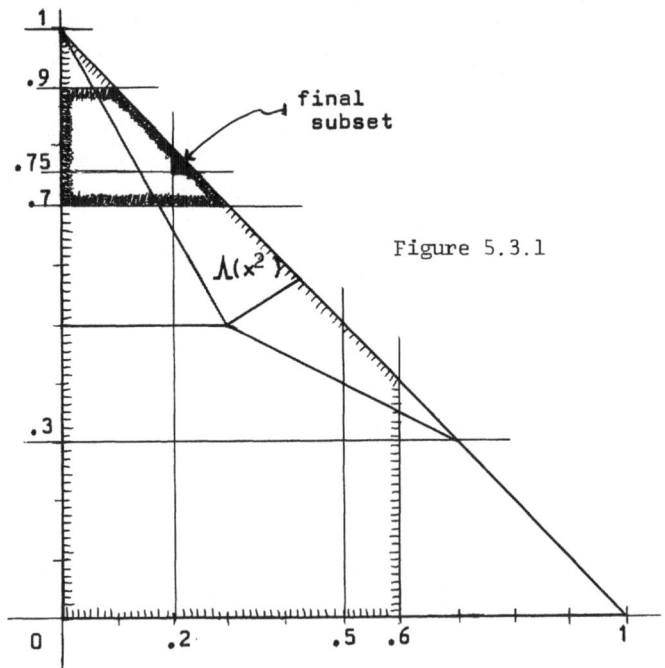

Figure 5.3.1

Observe that initially we reduced Λ to $0 \leq \lambda_1 \leq .7$, $0 \leq \lambda_2 \leq .6$ and $.3 \leq \lambda_3 \leq 1$. There is no corresponding reduction in N_{ex} - so the additional information had no impact. Further we specified our weights as $.1 \leq \lambda_1 \leq .3$, $0 \leq \lambda_2 \leq .5$ and $.7 \leq \lambda_3 \leq .9$. This leads to reduced set $\{x^1, x^2\}$. If we would further limit our weights for example to $.1 \leq \lambda_1 \leq .2, .2 \leq \lambda_2 \leq .5$ and $.75 \leq \lambda_3 \leq .9$ then we would obtain x^2 as the solution. (More precisely the face of X containing x^2 would contain also the solution maximizing U - if the weights chosen reflect U correctly).

5.3.2. The Ideal Solution.

We shall denote a maximum of each individual component of $\theta(x)$ as:

$$\underset{x \in X}{\text{Max }} \theta_i (x) = \theta_i (\bar{x}^i) = \bar{\theta}_i, \quad i = 1, \ldots, \ell. \tag{5-3-1}$$

Then $\bar{\theta} = (\bar{\theta}_1, \ldots, \bar{\theta}_\ell)$ can be defined as the "ideal solution" at which all objective functions would attain their maximum feasible values. So, if there would exist $\bar{x} \in X$ such that $\theta(\bar{x}) = \bar{\theta}$, then such solution $\bar{x}$ would be also the maximum of any increasing utility function U. There would be no decision problem. The ideal solution is however generally infeasible, $\bar{x} \notin X$.

Because of this prominent role of the ideal solution, we can argue that the decision maker, instead of maximizing unknown (and possibly nonexisting) function U, is trying to find a solution which would be "as close as possible" to the ideal solution. Such a fuzzy statement of human purpose is probably more realistic than maximization of U.

Let us briefly discuss some possibilities of measuring the "closeness" to the ideal solution. The fuzziness of "as close as possible" can be simply interpreted and measured if only a single dimension, the ith criterion, is considered at a time. The degree of closeness of an $x^j \in N$ to $\bar{x}$ with respect to i is defined as

$$d_i (x^j), \quad 0 \leq d_i (x^j) \leq 1, \tag{5-3-2}$$

$$i=1, \ldots, \ell, \quad j = 1, \ldots, k.$$

Observe that for $x^j \equiv \bar{x}^i$ we assign $d_i(x^j) = 1$, the highest degree of closeness. As the difference $\bar{\theta}_i - \theta_i(x^j)$ increases for different $x^j \in N$ we see corresponding $d_i(x^j)$ decreasing toward zero. The assignment of $d_i(x^j)$ is not difficult because all $\theta_i(x^j)$ is not difficult because all $\theta_i(x^j)$ can be completely ordered and thus the preferences are explicit . We want to capture relative strength of these preferences in relation to the ideal point. Aside of subjective assessment of $d_i(x^j)$ we could utilize some formal functions:

$$d_i(x^j) = \frac{\theta_i(x^j)}{\bar{\theta}_i} \quad , \qquad d_i(x^j) = 1 + \theta_i(x^j) - \bar{\theta}_i \qquad (5\text{-}3\text{-}3)$$

or more complicated

$$d_i(x^j) = \frac{\theta_i(x^j) - \underline{\theta}_i}{\bar{\theta}_i - \underline{\theta}_i} \qquad (5\text{-}3\text{-}4)$$

where $\underline{\theta}_i = \text{Min } \theta_i(x^j)$, $i=1, \ldots, \ell$. Naturally, many more functions like those in (5-3-4) could be considered. Proper procedure would be based on an interactive refinement and precision of some function like those in (5-3-3) and (5-3-4).

Among some operations described [27] we find the <u>operation of concentration</u> very useful:

$$d_i(x^j) \equiv d_i^\alpha(x^j), \ 1 < \alpha \leq 2, \qquad (5\text{-}3\text{-}5)$$

where α is the power of $d_i(x^j)$. This operation reduces the degree of closeness relatively less for higher degrees and relatively more for lower degrees. Similarly, the <u>operation of dilation</u>, defined as in (5-3-5) for $0 < \alpha < 1$, has the opposite effect than that of concentration. Observe that concentration leads to <u>contrast intensification</u> (the differences between degrees are larger) and thus effectively reduces the fuzziness.

We summarize that by combining some functional form of $d_i(x^j)$ with subjective and interactive assessment via concentration and dilation we construct <u>fuzzy sets</u> $\{\theta_i(x^j),\ d_i(x^j)\}$ describing the closeness of any $x^j \epsilon N$ to $\bar{x}$ with respect to the ith criterion.

Next problem is to design similar measure of closeness with respect to <u>all</u> criteria. Similar to [27] we consider one rational interpretation of "as close as possible" the following rule:

$$\underset{j}{\text{Max}}\ \underset{i}{\text{Min}}\ d_i(x^j) \qquad\qquad (5\text{-}3\text{-}6)$$

Because of the fuzziness and the complexity of a typical problem we should concentrate on <u>eliminating "obviously bad"</u> <u>solutions</u> rather than on identifying the best ones. So, the procedure (5-3-6) should reject all solutions with their degree of closeness smaller than some predetermined level of aspiration, say .5. An example is given at the end of this section.

Another natural approach would be to minimize the distance between x^j and $\bar{x}$ in geometrical sense. Let us define the distance as:

$$\bar{d}_i(x^j) = 1 - d_i(x^j), \qquad\qquad (5\text{-}3\text{-}7)$$

and use <u>a family of L_p - metrics</u> which provides a wide range of geometric measures of closeness possessing some desirable properties. They are defined as

$$L_p(x^j) = \left[\sum_{i=1}^{\ell} \bar{d}_i^p(x^j)\right]^{1/p},\ 1 \leqq p \leqq \infty, \qquad\qquad (5\text{-}3\text{-}8)$$

where $\bar{d}_i^p(x^j)$ indicates the pth power of $\bar{d}_i(x^j)$.

$$\text{If } \underset{x^j \epsilon X}{\text{Min}}\ L_p(x^j) = L_p(\bar{x}^p), \qquad\qquad (5\text{-}3\text{-}9)$$

then $\bar{x}^p \epsilon X$ is called a <u>compromise solution with respect to p</u> and its criteria value image is $\theta(\bar{x}^p)$. It has been shown in [28] that $\bar{x}^p$ are nondominated for $1 \leqq p < \infty$, and at least one $\bar{x}^p$ is nondominated for $p = \infty$. So it is safe to replace X by N again.

Since we cannot assume all criteria to be of equal importance, we must use more general form of (5-3-8):

$$L_p \ (\lambda, \ x^j) = \left[\sum_{i=1}^{\ell} \lambda_i^p \ \bar{d}_i^p (x^j) \right]^{1/p} , \ 1 \leq p \leq \infty \ . \tag{5-3-10}$$

We could disregard the power $1/p$ in (5-3-10) $1 \leq p < \infty$ since the solutions $\tilde{x}^p$ would not be affected.

To understand the role of <u>distance parameter p</u> better we can substitute $w_i = \bar{d}_i (x^j)$, omit $1/p$, and rewrite (5-3-10) as :

$$L_p (\lambda, \ x^j) = \sum_{i=1}^{\ell} \lambda_i^p \ w_i^{p-1} \ \bar{d}_i (x^j) . \tag{5-3-11}$$

As p increases, more and more weight is given to the largest distance. Ultimately the largest distance completely dominates and for $p = \infty$ we get from (5-3-8) $L_\infty (x^j) = \underset{i}{Max} \ \{\bar{d}_i (x^j)\}$.

By minimizing (5-3-11) , given λ and all p, $1 \leq p \leq \infty$, we obtain <u>a compromise set C.</u> Obviously $C \subseteq N$ and thus another way to reduce N is suggested. As an approximation of C it is quite sufficient to work with $p = 1, 2, \infty$ only. A helpful graphical insight into relation between C and N can be gained from Figure 5.3.2.

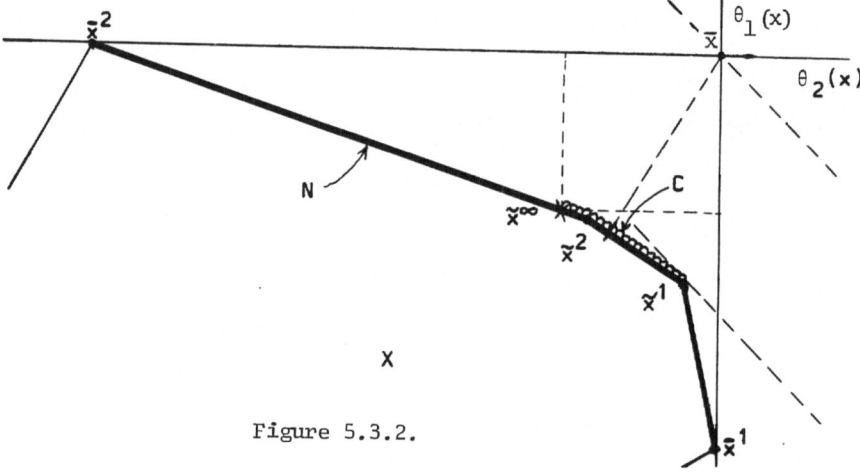

Figure 5.3.2.

<u>Example</u>. First we demonstrate (5-3-6) on the set of nondominated solutions obtained from (3-3-12). For simplicity let the degrees of

closeness be assigned according to (5-3-4).We get the following
table (5-3-12):

$d_i(x^j)$	x^1	x^2	x^3	x^4	x^5	x^6	
$d_1(x^j)$	.333	1	.333	0	.111	.111	
$d_2(x^j)$	.75	1	0	.25	.666	.666	(5-3-12)
$d_3(x^j)$	.5	0	1	1	.666	.666	
$\underset{i}{\text{Min}}$	.333	0	0	0	.111	.111	

Assuming that all criteria are equally important we would
choose x^1.

Similarly we could use distances (5-3-7)   and employ
L_p - metrics. Let us assume again that all criteria are equally
important and (5-3-4) describes fuzziness correctly. Then
we get the following table of distances (5-3-13):

$\bar{d}_i(x^j)$	x^1	x^2	x^3	x^4	x^5	x^6	
$\bar{d}_1(x^j)$	.667	0	.667	1	.889	.889	
$\bar{d}_2(x^j)$	.25	0	1	.75	.334	.334	
$\bar{d}_3(x^j)$	.5	1	0	0	.334	.334	(5-3-13)
$L_1(x^j)$	1.417	①	1.667	1.75	1.557	1.557	
$L_2(x^j)$	(.757)	1	1.445	1.563	1.013	1.013	
$L_\infty(x^j)$	(.667)	1	1	1	.889	.889	

The values of L_p - metrics are obtained from (5-3-11) with

$\lambda_i = 1$ for i and p = 1, 2. Observe that $\tilde{x}^1 \equiv x^2$. Obviously $\tilde{x}^2$
and $\tilde{x}^\infty$ are approximations since we considered extreme points only
but for the data of (5-3-13) we have $\tilde{x}^2 \equiv \tilde{x}^\infty \equiv x^1$. So the
compromise set is approximated by C= $\{x^1, x^2\}$. Obviously we
have to incorporate some measures of relative criteria importance
in our analysis.

5.3.3 Entropy as a measure of importance.

Throughout this study we have tried to indicate how multicriteria
decision making might be performed without direct assessment of
U. In section 5.3.1. we argued rather strongly against direct
assessment of weights either. Though the utility maximization is
not easily observed, <u>people do assign priority weights no matter</u>
<u>how imperfectly, fuzzily or temporarily.</u>

We suggest a methodology for determining priority weights which
would have the following properties:

(i) They would be dependent on a set of feasible
alternatives X (or N) and therefore sensitive to
any changes in X.

(ii) They would be determined objectively by
analysis of a given problem (and thus
reflect its particular structure) as well
as in interaction with the decision maker's
subjective assessment of importance.

For simplicity let us introduce new notation for $d_i(x^j) = d_{ij}$ (5-3-14)

Then we construct the following table:

ith criterion \ x^j	x^1	. . .	x^k	$\sum$
1	d_{11}	. . .	d_{1k}	D_1
. . . ℓ	. . . $d_{i\ell}$	. . .	. . . $d_{\ell k}$	. . . D_ℓ

(5-3-15)

We can interpret (5-3-15) a collection of ℓ fuzzy sets

$$d_i = (d_{i1}, \ldots, d_{ik}), \qquad (5\text{-}3\text{-}16)$$

which for each i provides a ranking of all x^j's in terms of closeness to the ideal point.

We shall attempt to offer a definition of weight as a measure of importance:

"A weight, assigned to the ith attribute as a measure of its relative importance for a given decision problem, is directly related to the average intrinsic information, generated by a given set of alternatives through the ith attribute, as well as to its subjective assessment."

EXAMPLE. Let us assume that it was assessed that profit has the highest weight of importance in a given hierarchy of criteria, say 1 for simplicity. The analysis of available alternatives indicated that they are all equally profitable. So the criterion receiving the highest weight would not allow to make a decision, it transmits no information to the decision maker. There are some other valuable criteria which were however excluded entirely because of zero weight. Our definition would assign 0 to profit automatically.

The introduced definition becomes operational only if the "average intrinsic information" can be measured. We observe that the set N is mapped into unit interval $< 0,1 >$ through (5-3-16). Class of all such mappings constitutes a vector

$$d = (d_1 , \ldots , d_\ell) \qquad (5\text{-}3\text{-}17)$$

To each $d_i \in d$ we assign a measure of its contrast intensity or entropy, denoted by $e(d_i)$.

In (5-3-15) observe that

$$D_i = \sum_{j=1}^{k} d_{ij} , \quad i = 1, \ldots , \ell , \qquad (5\text{-}3\text{-}18)$$

which is the _power_ of d_i. If N is a finite set, then traditional entropy measure can be written for our purpose as:

$$e(d_i) = -K \sum_{j=1}^{k} \frac{d_{ij}}{D_i} \ln \frac{d_{ij}}{D_i} \; , \tag{5-3-19}$$

where $K > 0$ and $e(d_i) \geq 0$. When all d_{ij} are equal to each other for a given $i, d_{ij}/D_i = \frac{1}{k}$, and $e(d_i)$ takes on its maximum value, say e_{max}. Obviously $e_{max} = \ln k$. So if we set $K = 1/e_{max}$, then $0 \leq e(d_i) \leq 1$ for all $d_i \epsilon d$. Such normalized entropy measure is useful for comparative analysis.

We also introduce _total entropy of N_, defined as

$$E = \sum_{i=1}^{\ell} e(d_i) . \tag{5-3-20}$$

Then a _measure of contrast intensity of the_ i^{th} _attribute_ is defined as:

$$\tilde{\lambda}_i = \frac{1}{\ell - E} \left(1 - e(d_i) \right) \tag{5-3-21}$$

Observe that by reducing N we could shift the ideal solution and thus change d_{ij}'s and then of course also $e(d_i)$, E and $\tilde{\lambda}_i$'s. So we can evaluate whether such reduction increases contrast intensity and thus adds decision relevant information. Similarly we can study the influence of adding or deleting any particular criterion. We can test any number of additional criteria because all components of N will stay nondominated no matter how much ℓ is increased. We might try to find such a combination of criteria which would give us the highest overall value of contrast intensity. If we denote the subjective assessment of importance of the ith attribute as w_i, dependent on social, cultural, traditional and environmental influences, then we can express our definition of a weight of importance as

$$\lambda_i = \tilde{\lambda}_i w_i \Big/ \sum_{i=1}^{\ell} \tilde{\lambda}_i w_i \quad , \; i = 1, \ldots , \ell . \tag{5-3-22}$$

EXAMPLE. Let us assume that we have three criteria θ_i which were assigned subjective weights w_i. There are four different alternatives available (nondominated). Relevant numerical values are summarized in (5-3-23):

w_i	$\theta_i(x^j)$	x^1	x^2	x^3	x^4	
.8	$\theta_1(x^j)$	7	8	8.5	⑨	(5-3-23)
.1	$\theta_2(x^j)$	⑩⓪⓪	60	20	80	
.1	$\theta_3(x^j)$	4	4	⑥	2	

Encircled are values of the ideal solution. Let us express degrees of closeness simply by using $d_i(x^j) = (1/\bar{\theta}_i)\,\theta_i(x^j) = d_{ij}$ from (5-3-3). Then we construct numerical equivalent of (5-3-15) in (5-3-24):

	x^1	x^2	x^3	x^4	$\sum$	
1	.778	.889	.944	1	3.611	
2	1	.6	.2	.8	2.6	(5-3-24)
3	.667	.667	1	.334	2.668	

Next we calculate $e(d_i)$ according to (5-3-19), $K = e_{max} = \ln 4 = 1.3863$. The calculations are given in table (5-3-25):

	d_{ij}/D_i			$d_{ij}/D_i(\ln\; d_{ij}/D_i)$			
	1	2	3	1	2	3	
x^1	.216	.385	.25	-.331	-.367	-.347	
x^2	.246	.231	.25	-.345	-.338	-.347	
x^3	.261	.007	.375	-.350	-.197	-.368	(5-3-25)
x^4	.277	.307	.125	-.356	-.363	-.260	
$\sum$	1	1	1	-1.382	-1.265	-1.322	

We get

$$e(d_1) = .997, \quad e(d_2) = .913, \quad e(d_3) = .954$$

and $E = 2.864$. Then $\tilde{\lambda}_1 = .022$, $\tilde{\lambda}_2 = .64$ and $\tilde{\lambda}_3 = .338$ indicate relative contrast intensities measuring intrinsic average information transmitted by each attribute. The weights of importance to be assigned are:

$$\lambda_1 = .153, \quad \lambda_2 = .555, \quad \lambda_3 = .292.$$

Let us use simple additive weight criterion to evaluate alternatives in (5-3-24) with both w_i's and λ_i's (and also $\tilde{\lambda}_i$'s):

	x^1	x^2	x^3	x^4
$\sum_{i=1}^{\ell} w_i d_{ij}$	.789	.838	.875	$\boxed{.913}$
$\sum_{i=1}^{\ell} \lambda_i d_{ij}$	$\boxed{.869}$	.664	.547	.695
$\sum_{i=1}^{\ell} \tilde{\lambda}_i d_{ij}$	$\boxed{.882}$	.628	.486	.647

So the traditional approach would recommend x^4 while our method indicates x^1 to be the best solution.

5.3.4. A Method of Displaced Ideal.

We have described several ways of reducing the set N. Let us summarize their main features:

(i) If the decision maker can express reliably a strict preference between any two elements of N, then the "unpreferred" solution can be removed.

(ii)   In the framework of linear programming the
       decomposition of the parametric space of
       weights is available. Fuzzy assessment of
       possible weight intervals then leads to
        reduction of N.

(iii) We can transform outcomes into degrees of
       closeness to the ideal solution with respect
       to a single criterion and then retain only
       solutions with the degree of closeness with
       respect to all criteria exceeding predetermined
       aspiration level.

(iv)   Find a compromise set C which is the subset
       of N of all solutions closest to the ideal
       solution with respect to one or more L_p - metric.

(v)   Using the entropy measure of importance we
       can discard those criteria which manifest low
       contrast intensity and therefore receive low
       weight of importance. Corresponding decrease
       in the number of criteria considered could lead
       to the reduction of N.

    The net result of discarding some elements of N (using any
of the above approaches) is the corresponding displacement of the
ideal point. Originally we subsitute X by N and considered all
solutions from X-N infeasible. The ideal solution for both X and
N is identical. The situation changes however when N is further
reduced to N^1 (or C). By this we construct new feasible set with
some of the original components of the ideal solution removed. Thus
the ideal solution is displaced closer to the new feasible set.
Since all our analytical information, etc. has been determined
in dependency on the ideal solution, they must be all recalculated
and reevaluated because of the displacement. We see that dynamic,
selfadjusting, interactive and iterative procedure can be designed.
Its iterative property of convergence to a single solution can be
best demonstrated graphically. Let us assume for simplicity that
only L_p - metric criterion is used for the reduction of N. We
also assume that the outcomes have already been scaled into intervals
< 0,1 > for all criteria. We may start with simplified two
criteria situation as in Figure   5.3.3.

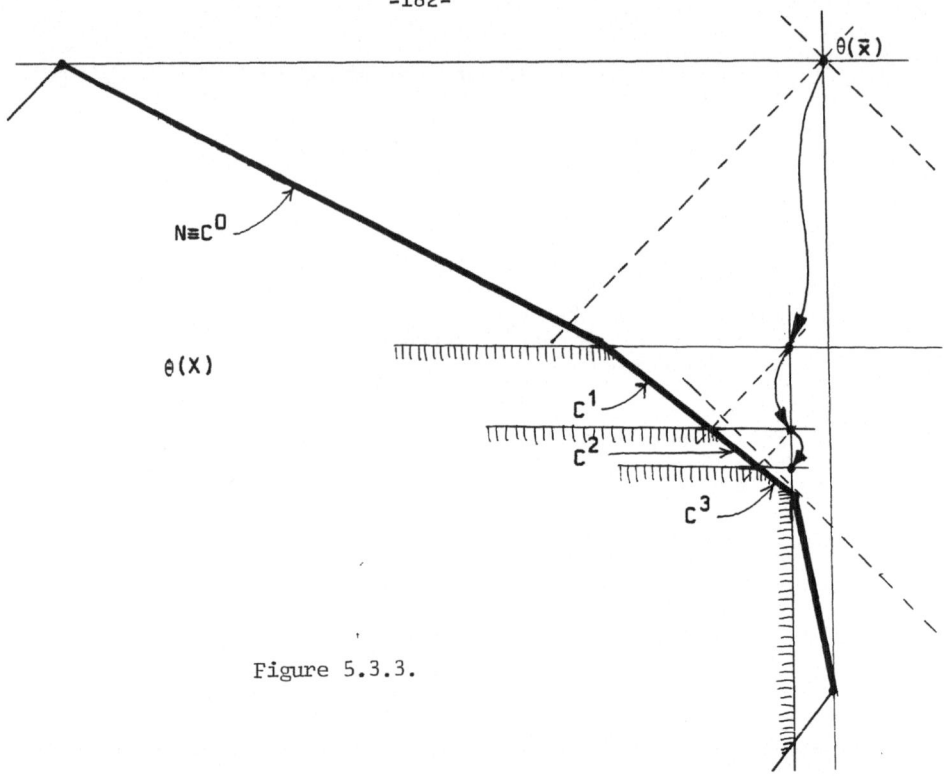

Figure 5.3.3.

Because each displacement of the ideal solution will result
in reevaluation of weights and because of combined effect of all
reduction methods we are most likely to observe more general path
of movement of the ideal solution.

Though the iterative process converges to a single point it
would not be wise to force the technique to such an extreme. The
displacements of the ideal solution will become progressively
smaller reflecting smaller returns for additional bits of information. Rather than seek for a single solution and thus impose
normative inflexibility on the decision maker, the procedure would
stop whenever resulting compromise set contains "few enough" alternatives to allow for the final decision to be made. Since by
adding more criteria the nondominance of any alternative is not
violated, these "chosen few" can be safely evaluated with respect
to any social, legal, moral, aesthetic and other aspect of this
complex world.

BIBLIOGRAPHY

1. Arrow, K.J., Barankin, E.W. and Blackwell, D., "Admissible Points of Convex Sets", In: H.W. Kuhn, A.W. Tucker (eds.), Contributions to the Theory of Games, Princeton University Press, Princeton, New Jersey, pp. 87-91, 1953.

2. Charnes, A. and Cooper, W.W., Management Models and Industrial Applications of Linear Programming, Vols. I and II, John Wiley & Sons, New York, 1961.

3. DaCunha, N.O. and Polak, E., "Constrained Minimization Under Vector-Valued Criteria in Finite Dimensional Space", Journal of Math Analysis and Applications, Vol. 19, pp. 103-124, 1967.

4. Gal, T. and Nedoma, J., "Multiparametric Linear Programming", Management Science, Vol. 18, No. 7, March 1972, pp. 406-421.

5. Geoffrion, A.M., "Solving Bicriterion Mathematical Programs", Operations Research 15, pp. 39-54, 1967.

6. Geoffrion, A.M., "Proper Efficiency and the Theory of Vector Maximization", Journal of Mathematical Analysis and Applications, Vol. 22, pp. 618-630, 1968.

7. Hadley, G., Linear Programming, Addison-Wesley, Reading, Mass., 1961.

8. Klahr, C.N., "Multiple Objectives in Mathematical Programming", Operations Research, Vol. 6, No. 6, pp. 849-855, 1958.

9. Klinger, A., "Vector-Valued Performance Criteria", IEEE Transactions on Automatic Control, pp. 117-118, 1964.

10. Koopmans, T.C., "Activity Analysis of Production and Allocation", Cowles Commission for Research in Economics, Monograph No. 13, John Wiley & Sons, New York, 1951.

11. Kuhn, H.W. and Tucker, A.W., "Nonlinear Programming", Proceedings of the Second Berkeley Symposium on Mathematical Statistics and Probability, pp. 481-492, University of California Press, Berkeley, California, 1951.

12. MacCrimmon, K.R., "Decision Making Among Multiple-Attribute Alternatives: A Survey and Consolidated Approach", Memorandum RM-4823-ARPA, December 1968, The Rand Corporation, Santa Monica, California.

13. Manas, J. and Nedoma, J., "Finding All Vertices of a Convex Polyhedron," Numerische Mathematik, Vol. 12 (1968), pp. 226-229.

14. Mangasarian, O.L., Nonlinear Programming, McGraw-Hill, New York, 1969.

15. Markowitz, H., "The Optimization of Quadratic Function Subject to Linear Constraints," Naval Research Logistics Quarterly, Nos. 1 and 2, March and June, 1956, pp. 111-133.

16. Pareto, V., "Course d'Economic Politique," Lausanne, Rouge, 1896.

17. Raiffa, H., "Preferences for Multi-Attributed Alternatives," Memorandum RM-5868-DOT/RC, April, 1969, The Rand Corporation.

18. Raiffa, H., Decision Analysis, Addison-Wesley, 1970.

19. Shepard, R.N., "On Subjectively Optimum Selection Among Multi-attribute Alternatives." In: Maynard W. Shelly, III, and Glenn W. Bryan (Eds.), Human Judgement and Optimality, John Wiley & Sons, 1964.

20. Von Neumann, J. and Morgenstern, O., Theory of Games and Economic Behavior, Princeton University Press, 1953.

21. Stoer, J. and Witzgall, C., Convexity and Optimization in Finite Dimensions I, Springer-Verlag, 1970.

22. Yu, P.L., "The Set of All Nondominated Solutions in Decision Problems with Multiobjectives," Systems Analysis Program, Working Paper Series, No. F71-32, University of Rochester, September, 1971.

23. Yu, P.L., "Cone Convexity, Cone Extreme Points and Nondominated Solutions in Decision Problems with Multiobjectives," Center for System Science, 72-02, University of Rochester, Rochester, New York, 1972.

24. Yu, P. L. and Zeleny, M., "The Set of All Nondominated Solutions in Linear Cases and A Multicriteria Simplex Method," Center for System Science, CSS 73-03, University of Rochester, 1973.

25. Yu, P. L. and Zeleny, M., "On Some Multi-Parametric Programs," Center for Systems Science, CSS 73-05, University of Rochester, 1973.

26. Zadeh, L. A., "Optimality and Nonscalar - Valued Performance Criteria," IEEE Transactions on Automatic Control, AC-8 (1963) 1, 59-60.

27. Zadeh, L.A., "Outline of a New Approach to the Analysis of Complex Systems and Decision Processes," In: Multiple Criteria Decision Making, Columbia: USC Press, 1973.

28. Zeleny, M. and Cochrane, J.L. (eds.), Multiple Criteria Decision Making, Columbia, S.C.: The University of South Carolina Press, 1973, p.816.

29. Zeleny, M. and Cochrane, J.L., "A Priori and a Posteriori Goals in Macroeconomic Policy Making," In: Multiple Criteria Decision Making, Columbia: USC Press, 1973.

30. Zeleny, M., "Compromise Programming," In: Multiple Criteria Decision Making, Columbia: USC Press, 1973.

31. Zeleny, M., "A Selected Bibliography of Works Related to the Multiple Criteria Decision Making," In: Multiple Criteria Decision Making, Columbia: USC Press, 1973.

<u>A P P E N D I X</u>

A1. A Note on elimination of redundant constraints.

We have noted that finding a nondominated extreme points of X, via direct decomposition of the parametric space, can be efficient only if nonredundant constraints of individual $\Lambda(x^i)$ can be identified. Each $\Lambda(x^i)$ is defined by as many linear inequalities as there are nonbasic variables in the simplex tableau. For instance, in the example of Section 2.5.1, we have seven inequalities for a polyhedron in two dimensional space. Many of these constraints are redundant and their identification might not be trivial. Linear programming subroutine, such as the one in (2-4-1) of Section 2.4, has to be employed. Introducing redundant constraint might lead to a dominated basis. Even if our goal is just a decomposition of the multiparametric space Λ, through the identification of adjacent decomposition polyhedra, nonredundant constraints must be identified and thus procedures of this type are generally inefficient, see e.g. [Gal, Nedoma, 1972].

Since the simplex method does not require a careful elimination of redundant constraints, but disregards them automatically, relatively little attention has been devoted to this problem.

One exception in the literature on linear programming is an article by J. C. G. Boot (1962),[*] dealing with some techniques for identification of redundant constraints. However, the method is not suitable for our purpose because we will have to use more refined definitions of redundancy in linear constraints.

Let the feasible set X is generated by a set of m constraints $A_i x \leq b_i$,

$$X = \{x \mid x \varepsilon E^n, A_i x \leq b_i, i = 1, \ldots, m\}.$$

D1. A constraint, say constraint 1, is <u>inessential</u> if, and only if, for all x such that

$$A_i x \leq b_i, i = 2, \ldots, m$$

also $A_1 x \leq b_1$.

D2. A constraint, say constraint 1, is <u>strongly redundant</u> if, and only if, for all x such that

$$A_i x \leq b_i, i = 2, \ldots, m$$

also $A_1 x > b_1$.

_____

[*] J.C.G. Boot: On Trivial and Binding Constraints in Programming Problems, <u>Management Science</u>, 8 (1962) 4, 419-441.

D3. Constraint 1 is <u>strongly redundant</u> if, and only if, there exists no vector x such that

$$A_i x \leq b_i, \; i = 2, \ldots, m$$

and $\quad A_1 x \geq b_1.$

<u>Remark</u>. The above definition may be restated as being true if there is no x such that

$$A_i x \leq b_i, \; i = 2, \ldots, m$$

and $\quad A_1 x = b_1.$

We shall call an inessential constraint which is not s-redundant to be a weakly redundant constraint.

D4. A constraint, say constraint 1, is <u>weakly redundant</u> if, and only if, there exists x such that

$$A_i x \leq b_i, \; A_1 x = b_1$$

and there is no x such that

$$A_i x \leq b_i, \; A_1 x > b_1$$

<u>Note.</u> The first part of this definition assures no s-redundancy; the second part the inessentiality.

In the traditional LP analysis all redundant constraints are dispensable. For the purpose of our problem only s-redundant constraints are superfluous. All essential and w-redundant constraints are operative in our computations.

We introduce some graphical examples to clarify the concepts. The shaded area is $A_i x \leqq b_i$, i = 2, ..., m and the constraint 1 is being explored.

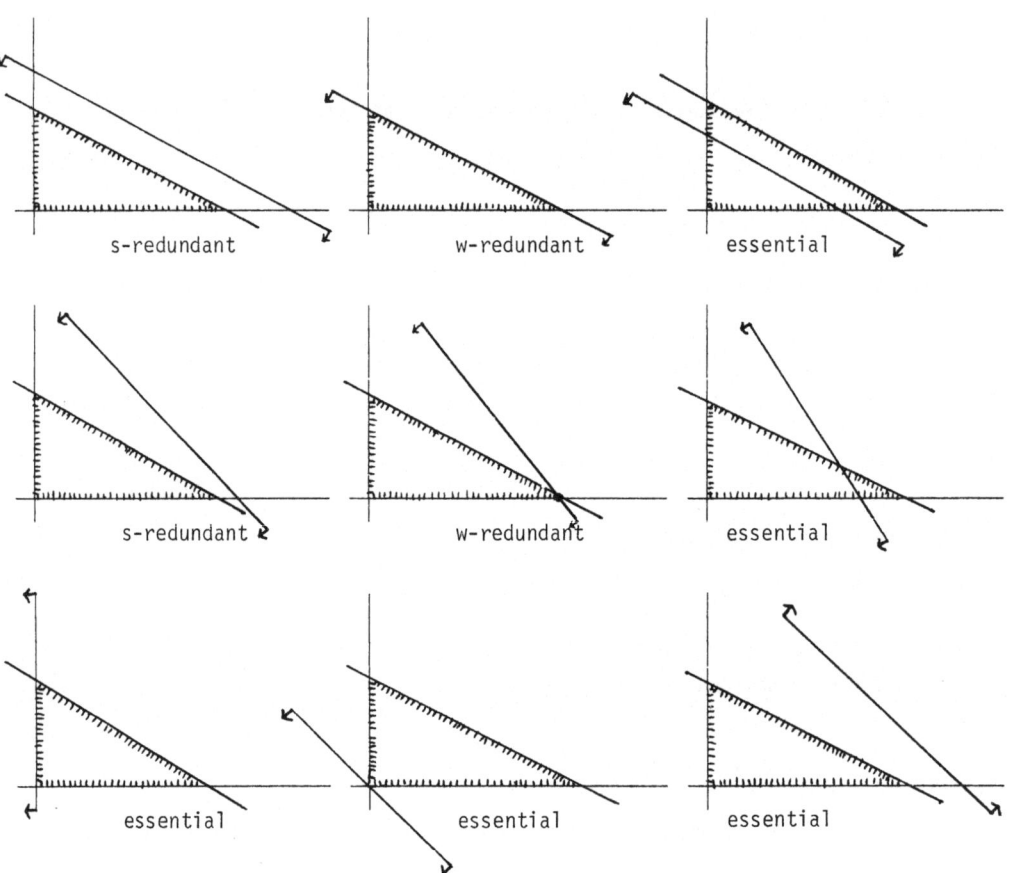

<u>D5.</u>   Constraint 1 is <u>essential</u> if, and only if, there is some x for which

$$A_i x \le b_i, \quad i = 2, \ldots, m$$

and $A_1 x > b_1.$

<u>Note.</u> If the set $\{x \mid x \varepsilon E^n; \; A_i x \le b_i, \; i = 2, \ldots, m\} = \phi$, then the constraint 1 is inessential and dispensable.

To determine whether constraint 1 is s-redundant, we check whether the system

$$A_1 x = b_1$$

$$A_i x \le b_i, \quad i = 2, \ldots, m$$

possesses a feasible solution. If it does, then 1 is essential or w-redundant; if it does not, 1 is s-redundant.

So we form

$$A_1 x + \bar{y}_1 \quad = b_1$$

$$A_i x \quad + y_i = b_i, \quad i = 2, \ldots, m$$

where y_i's are slack variables and $\bar{y}_1$ is an artificial variable. Solve

$$\text{Max} \quad - \bar{y}_1$$

s.t. $A_1 x + \bar{y}_1 \quad = b_1$

$\qquad\quad A_i x \quad + y_i = b_i, \quad i = 2, \ldots, m.$

If there are some constraints of the form $\ge$ or $=$ among the $i=2,\ldots, m$ constraints, then corresponding artificial variables must be appended.

Before solving the above problem we try to reduce the number of constraints entering the computations.

Strongly redundant constraints can be <u>dominant</u> and <u>nondominant</u>.

<u>D6</u>.   A strongly redundant constraint, say constraint 1, is <u>dominant</u> if, and only if, the axes intercepts of $A_1x = b_1$ are greater than those of some $A_ix \leq b_i$, $i = 2, \ldots, m$ (or if the axes intercepts of $A_1x = b_1$ are smaller than the corresponding intercepts of some constraint $A_ix \geq b_i$, $i = 2, \ldots, m$). Otherwise, the constraint is <u>nondominant</u>.

<u>Remark</u>. All w-redundant constraints are nondominant.

We can discard all dominant s-redundant constraints by using the following simple method:

1. Consider all constraints with $b_i > 0$, $i = 1, \ldots, m$. These can be divided into two groups: $\leq$ and $\geq$.

2. Divide each constraint in both groups by the corresponding b_i. Get thus new coefficients $\alpha_{ij} = a_{ij}/b_{ij}$, $i = 1, \ldots, m$.

3. a. Group $\leq$: if for any two constraints, say 1 and 2, $\alpha_{1j} < \alpha_{2j}$, $j = 1, \ldots, n$, then the constraint 1 is s-redundant and dominant.

    b. Group $\geq$: if for any two constraints, say 1 and 2, $\alpha_{1j} > \alpha_{2j}$, $j = 1, \ldots, n$, then the constraint 1 is s-redundant and dominant.

4. Delete all s-redundant dominant constraints.

We are left with constraints having $b_i = 0$, equality constraints, w-redundant, essential and s-redundant nondominant. All these will enter further computations.

We can graphically clarify the concepts:

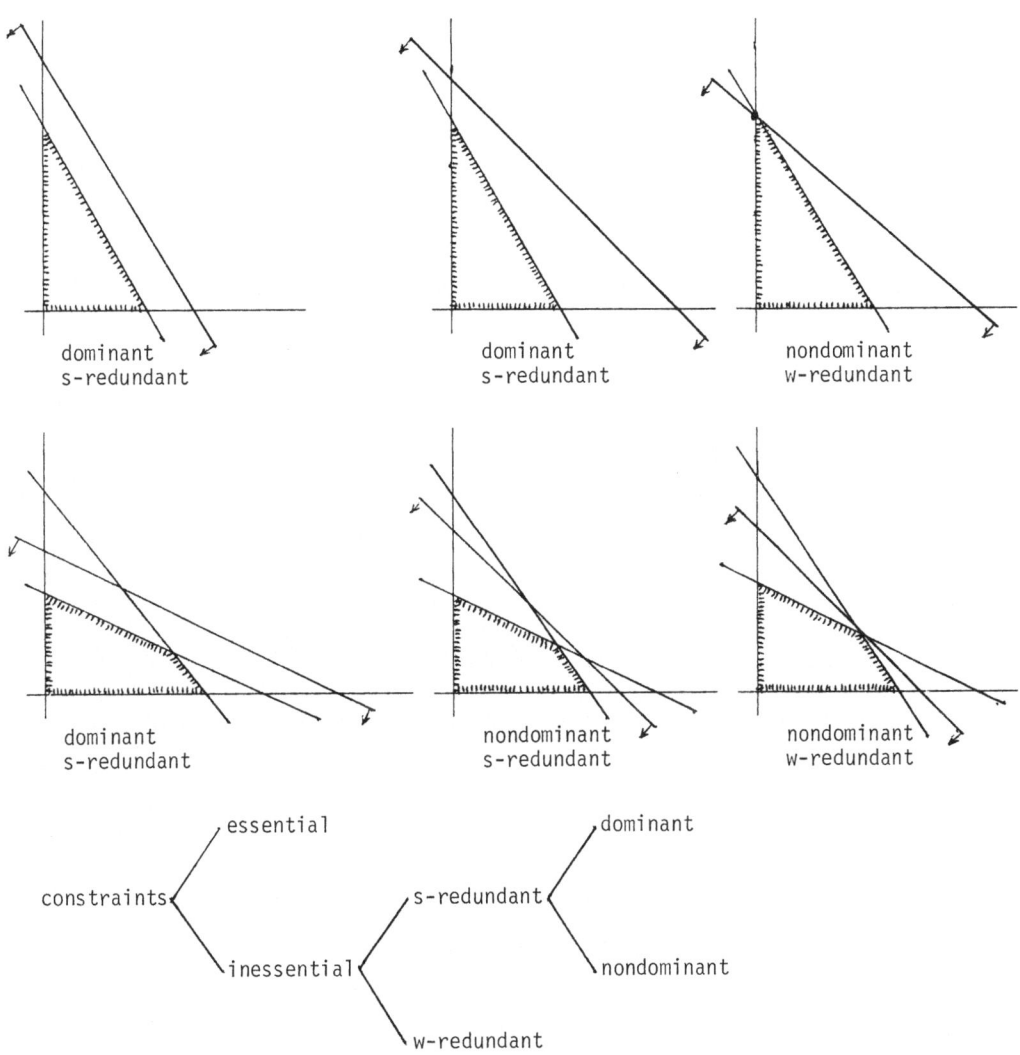

Example. Consider the following set of constraints and discard all s-redundant constraints.

1. $2x_1 + 2x_2 \leq 4$

2. $3x_1 + x_2 \leq 3$

3. $\frac{5}{2}x_1 + \frac{3}{2}x_2 \leq \frac{7}{2}$

4. $\frac{3}{2}x_1 + x_2 \leq 3$

5. $\frac{5}{2}x_1 + \frac{3}{2}x_2 \leq 4$

First, let us delete all dominant constraints by dividing all constraints by their right hand sides:

$$\frac{1}{2}x_1 + \frac{1}{2}x_2 \leq 1$$

$$1x_1 + \frac{1}{3}x_2 \leq 1$$

$$\frac{5}{7}x_1 + \frac{3}{7}x_2 \leq 1$$

$$\frac{1}{2}x_1 + \frac{1}{3}x_2 \leq 1$$

$$\frac{5}{8}x_1 + \frac{3}{8}x_2 \leq 1$$

We can see that $(\frac{1}{2}, \frac{1}{3})$ and $(\frac{5}{8}, \frac{3}{8})$ have both components smaller than $(\frac{5}{7}, \frac{3}{7})$ so the last two constraints may be deleted.

Consider

$$2x_1 + 2x_2 \leq 4$$
$$3x_1 + x_2 \leq 3$$
$$\frac{5}{2}x_1 + \frac{3}{2}x_2 \leq \frac{7}{2}.$$

Check for the 1 constraint:

$\bar{y}_1$	2	2	1	0	0	4
y_2	3	1	0	1	0	3
y_3	$\frac{5}{2}$	$\frac{3}{2}$	0	0	1	$\frac{7}{2}$
	-2	-2	0	0	0	-4

x_2	1	1	$\frac{1}{2}$	0	0	2
y_2	2	0	$-\frac{1}{2}$	1	0	1
y_3	1	0	$-\frac{3}{4}$	0	1	$\frac{1}{2}$
	0	0	1	0	0	0

The solution exists; constraint 1 is essential.

Check for the 2 constraint:

y_1	2	2	1	0	0	4
$\bar{y}_2$	3	1	0	1	0	3
y_3	$\frac{5}{2}$	$\frac{3}{2}$	0	0	1	$\frac{7}{2}$
	-3	-1	0	0	0	-3

y_1	0	$\frac{4}{3}$	1	$-\frac{2}{3}$	0	2
x_1	1	$\frac{1}{3}$	0	$\frac{1}{3}$	0	1
y_3	0	$\frac{2}{3}$	0	$-\frac{5}{6}$	1	1
	0	0	0	1	0	0

The solution exists; constraint 2 is essential.

Check the 3 constraint:

y_1	2	2	1	0	0	4
y_2	3	1	0	1	0	3
$\bar{y}_3$	$\frac{5}{2}$	$\frac{3}{2}$	0	0	1	$\frac{7}{2}$
	$-\frac{5}{2}$	$-\frac{3}{2}$	0	0	0	$-\frac{7}{2}$

y_1	0	$\frac{4}{3}$	1	$-\frac{2}{3}$	0	2
x_1	1	$\frac{1}{3}$	0	$\frac{1}{3}$	0	1
$\bar{y}_3$	0	$\frac{2}{3}$	0	$-\frac{5}{6}$	1	1
	0	$-\frac{2}{3}$	0	$\frac{5}{6}$	0	-1

y_1	0	0	1	1	-2		0
x_1	1	0	0	$\frac{3}{4}$	$-\frac{1}{2}$		$\frac{1}{2}$
x_2	0	1	0	$-\frac{5}{4}$	$\frac{3}{2}$		$\frac{3}{2}$
	0	0	0	0	1		0

The solution exists; actually the 3rd constraint is w-redundant since the other two constraints are satisfied as equalities.

A2. Examples of Output Printouts.

Problem (1).

$$v\text{-Max} \begin{cases} x_1 + 2x_2 - x_3 + 3x_4 + 2x_5 \quad\quad + x_7 \\ \quad\quad x_2 + x_3 + 2x_4 + 3x_5 + x_6 \\ x_1 \quad\quad + x_3 - x_4 \quad\quad - x_6 - x_7 \end{cases}$$

subject to:

$$x_1 + 2x_2 + x_3 + x_4 + 2x_5 + x_6 + 2x_7 \leqq 16$$
$$-2x_1 - x_2 \quad\quad + x_4 + 2x_5 \quad\quad + x_7 \leqq 16$$
$$-x_1 \quad\quad + x_3 \quad\quad + 2x_5 \quad\quad - 2x_7 \leqq 16$$
$$x_2 + 2x_3 - x_4 + x_5 - 2x_6 - x_7 \leqq 16$$

$$x_i \geqq 0, \quad i=1, \ldots, 7$$

```
--------------------- EXECUTION
       743
      ********
8F3.0)
  1.00000    2.00000    1.00000    1.00000    2.00000    1.00000    2.00000   16.00000
 -2.00000   -1.00000    0.00000    1.00000    2.00000    0.00000    1.00000   16.00000
 -1.00000    0.00000    1.00000    0.00000    2.00000    0.00000   -2.00000   16.00000
  0.00000    1.00000    2.00000   -1.00000    1.00000   -2.00000   -1.00000   16.00000
 -1.00000   -2.00000    1.00000   -3.00000   -2.00000    0.00000   -1.00000
  0.00000   -1.00000   -1.00000   -2.00000   -3.00000   -1.00000    0.00000
 -1.00000    0.00000   -1.00000    1.00000    0.00000    1.00000    1.00000
```

```
BASIS          VALUE
  5            0.79999998E 01
  9            0.00000000E-38
 10            0.00000000E-38
 11            0.79999998E 01
```

VALUES OF THE OBJECTIVE FUNCTIONS
    -0.16000000E 02   -0.24000000E 02   0.00000000E-38

                                          -0.40000000E 02

```
BASIS          VALUE
  1            0.16000000E 02
  9            0.48000000E 02
 10            0.32000000E 02
 11            0.16000000E 02
```

VALUES OF THE OBJECTIVE FUNCTIONS
    -0.16000000E 02   0.00000000E-38   -0.16000000E 02

                                          -0.32000000E 02

```
BASIS          VALUE
  1            0.79999998E 01
  9            0.32000000E 02
 10            0.16000000E 02
  3            0.79999998E 01
```

VALUES OF THE OBJECTIVE FUNCTIONS
    0.00000000E-38   -0.79999998E 01   -0.16000000E 02

                                          -0.24000000E 02

```
BASIS          VALUE
  4            0.53333333E 01
  9            0.10666667E 02
 10            0.53333333E 01
  3            0.10666667E 02
```

VALUES OF THE OBJECTIVE FUNCTIONS
    -0.53333332E 01   -0.21333333E 02   -0.53333333E 01

                                          -0.32000000E 02

```
BASIS          VALUE
  1            0.00000000E-38
  9            0.53333332E 01
  5            0.53333333E 01
  3            0.53333330E 01
```

VALUES OF THE OBJECTIVE FUNCTIONS
    -0.53333336E 01   -0.21333333E 02   -0.53333330E 01
                                          -0.32000000E 02

BASIS	VALUE
1	0.00000000E-38
9	0.00000000E-38
5	0.79999998E 01
11	0.79999995E 01

VALUES OF THE OBJECTIVE FUNCTIONS
    -0.16000000E 02   -0.24000000E 02   0.00000000E-38
                                          -0.40000000E 02

BASIS	VALUE
10	0.16000000E 02
3	0.00000000E-38
4	0.16000000E 02
11	0.31959999E 02

VALUES OF THE OBJECTIVE FUNCTIONS
    -0.48000000E 02   -0.32000000E 02   0.16000000E 02
                                          -0.64000001E 02

BASIS	VALUE
10	0.16000000E 02
1	0.00000000E-38
4	0.16000000E 02
11	0.31959999E 02

VALUES OF THE OBJECTIVE FUNCTIONS
    -0.48000000E 02   -0.32000000E 02   0.16000000E 02
      $IBSYS   -0.64000001E 02
      $IBSYS
      $IBSYS
      $IBSYS

COMPILE TIME	25083	TOTAL TIME	172866	MILLISEC
OBJECT PROG	5789	DATA STORAGE	3467	AVAILABLE
		CORE	336	SYMBOL TABLE	3128

Problem (2).

$$v\text{-Max} \begin{cases} 2x_1 + 5x_2 + x_3 - x_4 + 6x_5 + 8x_6 + 3x_7 - 2x_8 \\ 5x_1 - 2x_2 + 5x_3 + 6x_5 + 7x_6 + 2x_7 + 6x_8 \\ x_1 + x_2 + x_3 + x_4 + x_5 + x_6 + x_7 + x_8 \end{cases}$$

subject to:

$$x_1 + 3x_2 - 4x_3 + x_4 - x_5 + x_6 + x_7 + x_8 \leqq 40$$

$$5x_1 + 2x_2 + 4x_3 - x_4 + 3x_5 + 7x_6 + 2x_7 + 7x_8 \leqq 84$$

$$4x_2 - x_3 - x_4 - 3x_5 x_8 \leqq 18$$

$$-3x_1 - 4x_2 + 8x_3 + 2x_4 + 3x_5 - 4x_6 + 5x_7 - x_8 \leqq 100$$

$$12x_1 + 8x_2 - x_3 + 4x_4 x_6 + x_7 \leqq 40$$

$$x_1 + x_2 + x_3 + x_4 + x_5 + x_6 + x_7 + x_8 \geqq 12$$

$$8x_1 - 12x_2 - 3x_3 + 4x_4 - x_5 \leqq 30$$

$$-5x_1 - 6x_2 + 12x_3 + x_4 - x_7 + x_8 \leqq 100$$

$$x_i \geqq 0 , \; i = 1, \ldots , 8$$

```
--------------------- EXECUTION
    883
   00000200
F3.0)
  1.00000    3.00000   -4.00000    1.00000   -1.00000    1.00000    2.00000    4.00000
 40.00000
  5.00000    2.00000    4.00000   -1.00000    3.00000    7.00000    2.00000    7.00000
 84.00000
  0.00000    4.00000   -1.00000   -1.00000   -3.00000    0.00000    0.00000    1.00000
 18.00000
 -3.00000   -4.00000    8.00000    2.00000    3.00000   -4.00000    5.00000   -1.00000
100.00000
 12.00000    8.00000   -1.00000    4.00000    0.00000    1.00000    1.00000    0.00000
 40.00000
  1.00000    1.00000    1.00000    1.00000    1.00000    1.00000    1.00000    1.00000
 12.00000
  8.00000  -12.00000   -3.00000    4.00000   -1.00000    0.00000    0.00000    0.00000
 30.00000
 -5.00000   -6.00000   12.00000    1.00000    0.00000    0.00000   -1.00000    1.00000
100.00000
 -2.00000   -5.00000   -1.00000    1.00000   -6.00000   -8.00000   -3.00000    2.00000
 -5.00000    2.00000   -5.00000    0.00000   -6.00000   -7.00000   -2.00000   -6.00000
 -1.00000   -1.00000   -1.00000   -1.00000   -1.00000   -1.00000   -1.00000   -1.00000
```

BASIS	VALUE
9	0.64444444E 02
14	0.23111111E 02
11	0.11266667E 03
4	0.53333333E 01
13	0.18666666E 02
5	0.29777778E 02
15	0.38444444E 02
16	0.94666665E 02

VALUES OF THE OBJECTIVE FUNCTIONS

-0.17333333E 03	-0.17866666E 03	-0.35111111E 02
		-0.38711111E 03

BASIS	VALUE
9	0.58611110E 02
14	0.26611111E 02
11	0.11033333E 03
4	0.76666665E 01
2	0.11666667E 01
5	0.29777777E 02
15	0.43111110E 02
16	0.99333330E 02

VALUES OF THE OBJECTIVE FUNCTIONS

-0.17683333E 03	-0.17633333E 03	-0.38611111E 02
		-0.39177777E 03

BASIS	VALUE
9	0.57560282E 02
14	0.27347517E 02
11	0.11306383E 03
4	0.97021274E 01
6	0.11914894E 01
5	0.28453900E 02
15	0.19645390E 02
16	0.90297869E 02

VALUES OF THE OBJECTIVE FUNCTIONS

-0.17055319E 03	-0.17906383E 03	-0.39347517E 02
$IBSYS		-0.38896453E 03

COMPILE TIME	25900	TOTAL TIME	48866	MILLISEC
OBJECT PROG	5890	DATA STORAGE	3656	AVAILABLE
	CORE	46	SYMBOL TABLE	3128

A3.   The Program description and FORTRAN Printout.

Definitions.

NOV	— number of variables
NOB	— number of objective functions
NOC	— number of constraints
KUSE	— number of bases used
NOBZ	— (=NOB+1)the composite objective function is in-cluded
KAUX	— number of auxiliary bases stored
TAB	— tableau array
C	— objective functions array (initial)
Z	— objective functions array
IB	— status array of each variable (0=out of basis, 1=in the basis)
ID	— list of basic vectors
V	— value of basic vectors
X	— value of objective functions
INN	— list of bases previously searched
IAUX	— list of auxiliary bases

List of Subroutines.

(1) PRINIT

This prints out the simplex tableau and Z array if re-
quested.

(2) OBJVAL

This computes the value of each objective function.

(3) CHCOMP

This computes each element of the objective functions
array, Z.

(4) REMOVE

This performes the pivot transformation and changes
the basis.

(5) TEST 1

This tests whether any objective function is at its
maximum and whether alternative maxima exist which
would dominate the current basis.

(6) TEST 2

This tests whether a proposed basis has been used previously, and stores it in the list of bases previously
searched, if so instructed.

(7) TEST 3

This tests whether a proposed basis has been placed in
the auxiliary list previously and, if not, stores it.

(8) FORBAS

This selects the auxiliary basis "closest" to the current basis.

(9) DROP 1

This is used by FORBAS to delete a chosen auxiliary basis from the auxiliary list.

(10)TEST 4

This is used by FORBAS to test whether the chosen auxiliary basis has been used previously.

(11) CHOS 1

    This is used by FORBAS to select the auxiliary basis "closest" to the current basis.

(12) FEASBL

    This tests if the current basis is nondominated and, if it is, stores it in the file of nondominated bases.

(13) REMOV 1

    This is used by FEASBL to pivot in the subproblem tableau, used in FEASBL

```
C          THIS IS THE MAIN SUBROUTINE  FOR A MULTIOBJECTIVE LINEAR
C          PROGRAMMING PROBLEM.
C          THE NUMBER OF CONSTRAINTS IS LIMITED TO 12, THE NUMBER OF
C          OBJECTIVE FUNCTIONS TO 7, AND THE NUMBER OF VARIABLES
C          INCLUDING ALL SLACK AND ARTIFICIAL VARIELES TO 40
C          NOV# NUMBER OF VARIABLES
C          NOC# NUMBER OF CONSTRAINTS
C          NOB# NUMBER OF OBJECTIVE FUNCTIONS
C          NOBZ# COMPOSITE OBJECTIVE FUNCTION NUMBER#NOB & 1
C
C          WHEN THE CONSTRAINT IS LESS THAN OR EQUAL,   IEQ%J< # 0
C          WHEN THE CONSTRAINT IS EQUAL,                IEQ%J< # 1
C          WHEN THE CONSTRAINT IS GREATER THAN OR EQUAL, IEQ%J<# 2
C
      COMMON NOV,NOC,NOB,KAUX,KUSE,NOBZ,NOV1,TAB(12,40),V(12),
     1C(8,40),Z(8,40),X(8),ID(12),IB(40),IEQ(12),T(12,40),INN(300,3),
     2IAUX(200,3),FMT(12)
      COMMON/NDOMP/ NONDP
      DIMENSION VC(8)
      DIMENSION IM(40)
      REWIND 9
      NONDP=0
      READ (5,900)NOV,NOC,NOB
  900 FORMAT (2I2,I1)
      WRITE (6,990) NOV,NOC,NOB
  990 FORMAT (5X,2I2,I1)
      NOV1=NOV
      DO 5 I=1,8
      DO 5 J=1,40
    5 C(I,J)=0
      DO 6 I=1,12
      ID(I)=0
      X(I)=0.0
      DO 6 J=1,40
      IB(J)=0
      Z(I,J)=0.0
      T(I,J)=0.0
    6 TAB(I,J)=0.0
      KAUX=0
      KUSE=0
      NOBZ=NOB+1
      READ (5,901) IEQ
  901 FORMAT (20I1)
      WRITE (6,991) IEQ
  991 FORMAT (5X,20I1)
      READ (5,902) FMT
  902 FORMAT(18A4)
      WRITE (6,993) FMT
  993 FORMAT(5X,18A4)
      DO 9 I=1,NOC
      READ (5,FMT)  (TAB(I,J),J=1,NOV),V(I)
    9 WRITE (6,992)  (TAB(I,J),J=1,NOV),V(I)
  992 FORMAT (5X,8F10.5)
      DO 10 I=1,NOB
      READ (5,FMT)  (C(I,J),J=1,NOV)
   10 WRITE (6,992)  (C(I,J),J=1,NOV)
      DO 11 I=1,NOV
```

```
      DO 11 J=1,NOB
11 C(NOBZ,I)=C(NOBZ,I)+C(J,I)
      NOV1=NOV
      NOA=0
      K=1
      CALL PRINIT
      DO 15 J=1,NOC
      IF(IEQ(J).EQ.1) GO TO 15
      IF(IEQ(J).EQ.0) GO TO 13
      NOV1=NOV1+1
      TAB(J,NOV1)=-1.0
      GO TO 15
13 NOV1=NOV1+1
      TAB(J,NOV1)=1.0
      IB(NOV1)=1
      ID(J)=NOV1
      K=K+1
15 CONTINUE
      NOV2=NOV1
      NCV=NOV1
      DO 20 I=1,NOC
      IF(IEQ(I).EQ.0) GO TO 20
      NOV1=NOV1+1
      IB(NOV1)=3
      TAB(I,NOV1)=1.0
      ID(I)=NOV1
      K=K+1
20 CONTINUE
      IF(NOV1.EQ.NOV2) GO TO 66
      NOV3=NOV2+1
      NOM=NOV1-NOV2
      NOC1=NOC-NOM
      NOC2=NOC+1
      DO 60 I=1,NOM
      DO 35 J=1,NOV2
      DO 35 K=1,NOB
      DO 30 I1=1,NOC
      IF(ID(I1).GT.NOV2) GO TO 25
      IDI1=ID(I1)
      T(K,J)=T(K,J)+V(I1)*C(K,IDI1)
      GO TO 30
25 Z(K,J)=Z(K,J)+V(I1)
30 CONTINUE
      T(K,J)=T(K,J)-C(K,J)
35 CONTINUE
      IJ1=0
      DO 45 J=1,NOV2
      IF (IJ1.EQ.1) GO TO 45
      IF(IB(J).NE.0)GO TO 45
      IK1=0
      DO 40 K=1,NOB
      IF (IK1.NE.0) GO TO 40
      IF (Z(K,J).GT.0.0) GO TO 40
      IF (Z(K,J).NE.0.0) GO TO 38
      IF (T(K,J).GT.0.0) GO TO 40
38 IK1=1
40 CONTINUE
      IF (IK1.NE.0) GO TO 45
```

```
      JJ=0
      AMIN=100000
      DO 43 K=1,NOC
      IF (TAB(K,J).LE.0.0) GO TO 43
      VV=V(K)/TAB(K,J)
      IF (VV.GT.AMIN) GO TO 43
      AMIN=VV
      JJ=K
   43 CONTINUE
      IF (JJ.EQ.0) GO TO 45
      IDJ=ID(JJ)
      IF (IDJ.LE.NOV2) GO TO 45
      IJ=J
      IJ1=1
   45 CONTINUE
      IF (IJ1.NE.0) GO TO 46
      WRITE (6,904)
  904 FORMAT (5X,30H THERE IS NO FEASIBLE SOLUTION)
      STOP
   46 ICOL=IJ
      IROW=JJ
      DO 50 J=1,NOC
      IF (ID(J).LE.NOV2) GO TO 50
      IF (TAB(J,IJ).LE.0.0) GO TO 50
      IROW=J
   50 CONTINUE
      CALL REMOVE (IROW,ICOL)
      ID(IROW)=ICOL
      IB(ICOL)=1
      DO 51 K=1,8
      DO 51 J=1,40
   51 T(K,J)=0.0
   60 CONTINUE
C         AT THIS POINT ALL ARTIFICIAL VARIABLES HAVE BEEN REMOVED
      NOM=0
      DO 65 I=1,NOC
      DO 65 J=NOV3,NOV1
   65 TAB(I,J)=0.0
   66 CONTINUE
      NOV1=NOV2
      CALL OBJVAL
      CALL CHCOMP
      CALL PRINIT
      CALL TEST1
   67 II=0
      IJ=0
      AMIN=0.0
      DO 75 I=1,NOV
      IF (IB(I).GE.1) GO TO 75
      IJ=0
      IF (Z(NOBZ,I).LE.0.0) GO TO 75
      IF (Z(NOBZ,I).LT.AMIN) GO TO 75
      DO 70 J=1,NOB
      IF (IJ.NE.0) GO TO 70
      IF (Z(J,I).GE.0.0) GO TO 70
      IJ=1
   70 CONTINUE
      IF (IJ.NE.0) GO TO 75
```

```
      AMIN=Z(NOBZ,I)
      II=I
   75 CONTINUE
      IF (II.EQ.0) GO TO 85
      AMIN=.1E10
      IJ=-1
      DO 80 I=1,NOC
      IF (TAB(I,II)) 80,80,78
   78 AK=V(I)/TAB(I,II)
      IF (AK.GE.AMIN) GO TO 80
      IJ=I
      AMIN=AK
   80 CONTINUE
      IF (IJ) 81,81,82
   81 WRITE (6,905)
  905 FORMAT (//5X,19H UNBOUNDED SOLUTION)
      STOP
   82 IROW=IJ
      ICOL=II
      CALL TEST2(IROW,ICOL,0)
      IF (IB(ICOL).EQ.5) GO TO 67
      CALL REMOVE (IROW,ICOL)
      GO TO 66
   85 IF (NOB.EQ.1) STOP
      GO TO 186
   86 CONTINUE
C         AT THIS POINT THERE IS NO VECTOR THAT IMPROVES ALL OBJ. FUNC.
      DO 110 I=1,NOV
      IF (IB(I).EQ.1) GO TO 110
      AMIN=.1E10
      II=0
      DO 100 J=1,NOC
      IF (TAB(J,I).LE.0.0) GO TO 100
      VV=V(J)/TAB(J,I)
      IF (VV.LT.0.0) GO TO 100
      IF (VV.GT.AMIN) GO TO 100
      AMIN=VV
      II=J
  100 CONTINUE
      IF (II.EQ.0) IB(I)=2
  110 IM(I)=II
      DO 115 I=1,NOV
      IF (IB(I).GT.0) GO TO 115
      JJ=0
      DO  114 J=1,NOB
      IF (Z(J,I)) 114,114,113
  113 JJ=1
  114 CONTINUE
      IF (JJ.EQ.0) IB(I)=3
  115 CONTINUE
      NOVV=NOV-1
      DO 150 I=1,NOVV
      IF (IB(I).NE.0) GO TO 150
      I2=I+1
      DO 140 J=I2,NOV
      IF (IB(I).NE.0.OR.IB(J).NE.0) GO TO 140
      J1=IM(I)
      J2=IM(J)
```

```
      TH1=V(J1)/TAB(J1,I)
      IF (TH1.NE.0.0) GO TO 118
      IB(I)=3
      GO TO 140
118   TH2=V(J2)/TAB(J2,J)
      IF  (TH2.NE.0.0) GO TO 119
      IB(J)=3
      GO TO 140
119   DO 120 K=1,NOB
120   VC(K)=Z(K,I)*TH1-Z(K,J)*TH2
      IJ=0
      IK=0
      DO 125 K=1,NOB
      IF (VC(K).GT.0.0) IJ=1
125   IF (VC(K).LT.0.0) IK=1
      IF (IJ.EQ.0.AND.IK.EQ.1) IB(I)=3
      IF (IJ.EQ.1.AND.IK.EQ.0) IB(J)=3
140   CONTINUE
150   CONTINUE
      DO 151 I=1,NOV
      IF (IB(I).NE.3) GO TO 151
      CALL TEST2 (IM(I),I,2)
151   CONTINUE
155   DO 165 I=1,NOV
      IF (IB(I).GT.0) GO TO 165
      CALL TEST2 (IM(I),I,1)
165   CONTINUE
      J1=0
      DO 175 I=1,NOV
      IF(J1.EQ.0)GO TO 170
      IF (NONDP.EQ.0) GO TO 175
      IF (IB(I).GT.0) GO TO 175
      CALL TEST3(IM(I),I)
      GO TO 175
170   IF (IB(I).GT.0) GO TO 175
      IROW=IM(I)
      IC=I
      J1=1
175   CONTINUE
      DO 177 I=1,NOV
177   IF (IB(I).GT.1) IB(I)=0
      IF (IROW.EQ.0.OR.IC.EQ.0) GO TO 210
176   CALL TEST2 (IROW,IC,0)
      IF (IB(IC).EQ.5) GO TO 190
180   CALL REMOVE(IROW,IC)
185   CALL OBJVAL
      CALL CHCOMP
      CALL TEST1
186   CALL FEASBL (K)
      IF (K.EQ.0.AND.NONDP.GT.0) GO TO 190
      GO TO 86
190   IF(KAUX.EQ.0) GO TO 220
      CALL FORBAS(KKU)
      IF (KKU.EQ.1) GO TO 220
      GO TO 185
195   BIG=.1E10
      J1=0
      DO 200 K=1,NOC
```

```
      IF(TAB(K,IC).LE.0.0)GO TO 200
      IF(V(K)/TAB(K,IC).GE.BIG)GO TO 200
      BIG=V(K)/TAB(K,IC)
      J1=K
  200 CONTINUE
      IF(J1.NE.0)GO TO 205
      WRITE(6,906)
  906 FORMAT(5X,25H SOLUTION IS NOT FEASIBLE)
      STOP
  205 IROW=J1
      CALL TEST2(IROW,IC,0)
      IF(IB(IC).EQ.5)GO TO 190
      GO TO 180
  210 WRITE (6,1003) IROW,IC
 1003 FORMAT (//5X,5HIROW#,I5,10X,3HIC#,I5//)
  220 IF (NONDP.EQ.0) GO TO 999
      REWIND 9
      WRITE (6,1011)
 1011 FORMAT (1H1)
      DO 240 I=1,NONDP
      READ (9,1005) (ID(J),J=1,NOC)
 1005 FORMAT (8I2)
      READ (9,1006) (V(J),J=1,NOC)
 1006 FORMAT (8E15.8)
      READ (9,1006) (X(J),J=1,NOBZ)
      WRITE (6,1007)
 1007 FORMAT (    ///5X,5HBASIS,10X,5HVALUE)
      DO 230 J=1,NOC
  230 WRITE (6,1008)    ID(J),V(J)
 1008 FOPMAT (5X,I5,5X,E20.8)
      WRITE (6,1009)
 1009 FORMAT (///5X,33HVALUES OF THE OBJECTIVE FUNCTIONS   )
  240 WRITE (6,1010) (X(J),J=1,NOBZ)
 1010 FORMAT (5X,6E20.8)
  999 STOP
      END




      SUBROUTINE OBJVAL
C         THIS SUBROUTINE COMPUTES THE VALUE OF EACH OBJECTIVE FUNCTION
      COMMON NOV,NOC,NOB,KAUX,KUSE,NOBZ,NOV1,TAB(12,40),V(12),
     1C(8,40),Z(8,40),X(8),ID(12),IB(40),IEQ(12),T(12,40),INN(300,3),
     2IAUX(200,3),FMT(12)
      DO 20 I=1,NOBZ
      SUM=0.0
      DO 15 J=1,NOC
      ID1=ID(J)
   15 SUM=SUM+C(I,ID1)*V(J)
   20 X(I)=SUM
      RETURN
      END
```

```
      SUBROUTINE PRINIT
      COMMON NOV,NOC,NOB,KAUX,KUSE,NOBZ,NOV1,TAB(12,40),V(12),
     1C(8,40),Z(8,40),X(8),ID(12),IB(40),IEQ(12),T(12,40),INN(300,3),
     2IAUX(200,3),FMT(12)
      WRITE (6,900)
  900 FORMAT (//5X,16H SIMPLEX TABLEAU//)
      WRITE (6,901)
  901 FORMAT (1X,6H BASIS,2X,6H VALUE,7X,10H VARIABLES//)
      DO 100 I=1,NOV1,7
      IL=I+6
      IF (IL.GT.NOV1) IL=NOV1
      DO 90 J=1,NOC
   90 WRITE (6,902) ID(J),V(J),(TAB(J,K),K=I,IL)
  902 FORMAT (1X,I6,8E15.8)
      WRITE (6,903)
  903 FORMAT (1X)
  100 CONTINUE
      WRITE (6,904)
  904 FORMAT (///5X,20H OBJECTIVE FUNCTIONS //)
      WRITE (6,905)
  905 FORMAT (1X,7HOBJ. F.,2X,6H VALUE,7X,10H VARIABLES  //)
      DO 200 I=1,NOV1,7
      IL=I+6
      IF (IL.GT.NOV1) IL=NOV1
      DO 190 J=1,NOB
  190 WRITE (6,902) J,X(J),(Z(J,K),K=I,IL)
      WRITE (6,903)
  200 CONTINUE
      WRITE (6,906)
  906 FORMAT (/5X,19H COMPOSITE FUNCTION)
      DO 210 I=1,NOV1,7
      IL=I+6
      IF (IL.GT.NOV1) IL=NOV1
  210 WRITE (6,902) NOBZ,X(NOBZ), (Z(NOBZ,K),K=I,IL)
      WRITE (6,907) KAUX
  907 FORMAT (5X,5HKAUX#,I8)
      RETURN
      END


      SUBROUTINE CHCOMP
C         THIS SUBROUTINE COMPUTES THE VALUE OF EACH ELEMENT OF THE
C         OBJECTIVE FUNCTION ARRAY
      COMMON NOV,NOC,NOB,KAUX,KUSE,NOBZ,NOV1,TAB(12,40),V(12),
     1C(8,40),Z(8,40),X(8),ID(12),IB(40),IEQ(12),T(12,40),INN(300,3),
     2IAUX(200,3),FMT(12)
      DO 20 I=1,NOBZ
      DO 20 J=1,NOV1
      SUM=0.0
      DO 15 K=1,NOC
      ID1=ID(K)
   15 SUM=SUM+TAB(K,J)*C(I,ID1)
   20 Z(I,J)=SUM-C(I,J)
      RETURN
      END
```

```
    SUBROUTINE REMOVE(IROW,ICCL)
        THIS SUBROUTINE TRANSFORMS THE TABLEAUS AND ENTERS THE ICOL
        ELEMENT IN PLACE OF THE IROW ELEMENT IN THE BASIS
     COMMON NOV,NOC,NOB,KAUX,KUSE,NOBZ,NOV1,TAB(12,40),V(12),
    1C(8,40),Z(8,40),X(8),ID(12),IB(40),IEQ(12),T(12,40),INN(300,3),
    2IAUX(200,3),FMT(12)
     DI = TAB(IROW,ICOL)
     DO 10 I=1,NOV1
 10  TAB(IROW,I)=TAB(IROW,I)/DI
     V(IROW)=V(IROW)/DI
     DO 20 I=1,NOC
     IF (I.EQ.IROW) GO TO 20
     V(I)=V(I)-V(IROW)*TAB(I,ICOL)
     IF (V(I).LT.0.000001) V(I)=0.0
 20  CONTINUE
     DO 30 I=1,NOC
     IF(I.EQ.IROW)GO TO 30
     DO 25 J=1,NOV1
     IF(J.EQ.ICOL)GO TO 25
     TAB(I,J)=TAB(I,J)-TAB(I,ICOL)*TAB(IROW,J)
 25  CONTINUE
 30  CONTINUE
     DO 40 I=1,NOC
     IF (I.EQ.IROW) GO TO 40
     TAB (I,ICOL)=0.0
 40  CONTINUE
     DO 45 I=1,8
     DO 45 J=1,40
 45  Z(I,J)=0.0
     RETURN
     END




    SUBROUTINE DROP1 (KU)
        THIS SUBROUTINE DROPS THE KU BASIS FROM THE AUXILLARY LIST
     COMMON NOV,NOC,NOB,KAUX,KUSE,NOBZ,NOV1,TAB(12,40),V(12),
    1C(8,40),Z(8,40),X(8),ID(12),IB(40),IEQ(12),T(12,40),INN(300,3),
    2IAUX(200,3),FMT(12)
     IK1=KU
     IK2=KAUX-1
     IF (IK1.GT.IK2) GO TO 25
     DO 20 I=IK1,IK2
     I1=I+1
     IAUX(I,1)=IAUX(I1,1)
 20  IAUX(I,2)=IAUX(I1,2)
 25  IAUX(KAUX,1)=0
     IAUX(KAUX,2)=0
     KAUX=KAUX-1
     RETURN
     END
```

```
      SUBROUTINE TEST1
C         THIS SUBROUTINE TESTS TO SEE IF ANY OBJ. FUNCTION IS AT ITS
C         MAXIMUM AND IF IT IS , TESTS TO SEE IF ANY ALTERNATIVE MAXIMA
C         IMPROVES ANOTHER FUNCTION
      COMMON NOV,NOC,NOB,KAUX,KUSE,NOBZ,NOV1,TAB(12,40),V(12),
     1C(8,40),Z(8,40),X(8),ID(12),IB(40),IEQ(12),T(12,40),INN(300,3),
     2IAUX(200,3),FMT(12)
      DO 100 I=1,NOBZ
      MAX=0
      DO 10 J=1,NOV1
      IF (IB(J).EQ.1) GO TO 10
      IF (MAX.LT.0) GO TO 10
      IF (Z(I,J)) 10,7,8
    8 MAX=-1
      GO TO 10
    7 MAX=1
   10 CONTINUE
      IF (MAX) 100,11,11
   11 WRITE (6,906) I
  906 FORMAT (//5X,4H THE,I4,3X,35H OBJECTIVE FUNCTION IS AT A MINIMUM)
      IF (MAX.EQ.1) GO TO 12
      WRITE (6,907)
  907 FORMAT (  5X,32H THERE IS NO ALTERNATIVE MINIMUM    //)
      GO TO 50
   12 WRITE (6,908)
  908 FORMAT (  5X,29H THERE ARE ALTERNATIVE MINIMA//)
      DO 30 J=1,NOV1
      IF (IB(J).EQ.1) GO TO 30
      IF (Z(I,J)) 30,13,30
   13 DO 25 K=1,NOBZ
      IF (Z(K,J)) 25,25,14
   14 MAX=2
  909 FORMAT (//5X,14H OBJ. FUNCTION,I4,2X,12H IS IMPROVED //)
   25 CONTINUE
   30 CONTINUE
      IF (MAX.EQ.2) GO TO 100
   50 CONTINUE
  910 FORMAT (//5X,33H BUT NO OBJ. FUNCTION IS IMPROVED   //)
  100 CONTINUE
      RETURN
      END
```

```
      SUBROUTINE TEST2 (IROW,ICOL,IK)
         THIS SUBROUTINE TESTS TO SEE IF THE PROPOSED BASIS HAS BEEN
         USED PREVIOUSLY
      COMMON NOV,NOC,NOB,KAUX,KUSE,NOBZ,NOV1,TAB(12,40),V(12),
     1C(8,40),Z(8,40),X(8),ID(12),IB(40),IEQ(12),T(12,40),INN(300,3),
     2IAUX(200,3),FMT(12)
      DIMENSION IT(12),IS(12)
      IF (IK.NE.0) GO TO 101
      DO 10 I=1,NOV
   10 IF (IB(I).EQ.5) IB(I)=0
  101 CONTINUE
      DO 11 I=1,NOC
      IT(I)=ID(I)
   11 IS(I)=0
      IT(IROW)=ICOL
      DO 30 I=1,NOC
      MIN=100
      DO 25 J=1,NOC
      IF (IT(J).LE.0.OR.IT(J).GE.MIN) GO TO 25
      IJ=J
      MIN=IT(J)
   25 CONTINUE
      IS(I)=MIN
      IT(IJ)=0
   30 CONTINUE
      I1=0
      I2=0
      DO 40 I=1,NOC
      IF (I-4) 35,35,36
   35 I1=I1+IS(I)*10**(2*(4-I))
      GO TO 40
   36 I2=I2+IS(I)*10**(2*(8-I))
   40 CONTINUE
      IF (KUSE.EQ.0) GO TO 60
      IJ=0
      DO 50 I=1,KUSE
      IF (I1.NE.INN(I,1).OR.I2.NE.INN(I,2)) GO TO 50
      IJ=1
   50 CONTINUE
      IF (IJ.EQ.0) GO TO 60
      IB(ICOL)=5
      GO TO 99
   60 IF (IK.NE.0) GO TO 98
      KUSE=KUSE+1
      INN(KUSE,1)=I1
      INN(KUSE,2)=I2
      IB(ICOL)=1
      I1=ID(IROW)
      IB(I1)=0
      ID(IROW)=ICOL
      GO TO 99
   98 IF (IK.EQ.1) GO TO 99
      KUSE=KUSE+1
      INN(KUSE,1)=I1
      INN(KUSE,2)=I2
   99 RETURN
      END
```

```
      SUBROUTINE TEST3 (IROW,ICOL)
C         THIS SUBROUTINE TESTS TO SEE IF A BASIS HAS BEEN STORED FOR
C         FUTURE USE AND STORES IT IF IT HAS NOT BEEN STORED PREVIOUSLY
      COMMON NOV,NOC,NOB,KAUX,KUSE,NOBZ,NOV1,TAB(12,40),V(12),
     1C(8,40),Z(8,40),X(8),ID(12),IB(40),IEQ(12),T(12,40),INN(300,3),
     2IAUX(200,3),FMT(12)
      DIMENSION IT(12),IS(12)
      DO 10 I=1,NOC
      IT(I)=ID(I)
   10 IS(I)=0
      IT(IROW)=ICOL
      DO 30 I=1,NOC
      MIN=100
      DO 25 J=1,NOC
      IF (IT(J).LE.0.OR.IT(J).GE.MIN) GO TO 25
      IJ=J
      MIN=IT(J)
   25 CONTINUE
      IS(I)=MIN
      IT(IJ)=0
   30 CONTINUE
      I1=0
      I2=0
      DO 40 I=1,NOC
      IF (I-4) 35,35,36
   35 I1=I1+IS(I)*10**(2*(4-I))
      GO TO 40
   36 I2=I2+IS(I)*10**(2*(8-I))
   40 CONTINUE
      IJ=0
      IF(KAUX.EQ.0) GO TO 51
      DO 50 I=1,KAUX
      IF (I1.NE.IAUX(I,1).OR.I2.NE.IAUX(I,2)) GO TO 50
      IJ=1
   50 CONTINUE
   51 IF (IJ.NE.0) GO TO 99
      KAUX=KAUX+1
      IAUX(KAUX,1)=I1
      IAUX(KAUX,2)=I2
   99 RETURN
      END
```

```
   SUBROUTINE TEST4 (KU,II)
      THIS SUBROUTINE TESTS TO SEE IF A CHOSEN AUXILLARY BASIS
      HAS BEEN USED PREVIOUSLY
   COMMON NOV,NOC,NOB,KAUX,KUSE,NOBZ,NOV1,TAB(12,40),V(12),
  1C(8,40),Z(8,40),X(8),ID(12),IB(40),IEQ(12),T(12,40),INN(300,3),
  2IAUX(200,3),FMT(12)
   IA1=IAUX(KU,1)
   IA2=IAUX(KU,2)
   IA1=IAUX(KU,3)
   II=0
   DO 20 I=1,KUSE
   IF (II.EQ.1) GO TO 20
   IF(IA1.EQ.INN(I,1).AND.IA2.EQ.INN(I,2))II=1
 0 CONTINUE
   RETURN
   END




   SUBROUTINE REMOV1 (IR,ICO)
       THIS SUBROUTINE SOLVES THE SUBPROBLEM TABLEAU
    COMMON NOV,NOC,NOB,KAUX,KUSE,NOBZ,NOV1,TAB(12,40),V(12),
  1C(8,40),Z(8,40),X(8),ID(12),IB(40),IEQ(12),T(12,40),INN(300,3),
  2IAUX(200,3),FMT(12)
    COMMON/SUBPRO/ ATAB(8,30),CI(30),IC(8),IG(30),ZI(30),IE(30),NV
    DO 10 I=1,NV
    IF (I.EQ.ICO) GO TO 10
    ATAB(IR,I)=ATAB(IR,I)/ATAB(IR,ICO)
 10 CONTINUE
    ATAB(IR,ICO)=1.0
    DO 30 I=1,NOB
    IF (I.EQ.IR) GO TO 30
    DO 25 J=1,NV
    IF (J.EQ.ICO) GO TO 25
    ATAB(I,J)=ATAB(I,J)-ATAB(IR,J) *ATAB(I,ICO)
 25 CONTINUE
 30 CONTINUE
    DO 40 I=1,NOB
 40 IF (I.NE.IR) ATAB(I,ICO) = 0.0
    I=IC(IR)
    IC(IR)=ICO
    IG(I)=0
    IG(ICO)=1
    DO 50 I=1,NV
    SUM=0.0
    DO 45 J=1,NOB
    K=IC(J)
 45 SUM=SUM+CI(K)*ATAB(J,I)
 50 ZI(I)=SUM-CI(I)
 99 RETURN
    END
```

```
      SUBROUTINE  FORBAS (KKU)
          THIS SUBROUTINE SELECTS A BASIS THAT HAS BEEN STORED EARLIER
          AND IS CLOSER TO THE CURRENT BASIS THAN ANY OTHER BASIS STORED
          AND FORCES THAT BASIS INTO THE SOLUTION
      COMMON NOV,NOC,NOB,KAUX,KUSE,NOBZ,NOV1,TAB(12,40),V(12),
     1C(8,40),Z(8,40),X(8),ID(12),IB(40),IEQ(12),T(12,40),INN(300,3),
     2IAUX(200,3),FMT(12)
      COMMON /LOCAL/ IKA(12),IOUT(12),NOER,INA(12),IADD(200)
      DO 30 I=1,KAUX
      IADD(I)=1
      CALL TEST4 (I,II)
   30 IF (II.EQ.1) CALL DROP1(I)
      IF (KAUX.EQ.0) GO TO 98
    5 KKU=0
      CALL CHOS1 (KU)
      IF (KU.EQ.0) GO TO 98
      IADD(KU)=0
   10 IKK=0
      DO 25 II=1,NOER
      IK=0
      DO 20 I=1,NOER
      IF (IOUT(I).EQ.0) GO TO 20
      IF (IK.NE.0) GO TO 20
      IC=IOUT(I)
      IR=0
      DO 19 J=1,NOER
      IF (IR.NE.0) GO TO 19
      IF (INA(J).EQ.0) GO TO 19
      JJ=0
      J1=INA(J)
      AMIN=100000
      DO 18 K=1,NOC
      IF (TAB(K,J1).LT.0.0) GO TO 18
      IF(TAB(K,J1).GT.0.0)GO TO 16
      VV=0
      GO TO 17
   16 VV=V(K)/TAB(K,J1)
      IF (VV.GT.AMIN) GO TO 18
      IF (VV.EQ.AMIN.AND.ID(K).NE.IC) GO TO 18
   17 JJ=K
      AMIN=VV
   18 CONTINUE
      IF (ID(JJ).NE.IC) GO TO 19
      IR=J1
      INA(J)=0
      IK=1
      IROW=JJ
      ICOL=IR
   19 CONTINUE
      IF (IK.EQ.0) GO TO 20
      IOUT(I)=0
      CALL REMOVE (IROW,ICOL)
      ID1=ID(IROW)
      IB(ID1)=0
      IB(ICOL)=1
      ID(IROW)=ICOL
      IKK=IKK+1
      CALL OBJVAL
```

```
      CALL CHCOMP
   20 CONTINUE
   25 CONTINUE
      IF (IKK.EQ.NOER) GO TO 97
      WRITE (6,92)
   92 FORMAT (//5X,23HBASIS CANNOT BE ENTERED    )
      GO TO 5
   97 CALL DROP1 (KU)
      GO TO 99
   98 KKU=1
   99 RETURN
      END



      SUBROUTINE CHOS1 (KU)
C         THIS SUBROUTINE CHOOSES THE AUXILLARY BASIS THAT IS CLOSEST
C         TO THE CURRENT BASIS
      COMMON NOV,NOC,NOB,KAUX,KUSE,NOBZ,NOV1,TAB(12,40),V(12),
     1C(8,40),Z(8,40),X(8),ID(12),IB(40),IEQ(12),T(12,40),INN(300,3),
     2IAUX(200,3),PMT(12)
      COMMON /LOCAL/ IKA(12),IOUT(12),NOER,INA(12),IADD(200)
      DIMENSION IOU(40),IN(40)
      DO 5 I=1,12
      IKA(I)=0
      IOUT(I)=0
    5 INA(I)=0
      MIN=9
      KU=0
      DO 100 II=1,KAUX
      II1=II-1
      I1=KAUX-II1
      I2=IAUX(I1,1)
      I3=IAUX(I1,2)
      IF (IADD(I1).EQ.0) GO TO 100
      DO 20 I=1,NOC
      IF (I-4) 10,10,15
   10 I4= I2/(10**(2*(4-I)))
      IKA(I)=I4
      I2=I2-I4*10**(2*(4-I))
      GO TO 20
   15 I4=I3/10**(2*(8-I))
      IKA(I)=I4
      I3=I3-I4*10**(2*(8-I))
   20 CONTINUE
      IO=0
      IN1=0
      DO 30 I=1,NOC
      IJ=0
      DO 25 J=1,NOC
      IF (ID(I).NE.IKA(J)) GO TO 25
      IJ=1
   25 CONTINUE
      IF (IJ.EQ.1) GO TO 30
      IO=IO+1
      IOU(IO)=ID(I)
```

```
   30 CONTINUE
      DO 40 I=1,NOC
      IJ=0
      DO 35 J=1,NOC
   35 IF (IKA(I).EQ.ID(J)) IJ=1
      IF (IJ.EQ.1) GO TO 40
      IN1=IN1+1
      IN(IN1)=IKA(I)
   40 CONTINUE
      IF (IO.EQ.0) GO TO 100
      IF (IO.GE.MIN) GO TO 100
      MIN=IO
      KU=I1
      DO 50 I=1,IO
      IOUT(I)=IOU(I)
   50 INA(I)=IN(I)
  100 CONTINUE
      IF (MIN.EQ.9)  GO TO 99
      NOER=MIN
      IF (KU.EQ.0) GO TO 99
      KUSE = KUSE+1
      INN(KUSE,1)=IAUX(KU,1)
      INN(KUSE,2)=IAUX(KU,2)
      WRITE (6,90) IAUX(KU,1),IAUX(KU,2)
   90 FORMAT (5X, 9HAUXILLARY  ,5X,3I8)
   99 RETURN
      END


      SUBROUTINE FEASBL (K)
      COMMON NOV,NOC,NOB,KAUX,KUSE,NOBZ,NOV1,TAB(12,40),V(12),
     1C(8,40),Z(8,40),X(8),ID(12),IB(40),IEQ(12),T(12,40),INN(300,3),
     2IAUX(200,3),FMT(12)
      COMMON/SUBPRO/ ATAB(8,30),CI(30),IC(8),IG(30),ZI(30),IE(30),NV
      COMMON/NDOMP/ NONDP
      K=0
      DO 5 I=1,8
      IC(I)=0
      DO 5 J=1,30
      CI(J)=0
      IG(J)=0
      ZI(J)=0
      IE(J)=0
    5 ATAB(I,J)=0.0
      NC=NOB
      NV=0
      DO 20 I=1,NOV
      IF (IB(I).EQ.1) GO TO 20
      NV=NV+1
      ZI(NV)=-Z(NOBZ,I)
      IE(NV)=I
      DO 10 J=1,NOB
   10 ATAB(J,NV)=-Z(J,I)
   20 CONTINUE
      NV1=NV
      DO 30 I=1,NOB
      NV=NV+1
```

```
      ATAB(I,NV)=1.0
      IC(I)=NV
      IG(NV)=1
   30 CI(NV)=1.0
   31 II=0
      AMAX=0
      DO 35 I=1,NV
      IF (ZI(I).GE.AMAX) GO TO 35
      II=I
      AMAX=ZI(I)
   35 CONTINUE
      IF (II.NE.0) GO TO 36
C         THE BASIS IS NON-DOMINATED IF II≠0
      GO TO 70
   36 CONTINUE
      III=0
      AMIN=.1E10
      DO 50 J=1,NOB
      IF (ATAB(J,II).LE.0.0.OR.ATAB(J,II).GE.AMIN) GO TO 50
      III=J
      AMIN=ATAB(J,II)
   50 CONTINUE
C         THE BASIS IS DOMINATED IF III≠0
      IF (III.EQ.0) GO TO 51
      CALL REMOV1 (III,II)
      GO TO 31
   51 CONTINUE
      DO 60 I=1,NOC
      IF (TAB(I,II).LE.0.0) GO TO 60
      III=-1
   60 CONTINUE
      IF (III) 61,62,62
   61 WRITE (6,901)
  901 FORMAT ( 5X,24H SUBPROBLEM IS UNBOUNDED//)
      GO TO 99
   62 WRITE (6,902)
  902 FORMAT (//5X,30H ORIGINAL PROBLEM IS UNBOUNDED  //)
      GO TO 99
   70 NONDP=NONDP+1
      CALL PRINIT
      K=1
      WRITE (9,911) (ID(J),J=1,NOC)
  911 FORMAT (8I2)
      WRITE (9,912) (V(J),J=1,NOC)
  912 FORMAT (8E15.8)
      WRITE (9,912) (X(J),J=1,NOBZ)
   99 RETURN
      END
```

Vol. 59: J. A. Hanson, Growth in Open Economics. IV, 127 pages. 4°. 1971. DM 16,–

Vol. 60: H. Hauptmann, Schätz- und Kontrolltheorie in stetigen dynamischen Wirtschaftsmodellen. V, 104 Seiten. 4°. 1971. DM 16,–

Vol. 61: K. H. F. Meyer, Wartesysteme mit variabler Bearbeitungsrate. VII, 314 Seiten. 4°. 1971. DM 24,–

Vol. 62: W. Krelle u. G. Gabisch unter Mitarbeit von J. Burgermeister, Wachstumstheorie. VII, 223 Seiten. 4°. 1972. DM 20,–

Vol. 63: J. Kohlas, Monte Carlo Simulation im Operations Research. VI, 162 Seiten. 4°. 1972. DM 16,–

Vol. 64: P. Gessner u. K. Spremann, Optimierung in Funktionenräumen. IV, 120 Seiten. 4°. 1972. DM 16,–

Vol. 65: W. Everling, Exercises in Computer Systems Analysis. VIII, 184 pages. 4°. 1972. DM 18,–

Vol. 66: F. Bauer, P. Garabedian and D. Korn, Supercritical Wing Sections. V, 211 pages. 4°. 1972. DM 20,–

Vol. 67: I. V. Girsanov, Lectures on Mathematical Theory of Extremum Problems. V, 136 pages. 4°. 1972. DM 16,–

Vol. 68: J. Loeckx, Computability and Decidability. An Introduction for Students of Computer Science. VI, 76 pages. 4°. 1972. DM 16,–

Vol. 69: S. Ashour, Sequencing Theory. V, 133 pages. 4°. 1972. DM 16,–

Vol. 70: J. P. Brown, The Economic Effects of Floods. Investigations of a Stochastic Model of Rational Investment Behavior in the Face of Floods. V, 87 pages. 4°. 1972. DM 16,–

Vol. 71: R. Henn und O. Opitz, Konsum- und Produktionstheorie II. V, 134 Seiten. 4°. 1972. DM 16,–

Vol. 72: T. P. Bagchi and J. G. C. Templeton, Numerical Methods in Markov Chains and Bulk Queues. XI, 89 pages. 4°. 1972. DM 16,–

Vol. 73: H. Kiendl, Suboptimale Regler mit abschnittweise linearer Struktur. VI, 146 Seiten. 4°. 1972. DM 16,–

Vol. 74: F. Pokropp, Aggregation von Produktionsfunktionen. VI, 107 Seiten. 4°. 1972. DM 16,–

Vol. 75: GI-Gesellschaft für Informatik e.V. Bericht Nr. 3. 1. Fachtagung über Programmiersprachen · München, 9–11. März 1971. Herausgegeben im Auftag der Gesellschaft für Informatik von H. Langmaack und M. Paul. VII, 280 Seiten. 4°. 1972. DM 24,–

Vol. 76: G. Fandel, Optimale Entscheidung bei mehrfacher Zielsetzung. 121 Seiten. 4°. 1972. DM 16,–

Vol. 77: A. Auslender, Problemes de Minimax via l'Analyse Convexe et les Inégalités Variationnelles: Théorie et Algorithmes. VII, 132 pages. 4°. 1972. DM 16,–

Vol. 78: GI-Gesellschaft für Informatik e.V. 2. Jahrestagung, Karlsruhe, 2.–4. Oktober 1972. Herausgegeben im Auftrag der Gesellschaft für Informatik von P. Deussen. XI, 576 Seiten. 4°. 1973. DM 36,–

Vol. 79: A. Berman, Cones, Matrices and Mathematical Programming. V, 96 pages. 4°. 1973. DM 16,–

Vol. 80: International Seminar on Trends in Mathematical Modelling, Venice, 13–18 December 1971. Edited by N. Hawkes. VI, 288 pages. 4°. 1973. DM 24,–

Vol. 81: Advanced Course on Software Engineering. Edited by F. L. Bauer. XII, 545 pages. 4°. 1973. DM 32,–

Vol. 82: R. Saeks, Resolution Space, Operators and Systems. X, 267 pages. 4°. 1973. DM 22,–

Vol. 83: NTG/GI-Gesellschaft für Informatik, Nachrichtentechnische Gesellschaft. Fachtagung „Cognitive Verfahren und Systeme", Hamburg, 11.–13. April 1973. Herausgegeben im Auftrag der NTG/GI von Th. Einsele, W. Giloi und H.-H. Nagel. VIII, 373 Seiten. 4°. 1973. DM 28,–

Vol. 84: A. V. Balakrishnan, Stochastic Differential Systems I. Filtering and Control. A Function Space Approach. V, 252 pages. 4°. 1973. DM 22,–

Vol. 85: T. Page, Economics of Involuntary Transfers: A Unified Approach to Pollution and Congestion Externalities. XI, 159 pages. 4°. 1973. DM 18,–

Vol. 86: Symposium on the Theory of Scheduling and Its Applications. Edited by S. E. Elmaghraby. VIII, 437 pages. 4°. 1973. DM 32,–

Vol. 87: G. F. Newell, Approximate Stochastic Behavior of n-Server Service Systems with Large n. VIII, 118 pages. 4°. 1973. DM 16,–

Vol. 88: H. Steckhan, Güterströme in Netzen. VII, 134 Seiten. 4°. 1973. DM 16,–

Vol. 89: J. P. Wallace and A. Sherret, Estimation of Product. Attributes and Their Importances. V, 94 pages. 4°. 1973. DM 16,–

Vol. 90: J.-F. Richard, Posterior and Predictive Densities for Simultaneous Equation Models. VI, 226 pages. 4°. 1973. DM 20,–

Vol. 91: Th. Marschak and R. Selten, General Equilibrium with Price-Making Firms. XI, 246 pages. 4°. 1974. DM 22,–

Vol. 92: E. Dierker, Topological Methods in Walrasian Economics. IV, 130 pages. 4°. 1974. DM 16,–

Vol. 93: 4th IFAC/IFIP International Conference on Digital Computer Applications to Process Control, Zürich/Switzerland, March 19–22, 1974. Edited by M. Mansour and W. Schaufelberger. XVIII, 544 pages. 4°. 1974. DM 36,–

Vol. 94: 4th IFAC/IFIP International Conference on Digital Computer Applications to Process Control, Zürich/Switzerland, March 19–22, 1974. Edited by M. Mansour and W. Schaufelberger. XVIII, 546 pages. 4°. 1974. DM 36,–

Vol. 95: M. Zeleny, Linear Multiobjective Programming. XII, 220 pages. 4°. 1974. DM 20,–

Ökonometrie und Unternehmensforschung
Econometrics and Operations Research